Beyond The Open Well

The True Story of Bright Meadow and Desert Princess

Jean M. Hebert

AuthorHouse™
1663 Liberty Drive, Suite 200
Bloomington, IN 47403
www.authorhouse.com
Phone: 1-800-839-8640

First published by AuthorHouse 4/21/2008

ISBN: 978-1-4343-7366-3 (sc)

Library of Congress Control Number: 2008901916

Printed in the United States of America
Bloomington, Indiana

This book is printed on acid-free paper.

The characters and events in this book are from the lives of Jane McDaniel and Joyce West. Some names have been changed for the protection of those involved. The story is, however, true and factual in its content.

Book cover design by Chuck Gamble

For

Sharon Ann Colburn —Jane Alice McDaniel
and Shirley Maye Colburn—Joyce Mary West

Acknowledgments

I would like to thank the following people for their help in the creation of this book:

Jane McDaniel and Joyce West, for telling me their stories with such dignity and grace. Their wish to help others has given me hope for the future of mankind.

My sister, Sue McLaird, for the monumental task of reading and critiquing the manuscript, as it was being written. We managed to communicate via e-mail from my home in Wisconsin to hers in Alaska.

Ruth Sather, for giving me the encouragement I needed to continue with the project, and for giving me valuable suggestions for the physical structure of the book.

Peg Strand and Joanne Hebert, for their editing expertise and long hours spent with their red pens in hand.

Leone Laird, my mother, for reading the manuscript and giving me valuable suggestions.

Chuck Gamble, artist extraordinaire, for designing the book cover and resolving computer glitches for me.

Jean Hebert

Contents

Introduction

I guess everybody has a story to tell. We all have a past. We all have the struggles of the present. We all have hopes for the future. Life itself is a story and it seems to me, everything that happens to us is part of who we are and what we become.

This is a true story that chronicles the lives of two sisters over a span of six decades. Their story is fascinating and compelling. Early abuses and neglect negatively influenced their lives, even until today. In these pages, the sisters bravely talk about a subject that is too often kept secret.

It is their hope that by telling their story, they may shed light on the subject of abuse, and ultimately encourage other sufferers to overcome and live a prosperous life.

For me, the story began on a chilly November day. I answered the phone and heard Jane's voice, elaborately wrapped in a full Texas drawl, "My dad is dead. Can you come?"

"Of course!"

My own father was nearing ninety years of age and his health was failing. I could only imagine the pain of losing him.

I met Jane at the Cornell Funeral Home, and together we approached the coffin to look at the man lying there.

"Do you see that son-of-a-bitch?" Jane asked. "He's dead now. He can't hurt me anymore."

Sadly, I took Jane's hand. Silently, I gave her all the strength and support that I could muster. Hand in hand, we turned our backs to the coffin and slowly moved to where Jane's sister, Joyce, sat looking down at her folded hands.

As we approached, Joyce looked up, and said, "It's time to tell our story."

Jean M. Hebert

Book One...

Beyond the Beginning

Chapter One

The Open Well

Toward sundown on a patch of used up pasture, about a quarter mile south of the dilapidated farmhouse, Alan suddenly shouted to his little sisters, "STOP!"

As the boy skidded, bare feet first, rocks and dirt dislodged and fell into the water far below. His grasping hands found clumps of brown grass in his effort to stop himself.

A sharp blade of terror ran through the eight-year-old as he looked over his shoulder into the gaping mouth of an old open well. He lay there in the dirt, clinging to the grass as his legs and feet dangled above the black hole. With super human strength, he pulled himself back from the edge.

The two little girls came and stood over him. Eyes wide with fear, Shirley, almost seven, bent down and tenderly brushed a piece of dirt from her brother's cheek.

"Maybe this is where Mama and Daddy are going to throw us when they kill us," whispered Sharon.

Alan Colburn and his two little sisters knew only too well the threat of death. Many times they hid themselves under grungy threadbare blankets, hoping they could burrow deeply enough under the covers to be forgotten by their drunken parents.

Since early that morning, as the sun made a desperate attempt to pierce through the wall of gray clouds, Mama had been moaning and screaming. As usual, the screaming was mingled with Daddy's yells and the sound of dishes and furniture crashing against the walls.

In spite of the growling in her empty stomach, little Sharon still slept on her bed, amidst a mound of rancid smelling rags and dirty clothes. Alan and Shirley hoped their little sister would stay asleep until Mama and Daddy left for the tavern. One thing Mama said she couldn't stand was "a crying kid!"

Too soon, Sharon stirred and started to whimper. Alan and Shirley hushed the little girl and got her outside before they were noticed.

The children knew the safest place for them was either in the bedroom of the old house or outside, as far away from it as possible. Being "underfoot" was a punishable offense.

Once in the relative safety of the outdoors, Alan reached into his ragged pants pocket and produced a hunk of dry bread for Sharon. She was the smallest of the three and always hungry.

Four-year-old Sharon still had not learned to be quiet around Mama and Daddy. Her crying and begging for food would set off their volatile parents and all hell would break loose.

As the children ventured into the fields of the old farm, the late afternoon sun burst forth and with it came a bit of the joyfulness of the spirit.

Shirley and Sharon stopped to pick dandelions. Sensitive and guarded, Shirley fashioned hers into tiaras of yellow flowers. Angry and careless, Sharon gleefully popped off their little yellow heads with her thumbs.

Barefoot, bruised, and wearing their filthy ragged dresses, the girls were beautiful princesses with their dandelion crowns atop their heads.

Shirley, whose name means, "Bright Meadow," loved being outside in the sunlit pasture. Sharon, whose name means, "Desert Princess," strode with regal confidence across the field.

Alan, whose name means, "Handsome and Peaceful," led the way on his magical white steed. Pawing the ground and snorting loudly, swinging its huge head wildly from side to side, the imaginary horse and his master thundered across the countryside to defend the honor of the beautiful princesses.

In their secret kingdom there was no hunger. Servants spread feasts before them wherever they went. There was no fear. In this fantasyland, parents loved their children and protected them from pain.

But, in their kingdom, there was also an open well.

Shaken, the three children sat on the ground beside the well.

"They could dump us in here," Alan said thoughtfully. "No one would ever find us."

Alan had long ago become the protector of his sisters.

"I won't let that happen," he whispered through his teeth. "I won't let them kill us."

Silently, Shirley began to cry. Life was precious to her and she didn't want to die. Her strong will to live gave her the courage to fight each day against fear, physical pain, starvation, and neglect.

She had watched and paid attention to other children in school. She was sure there was a better way to live. She had seen the others come to school with nice shoes and clean clothes. They had pencils and lunch bags with food in them. She knew their parents helped their children with homework and tucked them into bed. Oh yes, Shirley knew there was a better way.

The children stayed in the field, beside the open well, until a silvery blanket of moonlight replaced the orange glow of sunset from the west. Only then did they dare to creep quietly into the old house and crawl under the bed.

Once the girls were settled, Alan rummaged through the kitchen to find some milk, bread and cheese. He brought the food to his sisters who were waiting for their first and only meal of the day. They ate until every crumb was gone. Then together they found enough warmth and comfort to fall asleep.

Chapter Two

Life with Grandpa

Shirley's very first memories were of living in Cornell, a small but thriving paper mill town in North Central Wisconsin. Her father, Hale Colburn, worked at the mill there for awhile. She must have been somewhere around three years old.

It's not clear if she truly remembered it, or if it's because of the pictures. In the pictures, the three Colburn children were all dressed up sitting in a rocking chair in the yard. It is clear that the photo was taken in Cornell because the house, in the background, is still standing today.

In one picture, Hale is holding baby Sharon. In another, Alan and Shirley are standing there looking cute. Even Esther, their mother, looked kind and loving. The family looked so happy and normal that you'd find it hard to believe the secrets that lurked in the shadows behind those pictures.

Their mother's sister, Aunt Sylvia, gave Shirley the pictures years after they were taken. Both Shirley and Sharon were already married when the pictures resurfaced. The pictures were one of the few mementos, besides the emotional scars, that remained from their early lives.

Hale didn't work at the mill in Cornell very long. Once again the loss of a job took them back to the farm at Turtle Lake, Wisconsin.

Grandpa Colburn's farm was a refuge for the little rag tag family. If life got too tough, Hale and Esther would run back to Turtle Lake to Grandpa Colburn's dilapidated little farm. For Hale, when life got too tough it usually meant the loss of another job or running short of money to buy beer.

Life on the farm was much more fun for the children than life on the road. At the farm, there were animals and fun places to play. It was easy to disappear into the barn or into the woods if it got too scary in the house. Alan felt a sense of freedom and safety at the farm. Each time they came back, he prayed things would go well so they wouldn't have to leave again.

Grandpa Colburn was an old and crusty man who basically ignored the kids. Living with him provided a few of the necessities not available on the road. At the farm, the children had food to eat and a few warm clothes in the winter.

The children felt safer at the farm as well. Once, while living with Grandpa Colburn, Shirley got an earache. Esther treated it by putting a piece of cotton in her ear. The cotton worked its way down into the ear canal where it festered and became terribly infected. The little girl was in pain for days until Grandpa took notice. He loaded Shirley up in his old Model A and took her into Turtle Lake to see the doctor. Minor surgery had to be performed to remove the putrid cotton. When the doctor was finished, he shook his head and plopped a bloody green blob onto his instrument tray.

Early on, Alan had become the protector of his little sisters. He took it upon himself to find them food and get them out of sight at the first sign of trouble. When their parent's violent tempers blew, the girls learned quickly to listen to their big brother and do exactly as he said.

Shirley and Sharon adored Alan. He was their hero. In the eyes of two little girls, he was big, strong, smart, loving and safe. They believed they would die if they didn't have their brother Alan with them.

Esther and Hale were married over eight years before they had the children. Hale was much older than Esther and felt he was ready to settle down and raise a family. The problem was that Esther hated being pregnant. She didn't like being sick and was mad when Hale tried to stop her from going with him to the tavern. She was terribly angry that he treated her like a child and tried to keep her from drinking while she was pregnant.

By the time Esther had given birth to three children, she was seething with hatred for Hale and she just couldn't find it in her heart to love her children. They made too much noise and demanded too much time and effort. In her darkest hours, she mourned her past and found her truth. She hated her children; they had drained the very life from her body.

She wanted her old life back where she was free to party with no responsibilities. Her head ached most of the time and the only comfort she found was in the bottle. She often thought of how her life would be if those kids were gone. In the dead of night, alone with her demons, Esther Colburn contemplated the murder of her children.

Esther had a ravenous appetite for food and drink. She was slowly morphing into a huge woman, growing fatter as her children starved. To Esther, the tavern presented an environment teeming with life sustaining elements such as beer, hot beef, candy bars, popcorn, peanuts, music and laughter. Oh yes…when Esther was at the bar, she was a happy woman.

There were things in the house that were not meant for the eyes of children. One afternoon, while they lived at the farm, they began snooping in the bedroom where their mother and father slept. Alan found a penis carved out of a piece of wood. He started to snigger and make fun of it. Suddenly his face turned white. He put the thing back, grabbed the girls by the hand and ran for all he was worth. He dragged those little girls into the other bedroom and pulled them under the bed, just as Esther and Hale stumbled drunkenly into the house.

The Colburn's were not clean people. Grandpa Colburn and his bachelor son, Jack, kept a messy house. Random stacks of dirty dishes, piles of dirty clothes and trash heaps were all over the place. There really wasn't a cleaned off chair to sit on. However, sitting atop a pile of old papers and clothing on a kitchen chair would actually bring the little girls to a manageable height when it came to mealtime—if, in fact, someone felt like cooking.

It was not unusual to find the engine from Grandpa Colburn's old Model A sitting on the table in the kitchen, leaking oil on the floor. Grease would be smeared all over the table and the smell of gasoline and motor oil added to the stench of the Colburn household.

Bathing was an event that did not happen often. A couple of times each summer, the old galvanized laundry tub would be put outside in the yard. Fear gathered the children in its clutches as they cowered just around the corner of the house, watching as Esther filled the tub with cold water. Then she brought the teakettle from the stove and splashed boiling water into the tub to take off the chill.

The rules of bath day were that Esther filled the tub only once and each person took their turn, youngest to oldest. That meant Sharon would go first and Grandpa Colburn would be last. That's how it went and no one argued.

Sharon lost her breath as she was unceremoniously dumped into the cool water. Then a scream rose from her throat as Esther grabbed the soap and roughly began washing her body. Esther was not careful about keeping the soap out of the little girl's eyes. Sharon screamed until her mother's nerves wore thin. Angrily, she grabbed the little girl and yanked her out of the tub. She threw her on a blanket, which was lying on the grass beside the tub.

Shirley, and then Alan, in turn, were practically thrown into the tub and scrubbed raw. They were old enough to bite their lips and not make a sound but the damage was already done. The tone of the day was set by the screaming child and the angry woman. Their mother would be in a vile temper for the rest of the day.

As soon as they could, Alan and Shirley scrambled to get back into their dirty clothes. They grabbed their little sister and disappeared into the barn while their mother took her turn in the tub.

The winter usually brought a reprieve from the dreaded bath. Esther believed it was not healthy to bathe at that time of year.

In spite of the baths and the smell of the house, the children were happy to live with Grandpa Colburn. They loved their grandpa. They thought he was a nice man, but they also understood that he was a mean drunk. When he was drinking, he didn't seem to have a worry in the world. It didn't matter to him that he was old, and when he was drinking, he'd pick a fight with anybody who'd fight back.

He picked a fight with Esther and demanded, "Get off your fat butt and do something around here."

He started in on Hale, saying, "Find a job and put some money toward living expenses."

With his face turning beet red and the veins in his temples about to pop, he yelled that he was tired of supporting everybody.

Grandpa Colburn was treading on thin ice when he criticized Esther. It was well known, especially by the family, that nobody told

Esther Colburn what to do. Predictably, there would be a row and soon the fight would escalate to include Hale.

One particular fight got so violent that Esther and Hale began hitting and slamming each other with uncontrolled fury. Hale bashed Esther into the red-hot potbelly stove. The stovepipe got knocked off and flames went shooting out into the room.

Hale got so mad about the stovepipe that he grabbed dirty dishes off the table and threw them at her. Esther was burned by the searing hot stove and bruised by the force with which she was shoved into it. But it didn't stop her. The fight went on.

The three terrified kids hid under the bed as Grandpa Colburn attempted to stop the fight. Suddenly Esther and Hale turned on him, and together, they kicked him until he crawled under the bed, where the children were trying to hide.

Esther went to the kitchen sink, moistened a dirty towel with cold water and began applying it to her burned chest. Without a word, Hale took her by the arm, and with an unusual tenderness, led her out to the old car. Together they drove to the hospital.

The next day the thing the three little children feared the most happened. They were off again to another place where Hale could find work for awhile.

Their fear was based on history. Without Grandpa Colburn nearby to protect them, they were fair game. Esther and Hale always blamed their children for their latest string of bad luck. If they had been good, Grandpa wouldn't have kicked the family out. If they hadn't eaten so much, they'd still be eating well at Grandpa's. If! If! If! If! If! The result of all those "ifs" was always the same. The family went back to life on the road.

Following a stay with Grandpa, the family would be forced to go without much food for several days while Hale waited for his first paycheck. The lack of money meant the lack of beer, which usually sent Esther to bed for a few days. Life on the road got back to normal quickly once the check arrived.

Chapter Three

The Farm Hand at Chippewa City

In the spring of 1945, Hale Colburn's search for another job took him to a farm north of Chippewa Falls, Wisconsin, at a place called Chippewa City. The huge, white, two-story farmhouse stood on the hill overlooking Lake Wissota. Down the hill, a few yards east of where O'Neil Creek emptied into the lake, stood a large red barn and several out buildings. One of those buildings was the house for the hired man, where Hale and his family found refuge.

The little house was only ten feet wide by fourteen feet long in size. It was built as a logger's warming cabin and had been brought down from the woods to serve as a hired man's place. The one-room building was meant to house a bachelor, so it was hardly suitable for a family with three children.

The Colburn's new home was barely distinguishable from the other out buildings clustered together along the lakeshore near the barn. Weathered gray tarpaper shingles covered the exterior of the little house and a stovepipe protruded through the roof. Curtain-less windows, dotted with flyspecks and covered in spider webs, graced the north and south sides of the building. A thick wooden beam had been rough-cut for use as a step in front of the only door, which faced west.

The door opened into the kitchen where the old black cook stove stood along with a small table and two straight-backed chairs. A kerosene lamp sat on the kitchen table. A bucket for drinking water took its place atop a series of boards attached to the wall for pots and pans, clean dishes, and food. An antique garbage disposal, called a slop pail, was kept in the corner by the door.

There was one bed against the back wall of the small room. A 4x8-foot piece of plywood had been attached to the north wall and extended to a 2x4 in the middle of the room. This was done in an effort to provide some privacy and divide the kitchen from the bedroom.

The walls inside the house consisted of 2x4 studs about a foot and a half apart. Cardboard had been shoved in between the studs and nailed to the rough wood sheeting, which provided limited insulation against the cold winds of Wisconsin winters. Horseshoe nails were driven into the studs in the bedroom area to hang clothing. Boxes against the wall served as storage for personal items.

The way to the bathroom was out the door, around the corner of the house past the granary and the icehouse, to the outhouse. For use during the night or for emergencies, a chamber pot was kept under the bed. The pot under the bed was the source of the unpleasant aroma that wafted through the house.

Although most of his children were grown and on their own, Louis Hebert, who owned the Chippewa City farm, still had two young sons living at home. Steve was six, and Louie Paul had just turned eight. They were overjoyed to have Alan Colburn living so near.

As a hand on the Hebert farm, Hale Colburn's family had plenty of food available to them. Whenever a cow or pig was butchered, the hired hands got some of the meat. The vegetable gardens, the potatoes, and corn from the fields were always free to them. The problem was…Esther didn't cook much. Esther drank! She only cooked when she was sober. Needless to say, the kids were usually hungry.

So Alan became the "cook" at the age of six. He was responsible to watch out for his sisters and find something for them to eat. He even baked a cake on top of the stove once. The cake wasn't pretty but the skinny little girls thought Alan was the best cake baker ever.

One afternoon, Steve and Alan were playing in the wood shed. Alan pulled out a piece of hard candy, which was wrapped in waxed paper. He offered it to Steve. He popped it in his mouth and started sucking on it for all it was worth. A few seconds later, Alan held out his hand and said he wanted the candy back. Steve spit it out and watched Alan wrap it up again and shove it back into his pocket. Alan didn't have much, but what he did have he shared. Steve wondered how many people Alan had shared that one little piece of candy with.

The Hebert brothers were lucky little kids. Their dad took them everywhere he went. When Alan came into the picture, they always asked if they could take their friend along.

The problem was Alan had to look after his sisters so he seldom had any free time. His mother was mean and foulmouthed when she was drinking and in a bad mood when she wasn't. Alan needed to stay around to take care of his little sisters and keep them as far away from Esther as possible.

All the kids, including Steve and Louie Paul, were scared of Esther when she was drinking. Her face would get beet red and her eyes would pop nearly out of her head. She'd drool when she yelled, and spit would spray from her quivering lips as she spewed every cuss word known to man. Her wild hair would be all over the place, sticking out in some places and matted to her head in others. Esther would throw whatever she had in her hand at whoever happened to displease her. Her children displeased her!

Often, Esther would stand at the front door of the little house looking wistfully across the O'Neil creek toward the Chippewa City Tavern. The sound of the jukebox playing loud music and the bright lights beckoned and said, "Come join us in the good life." Some people thought Esther Colburn was mentally retarded and maybe that was true. She seemed to have a lot of nonsense swirling around in her head.

On payday, Hale would walk across the bridge. Later, he'd come staggering back with a case of beer. He'd put that beer right up against the old black stove, which served as cook stove and heat source for the teeny house. Yes, Hale Colburn liked his beer warm. No one really knows how Esther liked her beer but it was well known that she liked it. Esther and Hale even turned in their WWII ration stamps for beer. They were drunks with children, and their children went without the necessities of life for the sake of a few cases of warm beer.

By autumn, Alan was old enough to start first grade. Steve would be a first grader, too, and he and Louie Paul were already enrolled in the Catholic parochial school. Mr. Hebert decided Alan should go to school with his boys. With permission from Hale and Esther Colburn, he made arrangements with the nuns and paid Alan's tuition.

Once Steve and Louie Paul found out that Alan would be going to school with them, the countdown began. Four more days to school;

three more days; two more days, until finally it was the night before school began. Neither of the boys slept very much that night. They were excited and scared all at the same time.

The Hebert brothers got up an hour earlier than usual, way before their mother could call up the steps to wake them. They jumped into their clothes and ran downstairs for breakfast. The night before they had carefully set out the new pencils and tablets their mother had bought for their first day of school.

Finally, their mother told them it was time to go outside and wait for the school bus. The boys ran out the door and found Alan already waiting at the mailbox. Louie Paul noticed that Alan wasn't wearing any shoes. He was only going to be in first grade so the older boy figured he probably didn't know that a person had to wear shoes to school.

Louie Paul told Alan to go back in the house and get his shoes on.

"I don't have any," Alan said with a big smile on his face.

As time went on, it became clear to everyone who knew him that Alan's big smile covered up lots of hurt.

Alan Colburn was the only kid who showed up at school with no shoes. None of the other kids made fun of him though. Everybody knew they would have to deal with the nuns if they teased him. Besides, Alan was a good mixer. He did what the other kids did. He fit in pretty well, and by the third day of school, he was wearing shoes.

That was because Steve had told his dad that Alan was barefoot. The next afternoon Mr. Hebert picked all the boys up from school and took Alan to the K&S Bootery, where he bought him a new pair of shoes.

All the kids who rode the school bus carried a lunch pail. All the kids, that is, except Alan Colburn. On the first day of school, the nuns shared their lunches with him. After that, they brought Alan his own lunch everyday. He would eat part of it and put the rest in his pocket to share with his little sisters when he got home.

One Saturday, when Alan was with Mr. Hebert and his boys, they went to the farm on Highway S. The boys loved to go over there because the railroad tracks crossed the road and ran past the farm buildings. In those days, many kids were very excited by the train and even wanted to be railroad engineers when they grew up. Steve and Louie Paul thought they were lucky to have a farm next to the train tracks.

On that particular day, Alan and Louie Paul went up on the road where the tracks crossed. They were playing around and found some metal plates on the rail bed, between the rails and the railroad ties. The boys got busy and hauled all those metal plates to the train tracks and carefully laid them across the rails, right where the train would cross Highway S.

The man who was renting the farmhouse turned the boys into the railroad company authorities. A day or two later, investigators arrived at the school and escorted Alan and Louie Paul out into the hall to interrogate them. The boys hadn't learned to lie very well yet so they admitted everything right there on the spot. A kid can really spill the beans if he thinks he's going to jail. What they really didn't understand was that their actions could have caused a disastrous train derailment. After the investigators pulled Alan and Louie Paul out of school three or four times and scared them sufficiently, the issue was dropped. Lesson learned!

One day. Louie Paul was out by the barn when he heard an animal howl coming from the little house. Suddenly, out of the door came Esther dragging a naked, two-year-old Sharon by the arm. The toddler had pooped her pants and was a mess from her neck to her knees.

"You shitty little son-of–a-bitch," Esther screamed as she tossed Sharon up into the air and threw her into the cold lake.

Louie Paul yelled, "Do you need some help?"

Finally, in one fleeting moment of sanity, Esther turned and walked into the lake with her shoes on. She grabbed little Sharon and dragged her up on shore. In spite of the look of surprise and confusion on her face, she had saved her little daughter from drowning.

Shirley also had her turn at an attempted drowning. One Sunday afternoon Hale and the kids were down at the water's edge. Mr. Hebert was in the barn when he heard a strange whimpering sound coming from the creek. He looked out the barn window and saw Hale holding four-year-old Shirley's head under the water. He was clearly trying to drown her.

In a panic, Mr. Hebert hollered and stopped Hale in his tracks. Little Shirley came up sputtering and gasping, while her drunken father tried to cover up for his actions. He tried to convince his boss that his daughter had fallen into the creek and he was merely trying to rescue her.

Mr. Hebert walked slowly up the path to the house. He told his wife what had just happened. They decided it was the end of having Esther and Hale at the farm.

Steve and Louie Paul watched the family leave. They wished Alan could have stayed around longer but their parents were relieved when the Colburn's drove away. Once again, Hale was forced to go back to Grandpa Colburn's farm at Turtle Lake.

Chapter Four

The Galvanized Washtub

Hale Colburn woke up with a headache—the price he paid for all the fun he'd had last night at Kings Tavern. He came wide-awake with a nagging feeling that something was wrong. When he felt like that, he hated his life, and he hated his wife. Most of all, he hated what he had become.

Through bloodshot eyes, he studied Esther as she slept. He felt disgusted at the dry rasping sound that came from her as she struggled to drag in her breath, and the blubbery wet flapping of her lips when she exhaled.

"She'll be out till noon," he thought to himself. "Better not mess with her today. It'll be safer to let her sleep it off."

It was an effort to get out of bed. Hale looked at the clock, and groaned, "It's 8:30. It isn't fair. She gets to stay in bed all day."

He almost reached over and socked her in the head. Then he realized, just in time, that he'd have to pay for it the rest of the day. She was mean when she was drunk or hung over. This morning she would probably be both.

Alcohol, or the temporary lack of it, could cause one to start to think. Hale was in a particularly pensive mood but wasn't sure why. He thought about the woman he married and wished with all his heart that he had never laid eyes on her. His mother always said Esther was trouble and she was right. Of course, he couldn't see it back then when there was still time to get out. Realization had come hard and when it hit, it hit him right between the eyes.

"My troubles all started when I met her," he whined to himself silently.

His head throbbed violently as he bent over to tie his shoes. The lace broke off in his hand.

"I can't even afford a decent pair of shoes," he sobbed at the downturn his life had taken. "It's her fault and those damn kids."

Hale thought about how he had been forced to move his family back in with his father on the old Colburn farm in rural Turtle Lake. He thought his brother Jack had it pretty easy—no responsibility and not a care in the world.

He couldn't quite understand why he'd lost his job at Chippewa City. He thought he had done well there. It was always the same story. Nobody appreciated how hard he worked and all too soon the job was over. If that wasn't degrading enough, he always had to go crawling back to his father, all because of that woman and those kids.

With an effort to crawl upward through the veil of dense fog that enshrouded his brain, Hale made an attempt to be fair.

"Those kids didn't ask to be born," he thought. "They deserve better than this."

He reached the kitchen just as the sheriff's car pulled into the yard.

"What now?" he moaned.

Hale took a quick inventory of his surroundings and decided it was safe to open the door to the officer.

"There's been an accident," the deputy said gravely. "Your father is in the hospital. I'm sorry to have to inform you that your brother Jack is dead."

The news didn't surprise Hale all that much. He wanted to shout, "I knew something was wrong when I woke up this morning."

But instead, he just mumbled, "Thank you, officer," and closed the kitchen door, leaving the deputy standing on the top step.

Hale needed a drink. It had been seven hours since his last one at Kings. He went to the cupboard over the old sink in the kitchen and took out a bottle of wine, looked at it, and shook his head. With tears running down his cheeks, in a moment on the fringe of sanity, he decided he would take action.

A determination he hadn't felt in years filled his soul as he opened the bottle and poured the red liquid down the sink. He couldn't think of what to do first. There was so much he needed to take care of, but he decided he was going to take care of it sober.

Hale stood at the sink watching the wine disappear down the hole. His brother Jack was no loss to him. They never did get along anyway. But if his father died, where would he go?

Everything had gone sour for Hale Colburn. Esther was a terrible wife and those three kids were always crying. He couldn't even look at them and they'd run away or burst into tears. It all got on his nerves.

He knew his father kept a gun under his bed. He had to find out, and find out fast if there were any bullets for that old gun. In the top drawer of the dresser in the living room, Hale found what he had been looking for. With a steady hand, he popped the bullets into the gun, and started for the door.

Alan was outside by the shed when he saw his dad stomp down the steps to the dirt path that led to the barn. Alan saw the gun. He backed up and flattened himself against the side of the shed. He hoped his father had not seen him there.

The hair stood up at the nape of his neck. Alan knew he and his sisters were in danger. He slid to the ground and crawled to the other side of the shed where his little sisters were playing in an old tire.

As soon as his father was in the barn, Alan grabbed his sisters and ran behind the house. There was an old galvanized washtub lying upside down amongst the long forgotten trash that littered the yard.

Bang! The children froze when they heard the sound of the gun.

"Oh, no," cried Shirley, "Daddy shot himself."

Sharon and Shirley clutched Alan by the leg of his dirty bibbed overalls. They were so scared; they almost threw up.

Bang! Another blast from the gun; this time followed by Hale's voice, "Sharon, Shirley, get out here. I know you're in there."

Alan knew what was up. His father wasn't going to shoot himself. He was out hunting for the girls.

Esther and Hale had tried to kill the girls before and this time Hale had a gun. Alan had seen the sheriff's car drive in and had overheard the deputy tell his father about an accident. The boy hadn't heard that his Uncle Jack was dead, but he knew that whenever Daddy got upset, somebody had to pay, and Daddy was upset.

Alan took action.

"Get under this washtub and don't come out," Alan told the girls. "We're going to play a game. No matter what happens, do not come out. Do you hear me?"

"Yes," said both girls at the same time.

They were scared but the idea of playing a game with Alan helped them feel safer. They crawled under the tub, ready to play the game.

"These are the rules of the game. I am the only one you can come out for," Alan said. "Even if Mama or Daddy call your names, threaten you, or offer you food or candy, don't come out! You could be under here for a long time, but don't come out until I come and get you," Alan warned them. "I'll get you the best food you ever ate when I come back for you."

"Okay," the little girls promised in wide-eyed unison.

After all, they were big girls now and they understood that it was wise to obey their big brother.

Alan only hoped his little sisters would remain quiet and not be fooled or coaxed from their hiding place. The children had played this game before when the girls were in danger, and they played the game well.

With his sisters safe in a place where his father would never think to look, Alan sidled away. He followed the trees and the tall grass along the edge of the yard. His goal was to reach the barn and hide where his father had already looked. If he could get there, he would be safe until his parents went off to the bar.

Bang! Bang! Bang! The zing of bullets hitting the barn and ricocheting off the metal cans and trash in the yard terrified Alan. He hadn't thought about his dad shooting at things in the yard. Maybe Sharon and Shirley were not as safe as he thought.

With his heart pounding hard, Alan burrowed deep into the hay pile and waited. He could hardly breathe it was so hot and dusty. He thought this just might be the end of the road. He wasn't sure if there was a God, but he decided it wouldn't hurt to say a prayer.

After awhile, the gun suddenly became silent. Everybody waited. Shirley whispered to Sharon to be quiet. It was dark under the washtub and not a very fun game to play. The girls waited for Alan to come and get them.

Soon they heard their father talking softly to them.

"Come out, girls," he said in a velvety voice. "I have some ham sandwiches from Bakers Tavern. You know the ones Mama and Daddy like to eat. I have some for you. Come out and get them."

Shirley held Sharon's hand and gave it a little squeeze.

"We have to wait for Alan," she whispered to her little sister. "He promised he'd bring us food. Alan always keeps his promise, remember?"

So the little girls waited and did not come out of their hiding place. They could hear their father cursing and kicking at things in the yard, but they never heard the shots from the gun again. They stayed under the washtub for a very long time. It was hot, dark, and cramped, but they were very brave.

At length, they heard their mother's voice and then the old Model A started up. The sound of the tires crunching on the gravel in the driveway told the children their parents were going away.

Five minutes after they heard the car leave, Alan lifted up the washtub and let them out. The sun was so bright it hurt their little eyes, blinding them for a moment. Their legs seemed to be stuck in a sitting position. Sharon fell over when she tried to stand up. They had been under the tub for over two hours.

The girls grabbed Alan and squeezed his rail thin body with all their might. They sobbed uncontrollably while their noses ran and their breaths came out in gasping hiccups of emotion.

"Good girls," Alan said. "We are all safe now. Come on," he coaxed, "Let's go inside and get something good to eat.

"I'm hungry," Sharon whimpered.

"Me, too," said Shirley as she wiped her eyes, straightened up her body and proudly led the way into the old farmhouse.

The children opened every cupboard door in the kitchen until they found the stash of peanuts and chocolate chips that Grandpa Colburn had hidden away. They also found Uncle Jack's bag of potato chips, behind the pots and pans. Alan knew he would be beaten within an inch of his life if they touched those treasures, but he didn't care today. His sisters had obeyed him and stayed alive. They deserved a special treat. To his immense relief, they all were out of danger for the time being.

Sharon loved chips and Shirley loved chocolate. Alan gave each girl a handful and carefully put everything back just the way he found it. Silently, he prayed that Grandfather Colburn and Uncle Jack wouldn't be able to tell they had been raided.

Chapter Five

The Castle and the Dead Man

Grandpa Colburn came home from the hospital the day before Uncle Jack's funeral. Mostly he just had a bad bump on his head and a black eye.

The kids didn't know what a funeral was but they did know better than to ask. They pretty much stayed out of the way and listened. They learned that, "Uncle Jack wasn't any good anyway." They learned that, "He never knew what hit him." They learned that, "He looked natural in the casket." They learned that, "It cost a lot of money to give somebody a proper burying."

Uncle Jack was laid out at the funeral home in Turtle Lake. Alan was very interested in what a real dead body looked like, but it was decided the children would not go to see him. Esther decreed the kids should stay home and not get under everybody's feet at the funeral parlor. Shirley was glad she didn't have to go see Uncle Jack all "dead and stuff." She declared she would shut her eyes so she wouldn't have to look.

The day after Uncle Jack's burial, Grandpa Colburn told Hale they would have to leave. He said the funeral was too expensive and he couldn't afford to feed Hale and his family any longer. Esther and Grandpa got in a fight and he slapped her across the mouth. That was the end of that. The family was packed up and driving out of the yard in less than an hour.

Hale had known about a job opening in St. Paul, Minnesota, for sometime now. He had been keeping the job in mind in case they got kicked out of his father's house again. With his head held high, he drove down the driveway to the road, turned left, and headed to Minnesota.

The children sat in the back of the old car with all of their belongings that didn't fit in the trunk—packed and stuffed all around them. Their huge scared eyes stared straight ahead all the way to the Wisconsin-Minnesota border. Fear kept them quiet and off the minds of their parents.

Both Hale and Esther had a bottle of beer for the road. Esther ranted until her bottle was empty and then she fell asleep in the front seat. Her head lolled from side to side and her lips flapped as she snored. Once she was asleep, her husband hummed softly as he drove along. The children noticed that he was in a fairly good mood. His mood helped ease their fright.

It grew dark and cold as they drove toward their new home. Hale knew of a wayside park a couple of miles inside the Minnesota state line. When they reached it, he pulled in and the family spent the night in the car. Thankfully there was an outhouse and a water pump in the park. It was hard for the children to fall asleep with fear in their hearts and no food in their bellies.

They got on the road again as soon as the morning sun rose above the horizon. By mid-morning, the family had arrived at their destination. Hale and Esther rented a place in an old hotel on Rice Street. Their new home was only one-and-one-half blocks west of the state capital building, in Saint Paul.

They moved their sacks of clothing and belongings into an efficiency apartment on the second floor of the hotel. There was only one bathroom at the end of the hall, which had to be shared by all the people who lived on the second floor. At the back of the building, a rickety open stairway extended down to the alley. The family was told to use the outside stairway and not come down through the lobby of the hotel.

There was a big mud puddle behind the hotel that never dried up the entire time the family lived there. The children loved to watch the ducks splashing around in the puddle, and they splashed in the puddle lots of times, too.

Hale came home from work the first day and told Esther of a position that was open for a woman. Esther decided to give it a try. The next morning both parents drove away together.

The kids didn't know what to do first, so they just went out on the sidewalk and started exploring. They kept the hotel in sight that first day so they could find their way home again. A close call with a car and a beeping horn quickly taught them to stay on the sidewalk and keep their eyes open.

The first time they saw the capital building, Alan looked up at the green dome and said, "Some day I'm going to live in a castle like this."

"Can we live in it with you?" asked Sharon.

She just knew that if Alan said he'd have one, he would.

"How will you get to be a king?" Shirley asked him.

She also knew her brother could do anything. So the would-be princesses began making plans to move into a castle.

The children went to the castle every day and played around in the rotunda. In their imaginations, it was a magnificent place for three lost street urchins to be. The whole time they lived in St. Paul, nobody ever told them to quiet down or to get out of the building.

With Esther and Hale both working, you'd think there would be a noticeable improvement in their living conditions. The only difference seemed to be that Esther went to the little grocery store across the street more often. Between paychecks, when beer money ran short, she would sometimes stay home and cook a meal.

When Esther made a home-cooked meal, the children thought she was the best cook in the world. Their hungry little bodies would quiver in anticipation. Just the smell of real food cooking made their mouths water and their stomachs growl. The hungry children would eat until their tummies were so full they felt like they could split wide open. Of course, that didn't last long. As soon as the checks came, Esther and Hale would be gone again.

Now that she was a working woman, she could buy her own drinks. Esther didn't have to listen to Hale, or wait for him to take her out to the bar any longer. She could go to a tavern and drink until she threw up, if she wanted to.

On one particular day, Esther came home roaring drunk and sobbing. She locked herself in the community bathroom at the end of the hall, threw up on herself, and then passed out.

The landlord finally arrived, after receiving several complaints from the other tenants on the second floor. He tried the doorknob and began knocking and pounding. Then he hollered and tried to get the attention of whoever was monopolizing the bathroom.

With great frustration, the landlord knocked on every door on the second floor in an effort to discover who was in the locked room. When he rapped on the Colburn's door, Shirley opened it just a crack and looked out at him with huge frightened eyes. He asked if the person in the bathroom was her mother. She hid her face in embarrassment and fear, and let the door squeak shut.

The landlord yelled, "I'm calling the police to get her out of there."

As he stomped down the hall to the stairway, the children lined up with their backs against the closed apartment door, shaking in terror.

The scream of squad car sirens sliced through the wooden door, into the hearts of the three terrified children. Alan put his finger to his mouth to warn the girls to be quiet. They listened to the pounding of the officers' heavy boots, as they came running up the stairs. Then came the noise of splintering wood, as they broke down the bathroom door.

Unceremoniously, the policemen picked up the sticky, foul-smelling woman and hauled her away to jail. Esther was unconscious. For once in her life, she didn't put up a fight.

The landlord knocked on the Colburn's door again. He pointed a finger at Shirley and told her to go into the bathroom and clean up after her mother. The five-year-old was terrified.

She was afraid of her abusive, neglectful mother, but since it was all she knew, she loved her. Shirley was afraid if she didn't clean up the room, the policemen wouldn't let Esther come home again. So, while retching at the smell and sobbing for her mother, she did her best to clean the putrid bathroom.

Around three o'clock the next afternoon, Hale brought Esther home. One night in jail seemed to calm Esther down.

She said, "I want things to be different around here from now on."

Shirley thought Esther looked happy and contented as she prepared a wonderful supper of chicken and dumplings for her family. Everyone ate until their hungry bellies nearly exploded and the children smiled. After supper, Hale brought out a bottle of homemade elderberry wine.

Esther tried to resist but she couldn't sit there and let Hale drink by himself. Her newfound happiness and contentment was short-lived. By nine o'clock, the three Colburn children were again hiding under the bed.

In a dysfunctional family, the lines between loyalty and revenge sometimes become blurred. The Colburn children had always remained loyal to each other until the day Hale beat Alan and little Sharon with a razor strap. He punished them for something that Shirley had actually done. Shirley ran into hiding so his drunken anger was spent on her siblings.

Alan and Sharon were left draped across the bed, with their mangled bodies wracked in pain and their hearts seething with anger. Their learned behavior, from their past, was to misplace blame. Their rage was now directed at "the villain," Shirley.

After Hale left the apartment, Alan and his youngest sister sought their revenge. Barely able to walk, Alan went down the hall to the bathroom and filled the bathtub with water. Next, he lured Shirley into the bathroom and threw her into the tub. With a strength derived from uncontrolled anger, Alan and Sharon carried out the sentence. The executioners held Shirley's head under the water. Justice would be served.

Unknowingly, Esther was the one who saved her oldest daughter's life. She came staggering into the bathroom to use the toilet and began screaming at the kids.

"Get the hell out of my way."

Alan and Sharon ran as fast as their bruised and bloody bodies could carry them. Shirley jumped, soaking wet and gasping, out of the tub and ran in the same direction as her brother and sister.

Together they all hid under the bed in the farthest corner. Somehow they again came to understand the need to band together for protection and survival. In the end, fear of their parents was stronger than the need to seek revenge against each other.

It was obvious there was a lot of rage in the Colburn household. The children were punished regularly for offenses imagined or otherwise. They always tried to be quiet and good, but somehow they failed.

Once Esther got really mad at Sharon because she asked for some food and then started whining.

Esther said, "Shut your goddamn mouth or I'm going to kill you."

Sharon didn't shut up quick enough, so Esther grabbed her and threw her on the sofa bed in the living room. Then she started rolling it up with the little girl inside.

She was about to sit on the bed, most likely killing her daughter, when Alan jumped up and screamed, "I'm going to get the cops!"

Alan's threat stopped her before she actually sat down. Because of Esther's recent incarceration, she staggered, swearing and crying, into the bedroom. Alan unrolled the sofa bed and got Sharon out. The children all ran outside before their mother could get her hands on them again.

Esther didn't even remember her out-of-control behavior or how angry she had been at Sharon. No word was ever spoken about the incident and it was clear that she hadn't told Hale, because Alan didn't get punished.

With their parents away most of the time, the children were left to scavenge for food on their own. In the summer, fruit stands and vendors were set up on the lawn between the capital building and the sidewalk, running beside the busy street. An organ grinder and his monkey were regulars at the open-air market.

The monkey would eat cigarettes, paper, or just anything at all. The children fell in love with the little monkey who was all dressed up in his little red jacket and sported a cute red and gold hat on his head. He would sit on the organ grinder's shoulder, dance around, and make funny gestures. That monkey became their friend in more ways than one.

The hungry children soon realized that while the monkey was entertaining the people, they could steal bananas and other fruit since nobody paid any attention. They ate lots of bananas and fruit that summer and never got caught. A little monkey, in captivity himself, helped free them from starvation.

In 1947, the St. Paul Museum was located on the capital grounds. The Colburn children often snuck into the museum and looked at all the artifacts. One day Sharon started crying. She said she was scared of the dead black man. She told her sister and brother that the dead man was burnt. Alan and Shirley went over to her and found her staring at a mummy with some of the cloth unwrapped on his foot. The toes were all dried up and black. It scared the kids half to death and they ran out of the building in terror. After that, the children went to the castle but stayed away from the museum.

Esther's sisters came for a visit while the family lived in the hotel on Rice Street. Aunt Sylvia was her real sister and Aunt Lydia was her half sister. Aunt Sylvia and her husband, Harold, and Aunt Lydia and her husband, Tony, brought food, clothing and toys for the children.

Alan, Shirley and Sharon didn't really know what it was like to get presents and be treated special. They loved it. The problem was, with the presents came the cousins.

The cousins were all teenage boys. That was the first time Shirley and Sharon experienced sexual abuse. The teenagers began to touch the girls in their private places. The little girls didn't know there was anything wrong with what the boys were doing to them. They thought it was all part of the game. The cousins were around thirteen or fourteen years old and the Colburn sisters were four and six.

The apartment was very small, so the sofa bed was in the living room and it was usually left open for somebody to sleep on. The cousins messed with Shirley and Sharon on the sofa bed, right in front of their parents. The adults were already passed out drunk and could have cared less that the boys were sneaking drinks and molesting the two little girls.

It was a mixed blessing to see Aunt Sylvia and Aunt Lydia. With one hand they delivered food, toys and clothes, and with the other hand, they delivered the cousins.

Chapter Six

In Hot Soup

"Be quiet and stay out of the way, if you know what's good for you today," Alan whispered a warning to his sisters.

Since dawn, the auctioneer and his crew had been at Grandpa Colburn's farm preparing for the auction that was scheduled for that morning. Without Uncle Jack to help with the chores, Grandpa Colburn just couldn't keep up with the work. He decided he was too old to be a farmer any longer and it was time to sell the machinery and livestock while he could still get something for it.

An autumn chill was in the air and a cold drizzle fell. The barefoot girls stood beside their brother in the shelter of the corn-crib, each clinging to a piece of his dirty overalls.

"What's going to happen today?" Sharon asked fearfully. "Are they really going to sell us?"

The question caused Shirley to burst into silent sobs. Her fragile shoulders shook and terror burbled up from deep inside her chest.

The family had come, once again, to live in Turtle Lake with Grandpa Colburn. On that morning, Hale, who was nursing a headache, was irritated that Grandpa Colburn had asked him for help with the auction. The night before the big sale Esther had explained to her children that Grandpa was tired of the cows and was going to sell them all.

She added, "I'm tired of you kids, too, and I just might let you brats go to the highest bidder."

Soon, neighbors and the people who had read about the auction in the paper began to arrive. They parked their cars and trucks along the road and walked up the muddy driveway.

The auction crew had arranged the farm implements in the yard for easy inspection. The brown and white Guernsey cows, on display in the barn yard, mooed and milled around as if to say, "What's up, and why all the action?"

The children watched with dread, as one by one the cows and old farm machinery were auctioned off. As each cow was led away and each rusty implement left the farm yard, they waited to see if it would be their turn next.

A man wearing a wide brimmed straw hat raised his hand.

"Sold," the auctioneer shouted, and he stepped forward to haul the last cow away from the farm.

As the final sale was made, Hale angrily stomped toward the rundown house. His headache wasn't any better and he was hungry.

When he saw Esther, he bellowed in a white rage, "You bitch, I have to work out there in the rain, helping the old man, and here you sit on your fat ass doing nothing. You get me something to eat and get it now!" he screamed.

The shivering children knew the script of this horror movie. They ran for cover and hid safely behind the house.

"You want supper? I'll give you supper," shouted Esther as she dumped whole unwashed tomatoes from the garden into a dishpan. Then she poured in some milk and put the pan on the open fire out in the yard. That done, she went back into the house.

Hale went out to the auctioneer's small mobile home trailer and sat down with the man and Grandpa Colburn to figure out the "take" from the day's sale. The auctioneer had a mug of strong hot spiked coffee, which he shared with Hale and his father. There were smiles all around as the man peeled off twenty dollar bills to settle up with the Colburn's.

Nearly an hour and several drinks later, Esther staggered out of the house with the remains of a loaf of bread, covered in green mold. She broke the bread into chunks and dumped the moldy green pieces into the now boiling tomatoes.

"Soup's on," Esther hissed menacingly through her rotting teeth.

Hale sloshed through the mud on his way toward his nice warm supper. He took one look at the foul looking red and green mess, slapped his wife across her smirking face and spun on his heels. He staggered briefly and then, with exaggerated dignity, walked to the Ford, revved it up, and drove away.

Esther screamed, "You can't leave without me."

She lumbered after the old car, swearing and crying incoherently. She stood at the end of the driveway for a moment, as though to compose herself. Slowly she turned and strode purposefully toward the hot dishpan still boiling on the open fire.

Carefully, Esther filled three bowls with the noxious mixture. Sweetly she called her children.

"Come and get it before it gets cold," she said in the nicest voice she could muster.

The children had had nothing to fill their bellies since yesterday and it was nearly sundown. Their mother sounded so pleasant and they were so hungry. Hesitantly, the three little ones came forward to get a nice warm bowl of soup. Their little hands shook with eagerness and hunger. They had not been sure if they would eat today.

Alan was the first to taste the soup. It was so hot it burned the inside of his mouth and it tasted terrible. Reflexively, the scalding liquid spurted from his mouth.

"You too good to eat the food God put before you?" his mother demanded as she grabbed a handful of hair and pulled his head around to face her. "You'll eat this," she screamed as she began shoving hot spoonfuls into his mouth.

The children were forced to finish their hot foul tasting supper. When the bowls were empty, Esther smiled at them. In her sweetest and raspiest voice, she told them to go inside and get washed up.

The children slowly walked to the house, glancing over their shoulders as they went. They were never sure, and never safe.

Her anger spent, Esther staggered down the driveway to the road, turned left and headed to town.

Out of immediate danger, Alan helped the little girls clean up as best he could. Their faces were washed and their clothes were wiped off. Shirley was crying because her mouth was burning and Alan was hoarse from gagging and coughing while his mother force-fed him.

"I feel sick. I'm going to frow up," gasped Sharon as a red tidal wave spurted from her little mouth. "Blood," she cried between spasms. "Am I almost dead?"

With great effort, the three sick children crawled into their nest of rags and dirty blankets under the bed. They soon fell asleep in the relative safety of obscurity.

Chapter Seven

The ABC's

The smell of autumn was in the air. Long red and gold streaks of light extended across the pale sky from the west as the late summer sun began to set earlier each evening.

The Grey children, who lived across the road from Grandpa Colburn, were excited. Summer was almost over and school would soon begin. To celebrate the beginning of another school year, the Grey's planned a roller skating party in the haymow of their barn. The Colburn children were invited. They didn't know what a roller skating party was since they had never been to a party of any kind before.

A few weeks before the skating party, Alan had been sent to a neighboring farm to work. The Jillisons lived about a mile from Grandpa Colburn. At the age of eight, Hale and Esther decided that he was old enough to go to work and learn to take care of himself.

When the day arrived, Esther and Hale were not home so Grandpa Colburn said the girls could go to the party. Sharon and Shirley excitedly ran across the road and up the long driveway to the red barn on the Grey farm. Once inside, they became too shy to speak. They looked around and saw many people whirling past them on roller skates. Everyone was having a wonderful time.

"I wish Alan could be here," said Sharon as she stood clutching her sister Shirley by the arm.

Alan always helped the girls feel safe. He always made things fun and they had never been without their brother before.

The girls stood alone by the door watching until a boy named John came up to them and offered each of them a pair of roller skates to wear.

Little by little, the girls began to get their skating legs. Soon, they were gliding along with the others in a large circle.

Their little faces were flushed with sweat and excitement. They had never had such a good time. Soda pop and other treats were spread on a table along the side of the barn wall. Food! The little girls were in heaven. Before long, they were just as excited as everybody else to be going to school.

The Colburn children had little experience with school. Their family moved with such regularity that attending school had been almost impossible. That fall, they happened to be living, once again, with Grandpa Colburn in Turtle Lake.

Life was not easy for Alan at the Jillison's. He was treated like a hired man but was expected to go to school every day. At 4:30 a.m. every morning, he had to help milk the cows, feed the heifers, and clean the barn. When those chores were done, he would wash his face, eat breakfast, and then walk two miles to the little one-room country school.

When school was over for the day, Alan walked back to the Jillison's and immediately began his evening chores. If he had homework to do, forget it, there was no time. All of his schoolwork had to be finished while he was at school or it wouldn't get done.

One of the advantages Alan had over his sisters was that he always had food to eat. Mrs. Jillison would pack him a lunch. He also had a new pair of overalls, two new shirts, and a sturdy pair of shoes. When the cold wind started blowing in the late fall, Alan was given a warm jacket to wear.

Once Alan left the Colburn family unit, the only time he was allowed to see his little sisters was at school. Alan worried about his sisters. He knew they were enduring beatings and starvation. He worried when they didn't show up at school. He worried when he saw them with welts, bruises, and open cuts on their bodies. He worried because they looked so thin and weak, and he knew that he could no longer protect them.

Still, Alan missed his family. He remembered the times when he and his sisters had done things together, like the time Hale moved the family to Ladysmith. While they were there, he and Sharon found some kittens, tied them up and threw them in the river. Then there was the time he found some old tires and talked Sharon and Shirley into getting inside them and rolling down the hill into the water. He was glad they didn't all drown.

He wondered if being naughty had caused him to be sent away from his family. He was terribly lonesome for his sisters and Grandpa Colburn. Alan felt so alone and sad at the Jillison's that he just wanted to go back home, and he wanted to go to the skating party.

The children attended a one-room country school. Schoolhouses in rural areas were placed just a few miles apart so no one would have too far to walk.

Usually the school was one big room with an entrance into a small hallway where the children hung their coats and put their boots. Lunch boxes were kept in the coatroom as well. If you were lucky, your school would have a library tucked into a corner somewhere.

A country school in Wisconsin always had a wood stove in the back of the room that needed to be stoked in the cold weather. There would also be a water bubbler that had to be kept full of drinking water. Black chalkboards ran across the front of the room behind the teacher's desk and all assignments were written on the blackboards.

There could be as few as twelve to as many as thirty children attending a country school. All grades, from first to eighth, attended the same school. The eighth graders did their math, while the first graders were at the front of the room in reading class and so forth.

The country school teacher had to prepare lessons in English, math, science, reading, spelling, and social studies for eight different grades each day, five days a week. On top of that, the rural schoolteacher was required to teach one period of music and one period of art each week. Then there were special events to prepare for, such as the Christmas program.

The older children were given the best jobs. When the duty list was posted, Alan always ran to see if his name was on it. It was an honor to prime the big metal water pump outside, or to pump the squeaky handle up and down until the pail was full of water, or to carry the water pail inside to fill the bubbler, or to carry wood from the woodshed to fill the stove.

The most coveted duty, however, was flag duty. Every morning, as the children loudly recited the Pledge of Allegiance, two students held the flag at the front of the room. Then they took the flag outside and ran it up the flagpole. The final duty of the day was to run the flag back down the pole, fold it into a tri-cornered bundle and stow it away for the next school day. The students never, ever, let the flag touch the ground.

One thing Sharon learned on her first day of school was that if she wanted to talk to the teacher, she had to raise her hand with one finger pointing up. If she had to go to the toilet, she would have to raise her hand with two fingers pointing up.

She also learned that the other children's lunches were kept beside the door in the hall behind the classroom. Students had to go through the hall to go outside to the outhouse.

Every day, just before lunch, Sharon would use the two-finger method of getting permission to leave the room without supervision. Once in the hallway, she would open somebody's lunch box and take out some food. She would make sure everything was left nice and neat in the lunch box.

Sometimes a kid would say, "Hey, my apple is missing," or "Hey, my cookie is gone." Usually no one said anything and Sharon would happily munch on her treat while she was in the outhouse. Sharon was clever and careful not to leave any crumbs on her face or her clothes.

Alan was walking back from the outhouse one day, when he saw Sharon come out of school and walk in his direction. She looked up and was surprised and embarrassed when she saw him. He immediately knew the reason for her embarrassment was the cookie she was already chewing.

Sharon began to run, but Alan ran faster.

He tackled her to the ground, and hollered, "Don't you ever steal," he said to her. "You are better than that. Even if you starve, I don't want to see you steal."

"But I can't stand lard sandwiches any more," Sharon cried. "Sometimes I'm so hungry, my legs don't work."

From that time on, Alan shared his lunch, from Mrs. Jillison, with his sisters.

The girls at school were hard on the Colburn sisters. They were teased about their clothes. They were teased because they didn't smell good. They were teased because they admitted they didn't have a dolly.

Shirley always dreamed that things were different. She dreamed that she had a doll to talk about. She dreamed that she had toys, and that Santa Claus would come to the Colburn house. She sat alone on the swings at recess and dreamed.

Alan, Shirley and Sharon didn't know much about Christmas. There was never a Christmas tree at the Colburn house and there was no such thing as Santa. When the kids at school talked excitedly about Christmas, the Colburn children just didn't really know what they were talking about.

Shirley and Sharon were absent from school so often that when school was closed for the holidays, they didn't even realize it. Once, the girls walked to school in the freezing cold only to find the doors locked and the school empty. Their parents didn't know it was Christmas vacation.

One bone chilling Tuesday morning, Esther Colburn grabbed the edge of the tabletop, and with both hands, hoisted her bulk to a standing position. Her head ached when she had to move that early in the morning.

"Why do I have to do everything?" she moaned. "That no-good husband of mine should be helping me get these two brats to school."

Hale and Esther had a visit from the teacher on Monday. Miss Glass had come with a message, "If Sharon and Shirley are not in school every day, you'll be arrested. It's the law. Children have to be in school every day," she warned.

"I don't know why some people just can't mind their own damn business," grumbled Esther as she took a step forward to yell at the girls. "It's not my fault they didn't get themselves to school," she griped.

"Get outta this house," she screamed.

Sharon and Shirley had been hiding under their bed for almost two days. Without Alan there to protect them, they didn't know what to do, so they did their best to remain unnoticed.

Their parents didn't have any money to go to the tavern and they were drinking Grandpa Colburn's home brew. That meant danger! Esther and Hale were drinking at home. The little girls were too afraid to come out of the bedroom until their parents fell asleep. Thus, no school.

That morning, Esther was screaming for the girls, "Get out here, and get to school."

Sharon and Shirley hesitantly moved toward the kitchen. There stood Esther with a grimace on her face and a belt in her hand.

Esther started whacking the little girls with the belt. She was very careful not to hit them on the hands or the face. As they tried to get past her, she tripped them and pushed them to the floor.

"You told the teacher that your mama and daddy abuse you?" Esther screamed. "You think you're abused, you little bastards? Get up and get to school. If I hear another word about this, I'll kill you both."

Sharon and Shirley ran out the door. They didn't have winter jackets and their shoes had holes in them. They had no mittens so they tried to wrap their hands in their sweaters as they ran the mile to the schoolhouse. The snowbanks were high and the wind whistled past their uncovered ears. Almost every morning the girls ran most of the way to school just to keep warm. However, on this particular morning, they ran to stay alive.

A frigid gust of wind mixed with snow, burst into the schoolhouse with the Colburn girls. Miss Glass looked up from her desk. All of the children turned around to see what was happening.

Alan jumped up from his desk and ran to his little sisters.

"They're almost frozen!" he cried.

Miss Glass rushed to the door and closed it on the blizzard swirling outside. Next, she dragged the little girls to the wood stove, which was stoked and busy sending warmth into the corners of the room.

The teacher tried to thaw out their frozen hands and feet. She sandwiched their little hands between her own and rubbed, trying to get the circulation back into them. As she worked, Sharon and Shirley cried. Their hands and feet were numb. As Miss Glass rubbed, the feeling started to come back, and with feeling came unbearable pain.

Miss Glass pulled their shoes and socks off in order to work on their feet. That's when she found the fresh welts and bruises on the girls' legs. She turned them around and looked at their backs. She saw what she was afraid to see. The girls had been beaten and the teacher saw that their bodies were excruciatingly thin. The girls were shaking, not only from the cold, but from starvation as well.

She asked Alan to get her bag from beside her desk. She opened it up and offered Sharon and Shirley each one-half of her ham sandwich. The girls grabbed the sandwiches and ate as if they had never eaten food before. A determination like none other gripped Miss Glass by the heart, and set the wheels in motion to help the little Colburn girls.

Chapter Eight

A Night on the Town

Sometimes the night was just so dark the stars and the moon wouldn't dare try to pierce the ebony curtain. On such a night, Esther and Hale Colburn loaded their two little girls into the old Ford, and headed for a night on the town.

Ever since Miss Glass had warned them about the kids being absent from school, Esther insisted on taking them along to the tavern. She didn't want someone coming to the house and finding Shirley and Sharon alone.

Esther was not planning to spend anymore time in jail. The night she spent in jail in St. Paul was enough. She would never forgive Shirley for letting the landlord call the police. She vowed to get even with her somehow. Esther continually obsessed about revenge.

Hale drove up and parked the car right in front of Baker's Tavern in Turtle Lake. He was hungry for one of their famous hot beef sandwiches. He just wished Esther hadn't insisted on bringing those kids along. Now he would have to fork over more money for a hot beef for them, too. If he didn't, his drinking buddies would call him cheap.

The two little girls couldn't believe their good fortune. Mama and Daddy wanted to take them along. Maybe Mama and Daddy did love them after all. For the moment, life was good.

Sharon and Shirley felt like real princesses. They were given a bottle of Orange Crush soda pop to share. First, Shirley took a sip, and then Sharon took a sip. They continued sharing the bottle until the soda was gone.

Bar stools were made for spinning. The girls spun each other around, and jumped off the stools and then crawled up again. It was the most fun they'd had in a long time. The longer they were at the bar, the bolder they became. Soon, the little girls were running around like hoodlums yelling and knocking into things.

The bar was noisy. The adults were drinking and talking loudly while the jukebox blasted out country honky-tonk. Everybody was in a jolly mood. The girls watched Esther leaning on the bar and laughing with some people. They loved the sound of their mother's laughter. They rarely had the pleasure. Sharon and Shirley stopped running, stood still, and took in the sound of their mother's happiness.

Suddenly, Esther turned and stared at them. The look on her face was one of surprise. It was as if she had forgotten they existed. In her confusion, Esther shook her head and made a jerking movement in their direction with her upper body. The girls clung to each other and backed into the furthest corner from the bar.

They stayed quietly in the corner until Hale yelled, "Get in the car."

Once on the road, Shirley worried because her father was driving the car rather strangely. It was swaying from one side of the road to the other. Between yelling and trading nasty comments, Esther and Hale were chugging from a bottle. Shirley grabbed her little sister tight in her arms and waited in silent dread for something terrible to happen to them.

Suddenly, a car without taillights appeared in front of them. Hale didn't see the car soon enough and he ran full speed into the back end. The old Ford stopped with a bang, and Sharon was thrown onto the floor behind the driver's seat. Shirley ended up in a heap on the floor behind Esther.

The girls were scared and hurt but afraid to cry. They just sat on the floor of the back seat and waited for the storm they knew would come their way.

To their surprise, Hale and Esther didn't even care that the little girls were present. Hale tried to start the car over and over again. He pushed the button on the dashboard until the pathetic whining of the automatic starter ceased entirely.

Somehow through their haze, they understood that the police would be involved. Frantically, they began throwing opened wine and beer bottles out of the car.

Esther cussed at her husband, "God damn it, you bastard. I'm not spending another night in jail just because you can't drive."

Once the bottles were disposed of, Hale staggered over to the other vehicle and looked in the window. The man at the wheel wasn't moving. That scared Hale.

He began to rant, "That bastard in there looks dead."

Sharon wanted to see the dead man, but Shirley grabbed her and forced her to lie on the floor in the back seat. The girls heard the sirens and saw the swirling red light of the squad car. Shirley was sure the squad car was going to hit them, but it skidded to a halt just in time. The frightened little girls heard the gravel crunch as two policemen flung open their car doors and jumped out onto the road.

Rapid breathing, pounding hearts, and sheer terror riveted the little girls to the floor in the back seat of the stalled car. Within minutes, they could hear another siren and soon saw the swirling red lights of the ambulance speeding toward them. It was all so breathtaking their young minds couldn't comprehend what was happening.

The injured man in the other car was hauled into the ambulance and whizzed away, amid flashing lights and the ear-shattering wail of sirens. The little girls listened as the noise grew dim and finally disappeared into the cold Wisconsin night.

Esther and Hale talked, argued with, and cussed at the two policemen. Try as they may, they couldn't talk the policemen into believing they only had one beer. The little girls watched through the rear window of the wrecked car, as their mama and daddy were put into the back seat of the police car and driven away.

One of the policemen stayed behind with the two girls. He tried to talk to them but they were far too upset to answer any of his questions.

"Where are you taking my Mama and Daddy?" Sharon sobbed uncontrollably.

"Don't worry," the policeman said in a kind voice. "The social worker will be here in a few minutes."

The policeman dug into his pocket and produced a chocolate candy bar. He broke it in half and handed each of them a piece.

Soon a shiny new Nash Rambler pulled up beside the disabled Ford. A lady in a pretty blue dress stepped out of the car and spoke a few words to the policeman. The policeman introduced the social worker to the frightened girls. Then he told them they were going to Grandpa Colburn's house. Suddenly things didn't look so bad. They were going home.

Once inside Grandpa Colburn's house, the social worker looked around with her nose all wrinkled up. She looked like she'd smelled a skunk. The nice lady in the blue dress made several notes in her folder and then told the girls to get cleaned up and crawl into bed.

Sharon and Shirley were so tired they practically fell into their bed of dirty blankets and rags. They clung to each other and drifted off to sleep almost immediately.

The girls awoke in the morning to find Esther and Hale sitting on the floor beside them. They cringed and tried to get as far away as they could, but their mother assured them she wouldn't hurt them.

"We have to go to court in Baldwin today," Esther said almost kindly. "I want you to tell the judge that you want to stay with us. Tell him that you don't want to be taken away from us."

That was easy. The two little girls did not want to be taken away. They didn't really know what "taken away" meant. They only knew one way of life, and in the way of many abused children, they loved their mama and daddy. The girls imagined that Alan would come back and live with them, too. They wanted the Colburn family together again. Fear of the unknown was worse than fear of their abusers.

The terrified sisters left the courthouse in the back seat of a car, driven by a woman they had never seen before. Sobbing quietly, they clung to each other and wondered if being taken away meant they were going to be killed.

Sharon whispered hoarsely, "I feel like I'm going to fall into the open well."

Chapter Nine

Foster Care

Sharon woke up crying. Everything was so very strange in the quiet room and she had to go pee. Bad! Where was she and what was the terrible feeling of panic flooding over her?

A thin silver streak ran across the wall as the moon's light came filtering through the window. She crept out of bed and walked toward the door. Then she suddenly remembered where she was. This was the foster home.

She and Shirley had gone on a long car ride, which took them far away from their brother, Alan, and their parents. Fear enveloped her as her mind began its journey backwards. She wondered where Alan was and if he was safe.

Just as she stepped through the door to find the bathroom, a sleepy eyed woman came out of the bedroom across the hall. The woman wore a worn nightgown with a robe hastily thrown over her shoulders. Sharon watched the belt of the robe drag on the floor as the strange woman came toward her in the dim light.

"Get to sleep before you wake everybody up," the woman said in a menacing voice.

She pushed Sharon back into the moonlit bedroom.

Sharon was so scared of the woman that she couldn't think of her name or what she looked like in the daylight. Fear took away her need to go to the bathroom. She stood inside the bedroom door unable to move.

Then she heard her sister whisper, "Come here, and sleep next to me. I'll take care of you."

That was Sharon's introduction to her new home. A woman named Ellie, who worked at the grocery store in St. Croix, Wisconsin, was going to be her new mother. Ellie's husband, Don, a farmer, was her new dad.

For almost a year, the sisters lived in the three-story farmhouse with their foster parents. For the first time in their lives, Shirley and Sharon had a real bedroom of their own. Their new room had two windows with curtains, and a bed with clean sheets and blankets.

Even though they missed their brother terribly, they felt lucky to be in such a beautiful and clean place. Every morning they would get dressed and put on socks and shoes. Their morning ritual was a real luxury for two girls, who in the past, didn't even have shoes to wear.

Once dressed, they followed the aroma down to the kitchen, where Ellie was busy cooking breakfast for everyone. What a wonderful experience to have all the food they could eat set before them. Each morning there would be bacon, eggs, and biscuits—not to mention fresh milk with heavy cream floating on top, just waiting for Don and the girls to dig in. The girls began to gain some weight.

Shirley and Sharon had the task of setting the great big kitchen table that was covered with a pretty red and white tablecloth. Once the dishes were on the table, they would all sit down to eat.

After breakfast, the girls had to help with the dishes and get ready for school. That was a time in their lives of new experiences, which included their first ride on a school bus. Unlike the school in Turtle Lake, the school in St. Croix was too far away for them to walk, and therefore required transportation.

Since the sisters hadn't attended school much, it was hard to decide what grade level they should go into. Sharon was put into first grade and the teachers decided to put Shirley into third grade.

Sharon did not want to leave Shirley and go with all those new kids. She hated school because she had to sit for hours at a desk, instead of being free to run and play.

Shirley didn't like going to school, either. She had trouble with her studies and just couldn't seem to see the papers clearly. On top of that, she felt left out. Everybody already had their group of friends and she was not invited to join them.

At recess, Shirley would go to the playground and swing by herself. She wished she were somewhere else. She believed that if she wished hard enough, somehow, it would happen, and she'd miraculously be gone.

The new school sat on a very high hill. To get to the street below, people had to use steps that seemed almost straight up and down. There was a wire fence across the schoolyard with a gate leading to the stairs.

Sharon always wanted to go down those steps but the teacher said, "Any student who goes down those steps will be in big trouble."

When Sharon complained to her about the rules regarding the steps, Shirley said, "Don't you ever go near that gate because I'm afraid you might fall."

Sharon made her sister a promise that she would never forget about the steps.

One day, while out for recess, Sharon was playing with another little girl. After recess was over, the little girl told the teacher that Sharon had torn her coat. A note was sent home to Ellie. No one believed Sharon when she explained that she had not torn the other girl's coat. In the end, Sharon was sent to bed without her supper.

In the solitude of her bedroom, Sharon wondered why no one ever believed her. In the past, she had been punished with beatings, and had been denied supper. Now, in this beautiful new home, food was still being used as a punishment.

In anger, she decided she hated them all. She would show them! From that day forward, hatred and fear fueled the strength that carried Sharon toward survival. It had become clear to her. With Alan gone, the only person left who loved her was Shirley, and she loved Shirley back.

One day Ellie received a note from the teacher telling her that Shirley was having trouble reading. The teacher thought Shirley might need glasses. Ellie made an appointment with the eye doctor and took Shirley for an exam. The little girl was scared to death. She thought the doctor was going to take her eyes out of her head to examine them.

Shirley had a lazy eye and the doctor ordered a pair of glasses for her.

"Glasses!" Shirley was elated.

One of the most popular girls in her school wore glasses. Life was good.

For two weeks, Shirley eagerly anticipated the arrival of her glasses. When they finally came, she was bitterly disappointed. The doctor had put a patch over her right lens to help strengthen her lazy left eye.

Shirley thought she looked very ugly in her new glasses. Now instead of being popular, Shirley was teased and called the "one-eyed monster."

She decided to stay home from school and never go back. Ellie was having none of that nonsense, so Shirley made the best of her new look. She decided it was better to endure the teasing at school. She sure didn't want Ellie mad at her.

At Christmas time, Don and Ellie took the kids to the Balsam Lake School where his mother, Grandma Mabel, was a teacher. All the children stayed in the basement of the school while the adults made preparations for the Christmas program. A tall eighth-grade boy named Karl brought his black and white dog, Sparky, with him to the school. The dog was in the basement with the children, and because he was a spotted dog, the kids called him a "fire dog."

Some of the children played school and took turns writing on the blackboard, pretending they were teachers. Others played games of Tic-Tac-Toe or Hangman, while they waited for the adults to finish upstairs. Sharon and Shirley had never had so much fun.

Suddenly, Sparky started barking and Karl couldn't get him to be quiet. Then someone smelled smoke coming from a door to the left of the steps. A fire had broken out in the furnace room. A seventh grade girl named Ruth ran up the steps to tell her mother about the smoke. The adults came running.

One parent ran to the nearest house to call the fire department. A couple of parents made sure all the children were out of the building and safely inside the cars and trucks in the parking lot. Everyone else did their best to put the fire out.

The screaming sound of the sirens and the flashing lights of the fire truck and squad cars brought Sharon to a terrifying pitch of fright. She sobbed uncontrollably in Shirley's lap, as memories of other flashing lights and howling sirens came flooding back.

In time, Shirley was able to comfort her sister, and the crying and trembling ceased. Once Sharon was more comfortable, the girls watched what was happening right outside their car window. It was very interesting and fun to watch the firemen do their job. Sharon thought girls couldn't be firemen but she didn't care.

She said, "I'm going to be a fireman when I grow up and I'm going to have a fire dog, too."

The schoolhouse was damaged, but did not burn to the ground. Sparky was having trouble breathing and he had some singed fur on his back. Karl and his father put him in their pickup and drove him to the animal doctor. The day ended well. The school could be rebuilt, and none of the children were hurt. Karl's dog, Sparky, was credited with saving the lives of the children. The fire dog became a local hero.

When Alan moved in with the Jillison's, he was only eight years old. Now he would be eleven, and the girls had not seen their brother since they had been put in foster care.

One Sunday in early March, the Jillison's brought Alan to see his sisters. It was so good to see him that the girls couldn't stop looking at him. Ellie invited the Jillison's and Alan to stay for Sunday dinner. All Shirley and Sharon wanted to do was sit next to their brother and touch him.

During dinner, the Jillison's told the girls that their father, Hale Colburn, had hung himself. He was dead. Sharon, who would soon be seven, sat looking from Shirley to Alan to see how she should respond to the news. For some reason, she couldn't remember what her father even looked like.

Nine-year-old Shirley began to cry.

"I want to go to the funeral," she sobbed.

"It's too late. He killed himself right after Christmas," Mrs. Jillison said unsympathetically. "They buried him January first."

Alan sat with his head down as if he were studying his plate of food. No emotion came from him at all. His face and eyes looked cold as a stone.

Without raising his head, Alan said, "Ma killed him," his raspy voice forcing its way through his clenched teeth.

"Don't be silly, Alan. Where do you get these crazy ideas?" chided Mrs. Jillison, with a condescending smile on her lips. "Kids these days," she added, and followed her statement with a couple of clicks with her tongue.

The girls didn't know that this visit would be the last time they would see their big brother for many years to come. As Alan and the Jillison's walked to the car, Sharon and Shirley skipped along beside him, chattering away and making plans to see him soon. The girls stood in the drive, waving until the car was out of sight. Then they skipped back to the house, and happily went to play in their beautiful bedroom.

Later in the spring, Shirley and Sharon went on a field trip with their school to see the Ringling Brothers Circus. They had never seen anything so spectacular in their entire lives. They just couldn't contain their excitement.

They laughed hysterically at the antics of the many colorful clowns. They watched in awe as beautiful ladies, dressed in pink, twirled high above them on the trapeze.

Real live elephants walked in front of them, swinging their trunks high in the air. Big cats stood on their hind legs and did tricks to the crack of the lion tamer's whip.

Sharon imagined herself in a sparkling costume, bravely standing on the back of one of the beautiful white horses. She felt the wind in her hair as the beautiful white steed galloped around the ring, rearing and pawing the air in front of the cheering crowd.

Shirley had never tasted popcorn before and the smell of it made her mouth water. The girls nearly died when the teacher handed each of them a box of popcorn.

The sisters loved everything about the circus. To this day, the Ringling Brothers Circus remains one of Shirley's most cherished childhood memories. Sharon decided that heaven couldn't even be this good, as she watched all the acts gather together for their final bow.

Once school was finally out for the summer, Shirley and Sharon would often go out and play in the hayfield, while the men cut the hay. They would get to ride on top of the hay, as the horse-drawn wagon slowly rolled to the barn. Once in awhile, Don would let them ride on the backs of the big draft horses. Sharon always pretended she was riding in the circus when she was on the back of one of the horses.

Shirley secretly imagined she was a beautiful princess, riding toward her brother who lived in the castle.

Though the girls were in a beautiful home with plenty of food and clothes, they still could not relax and just enjoy themselves. They never quite knew when trouble would strike, but they knew it always would.

One morning, while Ellie fixed breakfast, she accused Shirley of eating the last piece of pie. Shirley denied it and told Ellie that repeatedly. Little Shirley was telling the truth, but Ellie thought she was lying and being sassy. All at once, Ellie grabbed a plastic pancake turner with holes in it and hit Shirley across the face.

The loud slapping sound cracked like a bullwhip, while the holes in the spatula made permanent marks on the right side of Shirley's face. She never made a sound, but the tears came streaming down her swelling cheek.

When the girls finally left the kitchen and went to their room, Shirley cried and so did Sharon. Later that day, it was revealed that Don had helped himself to that piece of pie before he went to the barn to do his morning chores. No one ever said, "I'm sorry."

Shirley and Sharon often talked about running away. They wanted to try to get back to Turtle Lake and find their brother, Alan. They wanted all three of them to be together, forever. They wanted to be with Alan so much that it nearly killed them to think of him.

The one time they tried running away, they packed their meager treasures into a sack and got ready. As they were sneaking out of the house, the sky opened up and it began to pour. Wild streaks of lightning flashed and crackled across the blackened sky. Great booms of thunder pierced their little hearts with fear. After that, they were afraid to run away again.

Usually on Saturdays, Ellie and Don went to St. Croix to shop for groceries. They usually left the girls at home with Grandma Mabel. One Saturday while they were gone, Shirley and Sharon were playing outside. What started out as simply making mud pies, turned into the fun game of, "Who can smear the most mud on the side of the house?" Boy, when Ellie and Don came home, the girls were really in for it.

"If you want to wallow in the mud like the pigs, you can stay with them!" Ellie screamed when she saw their handiwork.

The girls had been warned never to go into the pigpen. Ellie had said the mama pig would kill them if she ever got hold of them.

"Please, please, please," the terrified little girls cried and begged. "We won't do it again. Please don't throw us in with the pigs."

Violently, Ellie grabbed the girls by the arms and literally dragged them to the pigpen. She dumped them unceremoniously over the fence into the muddy space. They landed on top of a mama sow and her new little piglets.

In a panic, they scrambled to the little shelter on the side of the pen, which had been constructed as a shelter for the piglets. The big sow tried to grab the girls as they scrambled into the shelter. They huddled together in terror.

They soon realized that the mother pig was too big to get into the shelter. They calmed down and eventually began to enjoy the antics of the little piglets. Those baby pigs were so cute and pink. Sharon wanted to touch them. They would come close enough for her to reach out and touch them, but the minute she did, they would squeal, jump sideways, and fall all over each other to get back to their mama.

Somewhere deep in her seven-year-old brain, Sharon knew Jack, the farm dog, would protect them. He could create a diversion so they could get out of the pigpen without the sow eating them. The little girls called and called until the dog came leaping over the fence and into the pigpen. The mama sow took after Jack and forgot all about the two girls huddled in the little shelter. Jack's repeated barking soon became a yelping for help, as the mother pig charged him again and again.

Don came running over to see what was wrong with Jack. He was so mad when he saw that the girls had put his dog in such danger that he took them out of the pigpen and hauled them roughly into the house. He threw them into a closet and locked the door. It was dark in there and the little girls were shaking with fear.

Their history told them not to cry out, or the punishment would just get bigger. They also knew they would not get any supper. Chilled to the bone, the sisters just sat there shivering and holding onto each other. The smell of pig poop made them sick to their stomachs, and took away their appetites, anyway.

After that episode, Sharon and Shirley did everything they could to be invisible. They set the table on cue, made their beds, and kept their room clean. Ellie did not have to ask them twice for help, and they didn't say a word that would be taken as sass. They had made a decision to be so good that they would never be spanked, starved, or put in the dark closet again.

Ellie and Don responded very well to the perfect behavior of their foster daughters. Soon, things seemed to go well at the big white farmhouse in St. Croix. Don took to whistling while he worked in the barn and out in the fields. Sometimes Ellie could be heard singing and humming as she worked around the house. She didn't even complain about driving all the way to town to get to work at the grocery store.

A month or so after the pigpen incident, a lady came to the house carrying a baby boy, all wrapped up in a new blue blanket. The girls marveled at how cute and tiny he was. Shirley asked if she could hold him. The lady helped her sit on the couch and put the baby in her lap. Then she took out a bottle, and asked Ellie to warm it in a pan of water, on the kitchen stove. When the bottle was the right temperature, the lady handed it to Shirley, and helped the elated little girl feed the baby his bottle.

Shirley and Sharon soon found out why Ellie and Don were so happy. The lady was a social worker. She had brought the little baby boy to live, in foster care, with Don and Ellie.

The next day, Ellie sat the two girls down on the couch and told them, "You are going to a new home." Then she added, "Your new foster parents are colored people."

Neither Sharon nor Shirley had ever known a black person before, and they had no idea about them. The way Ellie sneered, they figured it was not a good thing.

The girls were not allowed to take anything with them.

Ellie said, "All of your clothes and toys have to stay here. The only things you can take are your shoes and the dresses the welfare lady will bring with her when she comes to take you away."

Shirley's dress was pink satin, and Sharon's dress was blue satin with a big white collar. The welfare lady brought one set of underwear for each of the girls, and a pair of anklets to match their dress.

The lady helped the sobbing girls put on their new dresses. Without saying goodbye, Ellie turned her back and picked up the baby.

"Remember the open well?" Shirley whispered to her sister. "I feel just like that."

The little girls clung to each other in the back seat of the strange car. They were afraid to look back, as they were driven away.

Esther and Hale Colburn,with Alan and baby Shirley. Taken in 1940.

Grandpa Colburn. All dressed up, outside the house in Turtle Lake.

Hale Colburn and baby Sharon.
Taken in Cornell in 1943.

Alan, Sharon, and Shirley.

Book Two...

Life as Joyce and Jane Buck.

Chapter Ten

Welcome to Cornell

It seemed like hours that the little girls rode in silence before they crossed a bridge and drove past a mill. Large chunks of wood fell from a stacker onto a huge pile. The car passed a sign with WELCOME TO CORNELL printed on it.

"We've been here before," Shirley told her sister, with authority. "We lived here when you were a baby. People here know us," she said, as relief washed over her, and some of the tension began to fade.

The girls sat up straighter in the back seat and watched as they drove under the railroad bridge, up a big hill, and then turned onto Main Street.

"I don't see the house we lived in, but this is the town," Shirley said quietly.

They passed many stores with cars parked in front of them. As they went past the stores, they noticed a park and a school. Across the street from the school, they began to see trees and pretty houses on both sides of the street.

The welfare lady pulled up and stopped the car in front of a large green house with two great big oak trees and a white birch tree in front. Several tall pine trees surrounded the huge front yard.

"This is where you are going to live," said the lady as she moved to open her car door.

Shirley and Sharon were afraid. All of the relief Shirley had felt a few minutes before had evaporated into thin air. She didn't want to get out of the car, but then she saw a black dog with its tail curled up over its back.

He was beautiful and he came straight up to the car wagging that curly tail.

From somewhere behind the house, a woman's voice called out to the dog, "Smokey, Smokey."

The girls peeked out through the car window and saw a white man and woman walking toward them. They were relieved to see that Ellie was mistaken. The people were white and the dog was black.

The welfare lady jumped out of the Nash Rambler as soon as it stopped moving. Her voice was raised in excitement as she called loudly to the man and woman approaching them. With a swoop, she flung open the car door and effectively removed the safety barrier between the little girls and these strange people.

Sharon and Shirley clung to each other and stared. The black dog, Smokey, jumped through the open car door into Shirley's lap and planted a big, wet, pink doggy tongue on her cheek. She let out a squeal of surprised delight and realized she had been holding her breath.

She smiled at Smokey and slowly reached out to stroke his gentle black head. Shirley Colburn felt her heart thaw a little. She began to imagine this was the home she had been dreaming of. Hesitantly, she climbed from the back seat of the car, never letting go of her little sister's hand. She was the oldest and it was her responsibility to lead Sharon into their beautiful new life.

The welfare lady took each girl by the hand and followed the man and woman to the big green house. Smokey continued to jump around and licked at the giggling girls as they followed the sidewalk to the front door.

When they reached the top step, the door opened as if by magic. A kind looking old gentleman opened the door and asked them to come inside.

He held out his hand to Sharon, and then to Shirley, and then said, "Hello, I am your Grandpa Bailey."

Grandpa Bailey smelled clean and was dressed like a picture in a storybook. He smelled and looked nothing like Grandpa Colburn. For Shirley and Sharon, it was a case of love at first sight.

Shirley and Sharon were introduced to their new mama and daddy. Mama's name was Hazel and Daddy's name was Ted. The girls looked at their new mama and saw tears shining in her eyes. They couldn't believe what they saw. Nobody had ever been happy to have them around before—not happy enough to cry about it, anyway.

Hazel offered them all a cup of tea and a piece of fresh baked cake. The girls trembled and their little mouths watered with anticipation. They were so happy to be in this beautiful green house, with this happy loving mother who baked super-delicious cake. They just knew life was going to be wonderful from this moment on.

Soon the welfare lady said it was time for her to go. Shirley couldn't wait for her to leave. She was scared to be in a new family, but even worse was the thought of the lady taking them away with her.

Ted told the lady he would walk her to the car and get the girls' bags.

"Oh, they don't have any bags. They only have the clothes they are wearing," the lady answered.

Hazel said, "Well, Ted, I guess we'd better take these girls downtown and get them some underwear and pajamas. The rest can wait until tomorrow when we have more time to drive to Chippewa Falls to shop for them."

Sharon and Shirley couldn't believe their ears. Their new mama was going to take them shopping and buy them new things to wear. They clung to each other and stared.

Cornell had a business district at the west end of Main Street. The street climbed steadily up hill toward the east until it leveled off a bit. An elementary school stood on the right and the city park sat on the left. Just past the school and park, lawns with trees and houses marked the beginning of the residential part of Main Street. At the east end of the residential area, forcing a decision whether to turn right or left, stood the Catholic church.

The house where they would live was in the residential part of Main Street, on the same side of the street as the school. Since the downtown shopping area was only a few blocks from the house, the new family set out for a nice afternoon walk. They went downtown to buy the necessary things for two little girls who had arrived with nothing but the clothes on their backs.

Ted Buck was a thin man with a slouched posture, who wore glasses and a look of importance. Hazel Buck was a tall, slim, well-dressed pretty woman, who spoke kindly to her husband. The girls were mesmerized as they watched and listened to their new mother and father. The contrast they saw between the Bucks and their real parents, Hale and Esther Colburn, was startling.

Sharon walked shyly beside her new mother, holding her hand for dear life, while Shirley held her new father's hand. They stared straight ahead. Shirley was afraid of the people around her. She was afraid to make a mistake and upset her new parents. She was afraid she would wake up and find this was only a dream.

It didn't take long for Hazel to select the pajamas, toothbrushes, and underwear the girls needed for their first night as her daughters. When the clerk rang up the items, Ted surprised them by adding two lollipops to the pile on the counter. Outside the store, their new daddy dug into the bag and gave Sharon a cherry sucker and Shirley an orange one. The girls sucked and smiled, smiled and sucked all the way home.

Smokey was waiting for them in the yard. He jumped around and circled them as they walked toward the front door. Sharon got tangled up and fell down on the cement sidewalk. Ted picked her up and carried her into the house. He set her down on a chair in the kitchen, while Hazel went to get a band-aid for her knee.

Shirley knew what would come next, so she closed her eyes and waited to hear the sounds of her new parents screaming that Sharon should be more careful. She waited to hear the sounds of Sharon being beaten with a belt for being careless. She waited, but the familiar sounds didn't come. Instead, she heard her new momma softly talking to Sharon, while she washed her knee and made it feel better.

Ted, Hazel, and Grandpa Bailey showed the girls around their new home. Shirley and Sharon couldn't believe their eyes. The rooms were filled with beautiful furniture and curious things that looked like they belonged in the St. Paul museum.

Fear began to take hold of them as they went from room to room. How would they be able to live in this house without breaking something beautiful? Sharon decided she would walk with her arms tight at her sides at all times. She had been told her entire life that she was clumsy and she didn't want a beating from her new mama and daddy.

Up the stairs they went, to the bedroom. It was small and cozy with new curtains and bedspread, just right for two sisters to share. Sharon and Shirley were breathless with excitement and happiness.

The only reprimand of the first day came at suppertime. The smell of delicious food made its way all around the big house. The new family sat down to a homemade dinner of roast chicken, mashed potatoes, gravy and corn. By the time their plates were full, and grace had been said, the girls were so hungry, they grabbed the food and began to shovel it into their mouths with their bare hands.

Ted let out a snort and Hazel almost choked. Sharon and Shirley didn't know a thing about table manners. In the past, they grabbed and ate whatever they could find. It didn't matter to them if they used a fork or not.

"Stop," said Ted in a loud voice. "We eat like ladies in this house."

He took his knife and whacked each girl on the back of the hand.

"Use your forks and slow down. That food isn't going anywhere."

The girls were stunned. They sat back in their chairs trying to disappear, and waited for the beating that was sure to come. Hazel only smiled at them and showed the two sisters the proper way to hold a fork. Then she gave them a lesson on the right way to use a knife to cut their meat.

After supper, Hazel asked Sharon and Shirley to clear the table while she washed the dishes. When that chore was finished, she told them to go into her bedroom and wait, because she and Ted had something very important to talk to them about.

The girls cautiously entered their new parent's bedroom and crawled up onto the bed. They were afraid of messing up the pretty satin coverlet, so they sat very, very still.

"I bet they are going to send us away because we ate like pigs," Sharon whispered.

"Or else they are going to beat us! Maybe we should run away now," Shirley whispered as she started to slide off the bed.

Just then, Hazel, Ted, and Grandpa Bailey walked through the door. Grandpa Bailey smiled at the girls. When Sharon looked into his kind blue eyes, she instantly relaxed. She felt safe when Grandpa Bailey was nearby. Shirley, on the other hand, was very frightened. She didn't trust anybody.

Hazel and Ted sat on the bed with their new daughters sandwiched between them. Grandpa Bailey sat quietly in a chair in a corner of the bedroom.

Hazel put her arm around Shirley and began, "We have made the decision to adopt you. You will legally become our daughters in about a year. Once we get through the first year, no one can take you away from us," she said kindly. "We want you to be happy here and we want you to be our daughters," she added.

"I have always wanted two little girls named Jane Alice and Joyce Mary, so we have decided to change your names," Hazel continued. "It is up to you to choose which name you want."

Shirley spoke up first. It was easy for her to choose. There had been a girl in her school in Turtle Lake named Joyce Armstrong. Joyce had been nice to Shirley and she wanted to be named after such a nice girl.

Sharon didn't care. She didn't want to change her name. If she changed her name, how would her brother, Alan, find her and save her if she got into big trouble? What if Esther tried to find her? Sharon secretly hoped Esther would decide she really did love her and would want her back.

Ted and Hazel did not detect the turmoil going on inside of Sharon. They took her silence for acceptance.

The night their new names were chosen, Sharon and Shirley "died." Just as the mythical bird, Phoenix, rose from the ashes of death, Joyce and Jane emerged with renewed hope, faith, joy, and fear.

With the help of their mother, they put on their new pajamas and brushed their teeth. Hazel and Ted followed them up the stairs to tuck them in and say good night. It took the sisters quite awhile to fall asleep. Their new bedroom felt very strange to them, as they practiced in the dark so they wouldn't forget their new names.

Thus, Sharon Ann Colburn, "Desert Princess," age seven years and nine months, became Jane Alice Buck. Shirley Maye Colburn, "Bright Meadow," age ten, became Joyce Mary Buck.

Chapter Eleven

One Year in Paradise

The world of happy living progressed like the gradual unfurling of tulip petals in the early spring. The sisters practiced their new names and quickly became Joyce and Jane. Eventually, joy began to replace sorrow, and hunger eased toward a forgotten memory.

Alan Colburn, however, would never be forgotten. Joyce wrote her brother's name on a piece of pink paper, which she placed with her most important possessions in her treasure box.

Jane said a silent prayer for her brother every night. She prayed that he would not forget her. She prayed he would come to see them. Sometimes her prayers would be answered and he would come to her in a dream. She didn't tell anyone. It was a secret time she shared with the brother she loved with all her heart.

On the Saturday after their arrival in Cornell, Hazel and Ted took their new daughters to Chippewa Falls on their first shopping trip. That trip was surely a trip to remember. The girls received more new things in two hours than their old family had bought in five years.

The first stop was J.C. Penney's, on the corner of Bridge Street and Grand Avenue. Neither of the girls had ever been inside a real clothing store before. They didn't quite know how things were done, so they just stood wide-eyed and stared.

They watched Hazel pick out a skirt and say, "Joyce, isn't this pretty?"

Then she held it up to Joyce to check the size. If it fit properly, she would put it atop the growing pile on the counter.

The girls nearly fainted with joy and disbelief when Hazel selected a colorful beaded Indian skirt for each of them. These were called squaw skirts and everybody at school had one. Joyce and Jane agreed their new mother had saved the best for last.

When the pile of clothing had become a mountain, Ted stepped up to the counter and took a small book from his pocket. He wrote in it with his pen, then tore out a sheet of paper and handed it to the clerk. She put their new clothes in several bags, and then gave him a long thin sheet of paper in return. That was all there was to it.

Their new daddy must be very important, because they saw that he didn't have to pay money for their things. He must be really popular because he just had to write something on a piece of paper and he could get whatever he wanted.

Hazel said she was hungry and asked if anyone wanted to stop for lunch at Skogmo's. Ted said he was ready to eat, and led the way to the café.

Again, Joyce and Jane didn't know what to do. They were so scared. They would have to eat in front of strangers, and they knew they didn't want to be reprimanded in public. The little girls clung to each other, and tried to disappear as they followed their new mama and daddy into the café.

The girls just stared at the waitress when she came to their booth and said, "Hi, my name is Sandy. I'll be your server. What can I get for you?"

"We will all have chicken and biscuits, chocolate milk for the girls, and black coffee for Ted and me," Hazel ordered.

Jane looked around the little café and wondered why everybody was so quiet in this tavern. The people sitting at the bar were drinking coffee instead of beer, and it smelled so different. Music was playing softly and the only noise came from plates clanging together as the dishwasher put them on the shelves. Nobody was swearing, and most of the people smiled if they noticed her looking at them.

Joyce whispered, "Jane, use your fork."

Hazel and Ted just smiled and ignored their poor table manners. When they were done with their main meal, the waitress brought them each a piece of banana cream pie.

Dessert!!! How good could life be?

The next stop was K & S Bootery, across the street from Skogmo's Café. Hazel wanted to go there because they had an x-ray machine. The machine helped parents be sure the shoes fit their child well.

Jane chose a pair of shiny black patent leather dress shoes, while Joyce's were red with a pretty narrow strap across the front. The clerk helped put the beautiful new shoes on their feet. Then she asked Joyce to step up on the platform and slide her feet into the slots in the front of the machine. Joyce got to look into one viewfinder and Hazel looked into the other. When the clerk pushed the button, Joyce and her mother both saw the bones of Joyce's toes snuggled into her brand new red shoes.

"These fit just fine," said Hazel.

Joyce grinned with sheer joy.

"Jane, it's your turn," she said as she helped her little daughter put her feet into the slots.

Jane was always inquisitive. She couldn't help herself. She reached over and pushed the button herself. Both Hazel and the shoe store man laughed at her. She felt very special as she looked at her feet inside her new black shoes.

"We'll take them," said Hazel, as Ted stepped up to the counter and wrote on another piece of paper.

"Do you want to wear them?" asked the man.

Hazel nodded and her daughters grinned. Their feet took wing as they danced up the street to the waiting car. Nobody in the world had prettier shoes than Joyce and Jane Buck.

As Hazel and Ted loaded the bags into the car, the two little girls cautiously walked over to them and hugged their legs.

On the way home to Cornell, the girls fell asleep in the back seat of the car. They were totally contented and their fears were leaving fast. They were thankful for the kind people who were going to adopt them.

The girls were told they had a one-year waiting period before they could be adopted. At the end of the probation time, they would go to court and legally become Joyce Mary and Jane Alice Buck. Joyce and Jane vowed they would be good and they would make sure that Hazel and Ted would still want them when it was time to go to court.

That was a magical year. Joyce took a calendar and marked off each day that went by on the yearlong quest to legally becoming Ted and

Hazel's daughters. The two young princesses soon learned that the way into this family hinged on good behavior and complete submission.

Hazel and Ted kept the girls close to them. They seldom let them even play with the kids in the neighborhood. Hazel worried that her new daughters would be hurt. She also worried that they would misbehave in front of her friends. Hazel cared very much what the neighbors thought.

Ted was very sweet to the girls. He watched over them like an old mother hen. He decided what they should eat, wear, and how they should have their hair cut. Sadly, as the probationary year went on, Ted gradually broadened his control over the sisters.

As his attention to their needs expanded, the love and trust they felt for him grew. In time, the sisters did everything their father asked, without question. Ted began to call Joyce, "Pumpkin." She loved it and felt very close to him when he called her by that special name.

Soon the girls were so secure in his love that they began to forget about the life they had left behind. The longing they felt for Esther, Hale, and Alan began to vanish. Ted became the daddy whom they loved.

Hazel truly loved her new daughters. She loved it that Jane smiled almost all the time. She began to call Jane "Sunshine." The nickname made Jane smile even more. Hazel sewed dresses and baked cookies especially for the girls. She pulled them up onto her lap, and hugged and kissed them whenever she could. She smiled often and she smelled like home baked bread. Hazel became the mama whom they loved.

Even now, school was not the favorite place for either of the girls. Joyce was put in the fourth grade. However, after a short time, the teacher realized she should be at the third grade level. She had missed so much school when she was with her other family that she had to struggle with her studies everyday, just to keep up.

Jane became a first grader, again. She did well, but she found it very hard to sit still for all those hours. She would rather be outside playing with Smokey in the big tree-lined yard.

On one particular Thursday morning, exactly one year and three days after Sharon and Shirley had arrived in Cornell, Hazel called up the steps to remind the girls to put on their satin dresses and their new shoes. Today was the big day. Today they would legally become Joyce Mary and Jane Alice Buck.

Joyce hadn't slept well the night before. She was scared to death that her new mama and daddy might decide not to go through with the adoption. She knew she had been good, but she also knew that grownups were not to be trusted.

Jane had slept like a log. She didn't have a care in the world. Today she would legally become the daughter of Hazel and Ted Buck.

Breakfast was on the table when the girls bounced into the kitchen. The soon-to-be mama and daddy were dressed up in their church clothes. Boy, did they look fancy. Hazel had lipstick on, and she wore some sparkly combs that held her hair back at the temples. Ted wore his best suit and prettiest tie. This was a special day, indeed.

The trip that morning was uneventful. The girls sat in the back seat of the car and looked out at the farms. They watched the water go by as they drove along the winding River Road to the courthouse in Chippewa Falls.

As Ted drove past Chippewa City, Joyce pointed at a little house beside a big red barn.

"Do you remember when we lived there?" she whispered.

Jane shook her head no, and Joyce smiled. That life was gone now. *By the time we go to bed tonight,* she thought to herself, *we'll be Daddy and Mama's real daughters.*

The courthouse seemed big and scary to the little girls.

"It isn't as big as the castle in Saint Paul," Jane said shyly.

Joyce grabbed Jane by the hand as they followed their parents up the steps into the big building. The little girls clung to each other the same way they had a year ago when they first climbed the steps to their new home in Cornell.

The family sat quietly on one of the benches that lined the hallway outside the courtroom.

Finally, a lady, with her hair caught up in a tight bun at the nape of her neck, called out, "Edmund Buck."

They all stood and followed her into the room. The lady introduced them to Judge Riley. He looked Ted and Hazel straight in the eye.

"Have you decided to formally adopt Joyce Mary?" he asked.

"Yes," said Ted and Hazel in unison.

"Have you decided to formally adopt Jane Alice?" Judge Riley asked.

"Yes," both Ted and Hazel said again.

"Any questions or comments?" the judge asked.

"No, Your Honor," answered Ted.

"Do you girls want to be adopted by Mr. and Mrs. Buck?" the judge asked, looking directly at Joyce and Jane.

"Yes," said both girls at the same time.

"Then it shall be done. Here Mr. and Mrs. Buck, would you please sign your names on this line?" asked the judge.

That was basically all there was to it. Joyce and Jane smiled at each other. Their new mama hugged them both at the same time. It was a joyous day in the life of the new Buck family.

Hazel asked if anybody wanted to walk down the block and have an ice cream cone from Olson's Dairy.

"Yippy! Skippy! Ice cream," shouted Jane.

She thought Olson's had the best homemade ice cream in the world. Jane chose chocolate and Joyce selected strawberry. Hazel and Ted both got vanilla cones.

On the way to the car, Daddy asked if the girls wanted to ride through Irvine Park and see the animals on the way home.

"Can we get an ice cream cone for the animals, too?" asked Jane.

The entire official Buck family laughed.

Chapter Twelve

Welcome to the Family

The next Sunday, after church, Ted and Hazel's friends and relatives were invited to a party to celebrate the adoption of Joyce and Jane. The girls were so excited they could hardly sit still in church.

At the point in the service where the minister asked if there were any celebrations or concerns, Hazel stood and announced that the adoption was now final, and Joyce and Jane were officially her daughters. The smiling congregation clapped and the people sitting behind them patted both girls on the shoulders. When church was finally over, people swarmed around the happy little girls. One man reached into his pocket and gave each of them a shiny new quarter.

Joyce was happy, but shy and reserved. She stood back and smiled as her little sister, Jane, chatted and shook hands with everyone who came up to congratulate them.

Filled with the wonder of true happiness, the girls skipped along beside their parents, eager to get home and have their party begin.

To say the party was a bitter disappointment would be an understatement. All of the guests were old. There were no young people to play with, and the girls were expected to sit quietly as the people talked about olden times.

"Be seen and not heard, and for heaven's sake, smile," Hazel ordered.

Joyce and Jane sat beside their mother, with smiles plastered on their little faces. They opened gifts, and cards with money inside. They thanked each guest properly. The cake and ice cream was eaten without spilling a drop. But, their behavior was not good enough to suit Hazel and Ted.

When the party was over, and the last guests had said their good-byes, Hazel began, "Why can't you girls be good like Kathy across the street?" she said in a scolding voice. "Why do you have to embarrass me at every turn?" she cried.

Ted joined his wife in talking about the party and how terrible their daughters had behaved. He was upset beyond words that they had given a home to such unworthy girls.

Joyce and Jane sat in a chair together and hung their heads. They tried to understand what had changed. For the past year, they were perfect in their parent's eyes. Then suddenly today, they were a disappointment.

"Leave them alone," Grandpa Bailey grumbled almost under his breath. "They acted just fine," he said in an attempt to intervene.

"You can just go to your room," Ted yelled menacingly at the older man. "This is not your business."

The girls' mouths flew open in surprise and they stared in shock, as Grandpa Bailey walked slowly to his room and quietly shut the door. The sisters were very confused because they couldn't figure out what they had done wrong. They were also worried about Grandpa Bailey. He had come to their defense, and then had been scolded and sent to his room like a child.

Hazel was so worked up that she sent the sisters to bed without any supper, as punishment for being naughty at the party. In the dark room, an old familiar rumbling came from their hollow stomachs.

Joyce was baffled that her loving father had been so mean to Grandpa Bailey. She hadn't seen that side of Ted before, but his actions reaffirmed what she already knew. *Adults cannot be trusted.* In despair, she turned her face into the pillow and cried herself to sleep.

Jane did not want to go to bed hungry again. She had come to believe that part of her life was over. Stubbornly, she laid flat on her back without moving a muscle. She let shreds of hatred and fear build within her.

Chapter Thirteen

No, Daddy! No!

Saturday night was bath night at the Buck house. Hazel had arthritis in her hands and wrists, so when the girls came to live with them, she found it hard to wash their hair in the kitchen sink. Ted cheerfully became the official hair washer.

Every Saturday night he would wash their hair in the sink. When that chore was finished, the little girls would run to the bathroom, where Hazel would have a nice hot bath waiting for them.

The next step in the ritual was to hop on their parent's bed to say prayers and listen as their daddy read from the Holy Bible. Ted and Hazel would then take the girls up the steps to their room and tuck them in bed for the night.

Some nights Joyce and Jane would have trouble falling asleep. They would lie in bed, whisper, and giggle.

On those nights, Ted would call up the stairs, "Quiet down! I'll come up there and quiet you down myself," he would threaten.

Once the adoption was final, Ted systematically began his seduction as he carried out his threats. The sisters would hear his yelling voice from below, and soon, they would hear his tread on the steps.

The first time they heard him on the stairs, the sisters were scared to death. They thought they were in for a terrible beating for being noisy. They also thought if they were bad, their daddy wouldn't love them anymore.

In fear, Jane closed her little eyes and rolled over to face the wall. She did not move a muscle. She was very good at playing dead. Joyce was fully awake and looking, wide-eyed in terror, as Ted entered the room.

Something was very different this time. Ted did not yell at them. He tiptoed slowly to their bed and began talking quietly to Joyce.

Gently, he told her, "I have to go to work in the morning. You have to be quiet so I can get some sleep. You must be quiet so you don't wake up Mother."

As he talked, he moved closer to Joyce's face. Soon, his voice was lowered to a whisper, and he was on his knees beside the bed. As he talked, he worked his hand under the covers until his palm rested on her chest. He kissed her full on the lips. With fingertips as soft and light as a feather, he caressed her dormant breasts.

"No, Daddy! No!" Joyce pleaded as his hand moved lower on her body. "Jane is awake. She'll hear us!"

"No, she won't," Ted panted. "It doesn't matter, anyway. I'm not doing anything wrong. I'm doing this because I love you."

Joyce was so scared that she became rigid. The little girl lay there stiff and terrified, letting her father's hand travel where it may.

When he was finished, he warned, "Remember, this is just between you and me. It's our little secret," he said, as he quietly left the room.

Joyce turned her head and sobbed soundlessly into her pillow. She hoped with all her might that her sister was asleep.

After that night, he came often, though he didn't ever stay long.

Each time, Joyce would beg him, "Please, stop."

Each time, he would tell her, "I love you the most, and I'm not doing anything wrong." He cajoled her, "The love we share is private, and it isn't anybody else's business."

Still, after every visit, he would remind her not to tell anyone. Then he began to hint that he would have to hurt her little sister if she told.

A little while after the seduction began, Ted started complaining that it was too hard to wash the girls' hair in the sink. He decided it would be easier to rinse the shampoo out of their hair if they were in the shower.

He reasoned with Hazel, "Bath night shouldn't take so long. If the girls could shower instead of taking a bath upstairs in the tub, the job could get done quicker."

The shower was in the basement. Hazel decided that it would be fine as long as the girls wore their swimsuits while he washed their hair. She thought when Ted was finished with their hair, the girls could close the shower curtain, remove their suits, and then shower. It was Hazel's idea and it played right into Ted's plan.

From then on, every Saturday night, Ted took the girls down to the basement with their swimsuits on. After their hair was washed and rinsed, they would close the shower curtain, and remove their swimsuits to take their showers.

Sometimes he would wash their backs before they took off their swimsuits. When they were finished washing and rinsing off, they would turn off the water. Then he would pass their towels through the side of the shower curtain. The girls would wrap the towel around them and run upstairs to the bedroom to put on their pajamas.

Ted was their father. Joyce and Jane began to feel comfortable being naked around him. He was careful to make it seem that he was not interested in looking at their nude bodies, but the seduction slowly progressed.

Soon, their father started washing more than their backs.

He said, "Let me do it! I can wash you better, faster, and waste less water, then when you wash yourselves."

Once he convinced Hazel to let the girls go to the basement with him for their baths, his trips to the bedroom became fewer.

Ted went about the task of molestation very methodically. It took a lot of patience to groom the sisters into being comfortable with him touching them and seeing them naked. They knew he was watching them and touching them. They thought it was how families did things. They just didn't know, and besides, it felt good.

Chapter Fourteen

The Pattern

According to the Merriam-Webster Dictionary, the word pattern is defined as an ideal model. If you look further, it also defines pattern as a sample of a person's behaviors or characteristics.

A pattern had been developing in the Buck household for sometime now. It was a pattern which society would not consider an ideal model. Instead, it was a pattern of criminal behaviors and characteristics.

Ted would sexually abuse the girls and then control their every move to protect his dirty secret. He played on Hazel's weak nature to make sure she remained too cowardly to act on her suspicions—if she had any. Next, he promoted civic duty. He knew if Hazel believed they were pillars of the community, she would be too proud to blow the whistle and let the town know what was going on behind closed doors. He also planted the idea that Joyce and Jane were liars, just like their real parents, Esther and Hale Colburn. This was truly an evil pattern of deceit.

When sexual abuse became a way of life, religion came into the house. Suddenly, Ted Buck got religion. He became a deacon of the church, joined the Masons, and became important in Hazel's eyes. She was very proud to have a righteous, religious man for her husband. She could now show the town she had chosen her man well.

Ted was patiently gaining control over his daughters. Very gradually, he had taken control over decisions concerning what they were allowed to do, and with whom they were allowed to do it.

Wearing slacks was out of the question. He wanted his daughters in skirts, since it made his invasions to their private parts less encumbered.

He decided how they should wear their hair, which he now was cutting himself. Most disturbingly, he kept the girls away from other people, lest they might forget and let his little secret slip.

Once in awhile, Hazel and Grandpa Bailey took the girls to a movie at the Cornell Theater. Ted chose the movies they were allowed to see. He made sure they were innocent and moral enough for his daughters.

Roy Rogers, with his horse Trigger, and Dale Evens and her horse, Old Buttermilk Sky, were a favorite. Jane loved to see Gene Autry and his wonder horse, Champion. On the radio, she heard Gene Autry tell everybody that he chewed DoubleMint gum. Jane didn't like the taste but chewed the gum, whenever she could. If it was good enough for Gene Autry, it was good enough for her.

A girl named Kathy lived across the street. Ted declared that it was okay for the girls to play with her as long as they stayed in the yard. They also were allowed to belong to a sewing club with a few girls who were daughters of Hazel's friends. They could go to each other's houses for an hour every Friday after school. The girls would talk, giggle, eat snacks, and sew. They eagerly looked forward to their sewing club each week.

Alan Colburn was now a teenager. His current foster parents were pretty decent, and they had helped him locate his sisters. The foster mother had made the phone call asking if they could come to see the girls. Hazel didn't know what else to say, so she said they would be glad to have him for a visit.

For a week, Jane and Joyce could hardly eat or sleep. They hadn't seen their beloved brother, in person, for over five years. They wondered what he looked like and if he would recognize them. They prepared homemade presents for him, with hands that were shaking with excitement.

The day finally arrived, and Alan stood before them in the flesh. He was so tall and so handsome.

The girls cried tears of sheer joy and hugged him until he yelled, "Uncle."

They couldn't keep their eyes off him and all they wanted to do was touch him. Their hearts were full of love, and their eyes glowed with emotion.

Ted didn't like what he saw. He didn't want his daughters reacting to anyone else in that way. He wanted that kind of emotion and love for himself. It had completely eluded him, so far. He feared that if he left the girls alone with their brother that they would tell him their secret.

The kids sat together on the couch with Alan in the middle. The foster mother took out her camera and shot a picture of the three Colburn children, together for the first time in so many years. One look at that picture and you knew how much they meant to each other; how much they had survived, and how strong they had become.

Hazel brought milk and cookies, and set the tray on the coffee table for them.

Then she kindly suggested to Ted, "Let's go to the kitchen and leave the kids alone for awhile."

Ted would have none of that. He insisted that he wasn't hungry.

When Hazel pressed him to join them in the kitchen, he blew his top and yelled, "I SAID, NO!"

The whole while Alan was visiting, Ted eavesdropped on their conversation. When the last sip of milk was gone, Ted stood up and announced that it was time for the visitors to be on their way.

The foster mother and Hazel walked into the living room with questioning looks on their faces. Ted was already walking to the front door, where he stood until the good-byes were said.

As Alan and his foster mother walked out the door, Ted told them, in no uncertain terms, "You're not welcome in this house again!"

Hazel tried to intervene, but Ted was stern.

Jane tried to run out the door and follow her brother to the car, but her father grabbed her and held on tight. Joyce and Jane both cried as they watched their dear brother disappear down the street, and out of sight.

Hazel was worried Ted's impolite behavior would ruin their reputation. She yelled and nagged until she was crying so hard she almost fainted.

Ted told her, "Shut up and go to bed," and she did.

However, she actually cried for several days because she was sure the word would get around that her perfect religious husband had acted so rudely.

Later that night, when Ted was kissing and touching the girls, he told them, "It's for your own good. If I had left you alone with that nasty boy, he'd probably start doing dirty things to you. I know how boys think, and it's my job to protect you from bad boys."

Joyce shut her eyes and allowed herself the delicious feeling of pure hatred.

For reasons she could not grasp, Hazel found herself disillusioned with motherhood in general. She found it to be a lot of work with very little return. As her children grew older, Hazel noticed they were growing more distant and unhappy. She read that girls often did that when they reached puberty, and she didn't like it. In her mind, the girls seemed to like Ted better, and no one noticed what she had sacrificed for them. Those girls were ungrateful, and they were tearing her life apart.

Hazel used to call Jane "Sunshine," but now it seemed as if she didn't smile very much. Hazel's little Sunshine used to tell her often how much she loved her. Now Jane acted as if she didn't even like her anymore.

Hazel used to call Joyce "Pumpkin," but Ted called her that now.

He told Hazel, "It's my special name for Joyce. I don't want you to call her that anymore."

The seeds of doubt had been planted, but she refused to go there. In spite of herself, Hazel began to dislike Joyce—almost to the point of hatred. It was as if something had happened that she just couldn't put her finger on. A nagging feeling that something was terribly wrong with her family hung just over her head. She thought that her husband was giving his love and attention to his daughter instead of her, his wife.

A little voice in Hazel's head, which grew louder as the years progressed, told her she had competition for her husband's love right under her own roof. She somehow knew she was losing the competition. She was the one being left out in the cold.

Even though she still had fond feelings for Jane, deep in her heart, she felt sorry that she had agreed to adopt either of the girls. The wish that they had adopted a little baby instead of two half-grown girls, began to dwell in her distraught mind.

Hazel began to feel depressed and she often cried. Sometimes she cried for no reason at all. She found herself feeling terribly unhappy with her life, and she realized she was alone in her unhappiness.

Joyce and Jane were very afraid because their parents had begun fighting regularly. They said terrible things to each other.

One time, their mother threatened, "I'm going to kill myself," and then quietly shuffled into her bedroom, crying.

Ted wore a smug look on his face for hours as he smirked, "I won that battle."

Ted began to treat Grandpa Bailey worse and worse. Hazel sided with her husband and made life miserable for her father. Often, the girls were told about how bad he was, and they began to believe it. Grandpa spent much of his time in his room, or sat in his chair in front of the TV. Basically, Grandpa Bailey just stayed out of the way. He existed from day to day, even though it was his house they all lived in.

Chapter Fifteen

The Prisoners on Main Street

Hazel was a firstborn and the only surviving child. She grew up in a fantasy world where she was treated like a princess. What little Hazel wanted, little Hazel got. As she grew into womanhood, she felt entitled. She believed she deserved to have the perfect marriage, the perfect house, and the perfect white picket fence.

The fantasy marriage of Hazel's dreams had proven to be a little too real for her liking. If she was honest with herself, she would admit that her husband was manipulative, sneaky and mean. She'd admit that the car and their clothing were all the material possessions they had in the world. She'd admit that everything else belonged to her father. However, Hazel never was honest with herself. She lived in her fantasy and put on a good show in town.

She was terribly unhappy and saw herself as the victim. Therefore, when she first heard of Ted's plan to take over ownership of her father's property, she was all for the idea. She decided owning the house would solve all her problems and would somehow make her happy again.

With her blessing, Ted had a transfer of ownership paper drawn up by an attorney. He brought it home one evening and tried to force Grandpa Bailey to sign it. Ted met with resistance from his father-in-law, so in a loud and menacing voice, he threatened the old man. He vowed he would put him in a mental institution if he didn't sign. Then in a softer tone, Ted promised that if he did sign the paper, he would be taken care of and allowed to stay in the house as long as he lived.

Grandpa Bailey's fear of standing up to the monster made him a prisoner in his own home, for the rest of his life. Once the paper was signed, he was no longer given any respect or consideration. He was told to keep his mouth shut or they would kick him out. He understood that he didn't have anywhere else to go.

Dale Bailey was not the only prisoner who Ted Buck kept behind the walls of the green house on Main Street. Joyce and Jane became isolated from all but home, church, and school. As their bodies grew and began to mature, Ted tightened the screws of domination over his daughters. Gradually, their world shrank to a four-block zone.

At home and at church, Ted had few concerns about being discovered. When the girls were at school, however, he worried that someone might see the signs of what he was doing. He feared that one of the girls might let it slip. Some of his co-workers at the paper mill had children in his daughters' classes. He began mentioning to them that his daughters were liars.

Soon, he was regaling the men with stories of the things the girls did and the lies they told. Anyone who was on lunch break with Ted would hear how the sisters couldn't be trusted to tell the truth. He let them believe the girls were a big disappointment, especially after he and Hazel had taken them in and given them everything. Ted told these stories to his Masonic Lodge brothers as well.

The stories made their way around the small town. Everybody believed the Buck sisters were liars. The kids at school were no exception. They treated the girls very poorly. Joyce was always the last one standing when the kids chose sides to play a game in physical education class. Sometimes, the girls in her class surrounded her, jeered, and poked fun at her in the hallways. She was bullied at school. In turn, she hated every minute that she was forced to attend.

Joyce had no safe place to go, since the grandfather who at one time protected her, was now a piece of the furniture. The mother, who had loved her in the beginning, now hated her, cried constantly, and put on a happy smile only outside their home.

Joyce felt alone and couldn't understand what she had done to deserve this punishment. The first year in Cornell had been paradise, and she had had such high hopes for a bright future. Now, she felt her spirit turn inward. She prayed for real acceptance and love from her parents, and not the physical kind of love that hurts.

Jane, on the other hand, was forward. When she was made fun of, she got even. She would threaten to punch anybody who said a bad thing to her. She tried to protect her sister in the same way. She became very good at telling people off. Her body language took on a "Don't mess with me" persona, and people left her alone.

When the townspeople learned that the girls were liars, Ted's mission was complete. He was relatively sure that he could safely increase his sexual activity with his daughters and not be detected. Who would believe two ungrateful little liars? After all, he and his loving wife, Hazel, had rescued them from a life of pure hell. They had sacrificed everything for their adopted daughters.

One afternoon, Grandpa Bailey was sitting on the front porch. It was during the time when the girls were encouraged to disrespect their grandfather. Jane sauntered onto the porch where Grandpa Bailey sat. He said something to her, and she lipped off to him.

Ted was in the living room and overheard the exchange between them. He stood up and walked right out onto the porch.

He stood over Grandpa Bailey, and told him in no uncertain terms, "Never speak to Jane like that again in my house."

Silently, Grandpa Bailey stood up and walked through the kitchen toward the basement. He opened the door and took down one of his guns, which were kept in gun caddies on the wall of the stairwell. He cocked the gun open, and reached for the bullets, only to find the container empty.

Ted knew the gun would be useless to the old man. He had taken the bullets when he had taken over the house. Ted had hidden the bullets away exactly for that reason. He anticipated a time when the old fool might snap.

Hazel saw what was happening and led the girls out the back door. They all ran down behind the garage near the alley. She was bawling. She told the girls to be quiet and not tell anybody about it.

The girls and their mother stayed behind the garage for several minutes. They waited, but they heard nothing. Joyce and Jane were very good at being quiet and hiding. They waited for the gunshots. All those old memories came rushing back—of Esther and Hale Colburn, and settled in the pit of their stomachs.

When nothing happened, they fearfully started to creep slowly back to the house. No one said a word or made a sound. Hazel hesitantly walked up the back steps and peeked inside through the window. She breathed a sigh of relief and swung open the door to the kitchen. She motioned for the girls to follow her inside.

The prisoner, Grandpa Bailey, sat in his chair, while Ted sat in another. They both acted as if nothing had happened.

With no bullets, Grandpa Bailey was now a totally defeated man. He appeared round-shouldered, old, and lifeless. His once kind smile was permanently removed from his ashen face. From that time on, Jane carried guilt for sassing her grandfather and causing him so much misery.

Joyce and Jane were very sure that if there had been bullets for the gun, their father would have been dead.

Chapter Sixteen

Out West, Here We Come

Several big red X's marched across the days of May on the kitchen calendar. Jane marked off the days until school would be out for the summer. As soon as school was over, Ted and Hazel had planned to take the family on a once-in-a-lifetime trip out west.

Hazel and Ted had prepared for that vacation since the winter snow began to melt. They had a huge map spread out on the dining room table, with all the places they wanted to stop circled in red. It was very exciting to look at the map and anticipate being in all those exotic places.

After the death of his parents, Ted had taken on the responsibility of caring for his siblings. The trip was planned so he could visit the brothers and sisters he had not seen since his marriage to Hazel, and his move to Wisconsin.

Joyce had never gone on vacation and was feeling afraid. She told her mother that she wasn't sure about the trip, and that she was scared to meet her new family.

Hazel looked at her with a hateful sneer on her lips and said, "We'll leave you home alone, if you don't quit trying to ruin the vacation before it even starts."

At dawn on the first Saturday morning in June, Grandpa Bailey, Jane, and Joyce squeezed into the back seat of the light green Chevy sedan, with their black dog, Smokey. Hazel settled into the front seat as Ted put the last suitcase into the trunk.

He slammed down the lid, slid behind the wheel, and announced, "Out west, here we come," and drove away.

Familiar landmarks flickered past the window as Ted drove out of town. The first destination was Duluth, Minnesota, where Ted had planned to stop for a breakfast of pancakes and bacon.

Ted wanted to be in Minot, North Dakota, before nightfall. When they arrived in Duluth, he hurried them through breakfast. There was barely time to use the bathroom before Ted had the engine running, and they hit the road again.

It wasn't long until Jane and Joyce started to get bored. Grandpa Bailey had fallen asleep immediately after breakfast. The girls were told to sit in the back seat and be quiet. Soon, they fell asleep, too.

Suddenly, the car came to a screeching halt. The unexpected stop propelled all of the bodies in the back seat forward. They rammed into the backs of Hazel and Ted's seats. Jane ended up on the floor with Smokey on top of her. Terror grabbed the girls and they started to cry. The last time they had come to a quick stop, and fallen onto the floor like that, was the day the authorities had taken them away from their real parents, Hale and Esther.

Ted was swearing loud and hard. Smokey had gotten carsick and had thrown up on the back seat. Ted was livid.

His face was beet red as he yelled, "It's your fault. I don't want you sleeping. From now on, you stay awake and keep an eye on that dog."

A blood vessel popped out at his temple as he screamed, "Now clean up this damned mess."

The girls grabbed tall grass, which was growing in the ditch alongside the road. They did their best to pick up the gunk, but they didn't have any way of washing off the smell. Ted rolled down his window and drove on through Minnesota. They stopped for lunch somewhere near the North Dakota border.

As soon as the car stopped, Joyce ran into the bathroom of the cafe, and unrolled a big handful of paper towels. She wet some of the towels, put some hand soap on them, and ran back to the car. Hazel yanked the paper towels out of her hand and scrubbed the back seat. Satisfied that she had cleaned the smell out of the car, Hazel joined the others as they ate lunch in the little restaurant.

Joyce and Jane soon learned that there wasn't much to do on a long road trip—sleep, eat, pee, watch the trees and tall grass whistle by the window, and clean up puke. The girls decided to take turns watching to make sure Smokey didn't get sick in the car again. One would sit on the seat and watch, while the other laid on the floor and slept.

Smokey wasn't the only one to get carsick. Jane took her turn. About a half hour before they stopped for dinner, she sat on the seat looking out the side window while Joyce slept on the floor. All that scenery speeding past took its toll.

Suddenly, she yelled, "I'm sick. I think I'm going to throw up."

Joyce's eyes flew open in time to see Jane's face hovering over her. Before Ted could stop the car, Jane's mouth erupted like a volcano. Joyce turned her head as quickly as she could, but she still felt the warm wet liquid running down the side of her face.

Jane was crying. Joyce was gagging.

Ted was yelling, "At this rate, we won't get to Minot before midnight. All the hotel rooms will be taken and we'll have to sleep in this car. I should have known better than to bring you worthless kids on this vacation," he yelled, his voice exploding like a bomb.

They sat still as statues, with puke dripping from them, as Ted pulled the car over. He slammed to a stop with a violent jerk. Hazel was crying and Grandpa Bailey pretended to be asleep. Jane and Joyce tried to clean up the mess, while Smokey took a potty break.

The night spent in Minot, North Dakota, was the first time the sisters had ever stayed in a motel. They were so excited they wanted to jump up and down on the bed, but the rules of the family were that children had to sit down and be quiet.

By dawn, they were back in the car and ready to take off for Kalispell, Montana. Ted came out of the motel carrying several wet washcloths, some towels, and an empty ice bucket. He vowed there would be no more puke messes in the back seat of the car.

"Throw up in the ice bucket and wipe yourselves off with these washcloths," he ordered.

A woman Hazel had gone to school with lived in Kalispell. Ted was on a mission to get to her house before nightfall. He thought they could stay with her instead of spending money on another motel room.

The second day of the trip was just as boring as the first. They drove for miles before they stopped for breakfast. Across the street from the diner was a small drug store. While the family finished breakfast, Ted walked over to talk to the pharmacist. He soon came strolling back to the diner with a package of carsickness pills in his hand.

Taking pills never seemed to be easy for Jane, but she took one and washed it down with several sips of orange juice. The pharmacist had told Ted to feed Smokey only at night, so he would have plenty of time to digest his food before getting back in the car. The new feeding schedule seemed to work.

Hazel had the address of her friend in her purse. At dusk, when they arrived in Kalispell, Ted asked the gas station attendant for directions. Hazel was happy and smiling while she told the family about her friend and how much fun they had when they were kids.

"They must be gone," said Hazel, as she opened the car door and started up the sidewalk to the dark house.

She pulled out a piece of paper from her purse and shoved a note into the crack between the door and the frame.

"Let's get a motel room for the night and stop back and see them in the morning," Hazel said, as she got back in the front seat of the car.

Ted gunned the motor and took off before Hazel had the door shut all the way. He was mad that he was not going to have free lodging for the night. Ted's anger hung over the little motel room all evening, like a thunderhead. The frightened girls crawled into bed and covered their heads with the blankets until they fell asleep.

Early the next morning, Ted was up and storming around the hotel room. He was packing up their things and getting ready to leave. Hazel was crying and said she wanted to see her friend before they left.

"I left them a note saying we were stopping," she whimpered. "I can't just leave town without seeing her. We came all this way."

Grandpa Bailey tried, one last time, to intervene on behalf of his daughter, as they piled into the sedan. Ted told him off and that was the end of that. The car, carrying the Buck family, went speeding west toward Arcata, California, where Ted's brother, Byron lived, very close to Humboldt Bay.

It was almost midnight, the third day of the trip, when they arrived at Uncle Byron's house. Ted was apprehensive because he hadn't seen his siblings for many years. Since their parents died and Ted had taken responsibility for his brothers and sisters, things had not been good between them. Lately though, his siblings had been responding better to his letters and phone calls. He decided it was time for this visit.

Uncle Byron invited them in. The girls sat on the couch, while Hazel and Ted talked with Uncle Byron and his wife. Joyce and Jane were so tired they had a hard time sitting upright. After an hour or so, it became apparent they would not be invited to stay overnight. Ted and his brother were having a disagreement of some kind. Ted tipped over his chair, stood up in a huff, and ordered his family to get back in the car.

One by one, the exhausted girls and their grandfather slouched out to the car and got in. Ted revved up the engine and pulled away from the curb. The car spewed dirt and gravel behind them as they roared up the street. Nobody said a word as Ted drove on. Finally, they saw a motel with a sign that said, "Vacancy."

The Buck family had just driven all the way from Wisconsin to the California coast. They had endured heat, boredom, bad smells, tight quarters, and carsickness. They still had not had a good visit with anybody.

Surprisingly, Ted and Hazel woke up in a pretty good mood the next morning.

Ted announced, "We'll be driving past the Pacific Ocean today."

He told them that he had gone swimming in the ocean once and he had really liked the experience.

Grandpa Bailey boldly said, "We should stop to let the girls put their feet in the ocean. This might be a once in a lifetime opportunity, and they may never see the ocean again."

Ted wasn't interested in spending the time that it would take for Joyce and Jane to "slosh" around in the ocean, but Grandpa insisted. Hazel joined her father. They didn't give up until Ted stopped at a rest area that advertised ocean access.

The ocean felt cold on their hot feet, but they squealed as the waves lapped at their bare legs. They tasted their wet fingers to find the water very salty. Grandpa, Hazel, and even Ted stood on the beach. They laughed as the girls ran and jumped up and down in the water along the sandy shore.

Grandpa Bailey told of a redwood tree that was big enough to drive a car through. It seemed almost impossible, but Joyce and Jane were in awe as they stared at the huge trees they passed. On the way through the redwood forest, Hazel spotted a little gift shop, where the girls were allowed to buy a redwood pencil for a souvenir.

Chapter Seventeen

The Evil Tool of the Devil

One look at the map and Joyce realized they were heading east again. What was the big deal about going out west anyway? None of the promises of fun and wonderful visits with family and friends had been fulfilled. Up to this point, her life had been a series of broken promises, hopes, and dreams. It wasn't likely to be different anytime soon. Another thing she realized was that going out west had given her an unexpected freedom from her father's unwelcomed kisses and touches.

Suddenly Hazel yelled, "Ted, where are we going?"

Ted didn't answer. He kept both hands on the wheel and drove on, looking straight ahead. Both girls looked at Grandpa Bailey and watched as he slowly shook his head. His shoulders indicated an "I don't know" shrug.

"You're going to gamble, aren't you," Hazel sobbed. "Ted Buck, you'll rot in hell."

The girls knew Ted's stories by heart—about his life before he married their mother and came to live in Cornell. He loved to tell how he had been a cigarette smoking, hard drinking cowboy, who was also a poker faced gambler.

Jane and Joyce believed him when he bragged about all the exciting times he had, and all the fast living he did as a young man. Hazel must have believed him, too, because when he finally announced that they were taking a side trip to Reno, Nevada, she started crying and preaching that gambling was the evil tool of the devil.

Hazel cried until Ted yelled, "Shut up."

The sisters sat in the back seat of the sedan and feared for their mortal lives, all the way to Reno.

Around noon, Ted pulled up in front of a restaurant. Hazel began crying wildly and said she wasn't going in because she heard there were slot machines everywhere in Reno. Jane and Joyce didn't want to go in either, then.

Grandpa Bailey spoke up and said he didn't think there would be anything wrong with going into a restaurant to eat lunch. Hazel was starving, so she grudgingly picked up her purse and took out her mirror. She put some face powder around her red eyes, pasted a smile on her lips, snapped her purse shut, got out of the car, and sauntered toward the building. They looked like any other happy family on a vacation, when they walked into the restaurant in Reno. They calmly slid into a booth by the window.

While they ate, Ted said that he was running low on money and wanted to gamble to win back some of the cash he had spent on motel rooms and meals. Hazel looked as if she was going to be sick, right there in the restaurant. Grandpa sat quietly for a few moments. Then he said he had brought some extra money along. In a desperate attempt to steer Ted away from the casino, he dug in his pocket and handed a wad of bills across the table. Ted took the money and his mood lifted. He was almost jovial as the family hopped back in the car and headed for Idaho.

Several of Ted's sisters lived in Glenns Ferry, Idaho. The first stop was to see his sister, Nona, and her husband, Pete. It only took a few minutes to see the writing on the wall. The adults were cool toward each other and their children stood at a distance and gawked. Jane smiled and took a step toward the kids, only to see them back away. Hazel grabbed her by the arm and told her to sit down.

Nona brought her oldest daughter, Norma, over to stand in front of Ted and Hazel. She told them that Norma was very responsible. She said she would like to take Joyce and Jane for a little walk and show them around. To the girl's surprise, their mother and father agreed to let them go.

It was a quaint little town on the banks of a fairly large lake. The children tossed stones into the still water and watched the ripples move away from the spot where they fell. When Norma decided it was time to go back to the house, she stood without a word and just walked away.

As they neared the house, they heard Norma's sisters and brothers playing in the back yard. The girls ached to join them and have as much fun as the others.

As they walked up the sidewalk toward the house, Ted stood and yelled to them, "Get in the car! NOW!"

Without another word, they got in the car and drove away.

In a huff, Ted drove across town to where his sister, Lulu and her husband, Ben, lived. Lulu and Ben were the best man and the matron of honor for Hazel and Ted when they were married. Lulu served a wonderful meal. Hazel gave her daughters dirty looks and motioned for them to wipe their mouths, the entire time they ate. The girls tried very hard to keep from embarrassing their mother with their table manners.

Hazel and Ted thanked his sister repeatedly for the nice supper and the wonderful time. It was the best the family had been treated by anyone on the whole trip. They were so pleased that they didn't even yell at the girls about their poor behavior.

After supper, the family left Lulu's to go to Ted's sister, Dora's, house. She and her husband, Doug, lived on the outskirts of town near the deserted one-room country schoolhouse where Ted had gone to school when he was a little boy. It was interesting for the girls to see the school and realize that their father had been a child once, too. It was fun to see where he had played and studied.

Dora was the oldest child in Ted's family. She had invited her brother to stay at her house while he was in Glenns Ferry. Ted was happy about that because it meant one less night in a motel. The problem was, Dora did not believe in adoption. She found Jane and Joyce quite inferior, and would not allow her children to play with them. She did not tire of talking about the fact that Hazel and Ted didn't know anything about these girls that they had taken in.

Grandpa Bailey took it as long as he could. He wasn't one to speak up and cause a fuss, but he said a few things to Aunt Dora that didn't sit right with her. Ted got involved in the ruckus and the next thing they knew, the family was on the way to the car. Off they drove to the nearest motel.

In the morning, Ted drove to the cemetery where his mother and father were buried. It was creepy to know that wherever they stepped, they were probably walking on top of a dead body. Jane found it interesting to hear her father talk about his parents.

After they left the cemetery, they drove several miles before they stopped for breakfast. Ted blew his top when he realized they had left Smokey's leash at the motel. He was beside himself with anger. Joyce wondered what the big deal was all about, considering it was only a leash. Both girls knew it was best to sit in the back seat of the car and not move a muscle.

Leaving Idaho, they took the long hot road to Utah. Another one of Ted's sisters, Daisy, and her husband, Rod, lived in Salt Lake City. They were Mormon's who had lots of kids. Ted was happy to leave Idaho. He told Hazel that Daisy was his favorite sister. He promised the girls they could swim in the Great Salt Lake. He said that with all the salt in the lake, they would be able to float.

Jane threw up again on the road to Utah and Grandpa Bailey slept most of the way. The girls whispered to each other that Grandpa wasn't having any fun. However, they noticed Hazel and Ted were treating him better on the trip then they did at home.

Joyce and Jane both thought the mountains, tall trees and blue skies of Utah, were beautiful, as was the Mormon Temple. They saw its six spires reaching toward the sky as they drove into Salt Lake City.

Daisy seemed genuinely happy to see her brother and his family. She hugged the girls and they were happy to be in her presence, but their cousins were another matter. Joyce and Jane were pretty much ignored by all of the kids. Hazel made things worse because she wouldn't let them leave her side. They stayed with Daisy and her family for three days and were never allowed to play with their Mormon cousins.

Daisy took them to see the breathtakingly beautiful Mormon Temple. It was not open to the public, but since Ted was her brother, Daisy was allowed to take them inside. Jane and Joyce thought they had never seen a more beautiful building. Even the castle in St. Paul, Minnesota, paled by comparison.

Daisy asked them to stand by the entrance and listen very carefully while she walked to the front of the temple. The front was so far away from them, that Daisy appeared to shrink to the size of a doll.

When she reached the altar area, she held up her hand to signal them to listen. Then she dropped a pin. The acoustics were so good in the temple, they could actually hear the pin drop. They all were terribly impressed.

The weather had taken a turn for the worse, with temperatures soaring into the high nineties. Everyone commented on the hot weather. It was so hot that Joyce felt dizzy and was afraid she would pass out. Daisy asked if she wanted to go back to the house and lie down for awhile. Joyce wanted to go back, until Ted offered to go with her. That's when she froze. She knew what her father had in mind, and she just couldn't move.

She told Daisy that she would be okay, but Daisy decided it was time for all of them to go back and rest for awhile. Joyce was so grateful that she could have hugged her. She wondered if Daisy understood.

Later in the evening, after another good meal, Daisy and Rod took them to ride the roller coaster. The stars were shining and the moon was bright as they went to the amusement park. The sisters had never gone on a carnival ride before. Jane shook with excitement, and she was ready to roll. Joyce admired her sister's forwardness and lack of fear, but she was scared to death.

Each girl was handed a ticket. Then a man helped them get buckled into a roller coaster car at the gate. Joyce held on for dear life, and screamed in terror as the car went fast and high above the Great Salt Lake. The lights below were beautiful as they bounced and danced off the surface of the lake. Joyce thought she was going to fall out and plummet to her death, but Jane just screamed for joy, with a huge smile on her face.

At dawn the next morning, the "happy family" piled into the car and said goodbye to Utah.

Chapter Eighteen

The Happy-Go-Lucky Girls

Once on the road again, Smokey threw up, and Ted's yelling caused Jane to throw up as well. It was not starting out to be a very good day. Grandpa Bailey just shut his eyes and checked out. The road from Salt Lake City, Utah, to Kemmerer, Wyoming, was the shortest stretch between destinations that they had experienced so far on the trip.

Ted arrived at his sister, Alice, and her husband, George's house just before lunch. They planned to stay with Alice for three days since her house was the largest. Alice thought they could visit the other relatives in the area during the day, and then come back to her house at night.

From the beginning of their stay, Alice and Ted did not get along. However, Ted was careful not to cross the line since he was tired of paying for motel rooms.

Joyce and Jane met their cousin, Kim, and instantly fell in love with her. Kim treated them like they were real people. She showed them her bedroom filled with all of her treasures. They laughed and giggled at her outlandish stories. Finally, they had found a relative who paid attention to them. The sisters didn't know it then, but Kim would eventually come to Cornell and have a huge impact on their lives.

Alice and Kim took their visitors to see Aunt Irene and Uncle Joe. They owned a dude ranch in Kemmerer. Jane was in heaven because the ranch was home to dozens of horses, and all the horses were tame and ready for greenhorns to ride.

The cowboys saddled up a couple of horses and assured the girls, "These old nags are as gentle as babies."

Joyce was scared to death, but Jane was eager to ride. After a few trips around the corral though, Joyce began to relax. She discovered that she loved riding horses.

The dude ranch had a sauna, so Irene, Alice, and Hazel all decided to use it. Since Joyce and Jane were not allowed to be out of Hazel's sight, they had to take a sauna, too. The girls didn't know they had to take off all their clothes to use a sauna. Joyce was terrified because she thought the men might come in. She didn't want any man to see her naked. She knew what that meant, and she was enjoying her freedom from roaming hands and sloppy kisses.

Ted's brother, Jess, and his wife, Janice, owned a sheep ranch and had invited the family for dinner. Their ranch held many wonderful surprises. Jess had several children who were eager to play with the girls, and Hazel let them play. Janice told them they were going to eat their dinner outside, in the field. All of the shepherds and ranch hands joined the family for dinner at the chuck wagon. It was just like the Roy Rogers westerns they had seen at the movies.

Everyone stood in line with their plates held out in front of them, as they worked their way to the rear of the wagon. The cook plopped food on each plate until they were almost overflowing with delicious smelling meat, beans, and potatoes. All of the kids got their plates full and then met under a tree to talk, laugh, and best of all, eat.

After supper, they played a bit more. Then reluctantly, they went back to stay at Alice's house for the night. In the morning, the girls sadly said goodbye to Kim and hopped in the car for a twenty-mile drive to visit Ted's brother, Nick, and his wife, Beale.

Nick and Beale had two daughters who were about the same age as Joyce and Jane. The girls liked their new cousins Linda and Marie a lot.

Ted said, "They're just happy-go-lucky girls. They think the world revolves around them."

Joyce and Jane had never spent time with happy-go-lucky kids before, and they thought happy-go-lucky was lots of fun. They wished they knew how to be happy-go-lucky girls.

During lunch at Nick's house, there was a feeling of tension around the table. Joyce and Jane worried that they may have done something wrong, but Linda and Marie just talked and laughed. They didn't seem to notice anything was amiss.

Suddenly, before lunch was even over, Ted stood up and sternly ordered, "Get in the car! NOW!"

He revved the engine, and once again, the car spun out with an angry man at the wheel. Away they went down the highway toward South Dakota.

Joyce had studied about the Black Hills, in school. She was very excited when Ted announced they were taking a side trip to South Dakota to see Mount Rushmore. She had seen pictures and now she would see it with her own eyes.

They began the long ride to the Black Hills. It was hot and bumpy for Jane, who was lying on the floor trying to sleep. All of a sudden, she threw up, but this time she helped Grandpa Bailey's shoes go from brown to a strange shade of green. Silently, Grandpa tried to help her clean it up without Ted finding out. The plan worked, only because Ted had his window open and was driving along with the wind blowing in his face. Grandpa Bailey did his best to help, but he was snickering pretty hard. He was tickled that they were pulling one over on Ted.

The Black Hills were pretty and the Bad Lands were beautiful, in a desolate and lonely sort of way.

Suddenly, Ted yelled, "There it is."

They all looked out the windows at the four presidents carved into the side of the mountain.

The workmen were building an observation platform and they had binoculars available for tourists to use. Joyce looked at the perfection of the carvings. Her mind was filled with wonder as she realized the toil and dedication it took to create that beautiful work of art.

Chapter Nineteen

Poor Aunt Annie

Funny, how a person can get used to anything if it happens often enough. On the long ride to Sioux City, Iowa, both Smokey and Jane threw up. The girls cleaned up the mess without so much as a mention of it, and Ted drove on as if nothing had happened.

Grandpa Bailey began to get excited. He had endured the whole trip just to spend some time at the last planned stop. He had been born and raised in Sioux City, and he was eager to show his granddaughters where he had lived.

Hazel smiled and hummed to herself as Ted drove the car into town.

"There's Uncle Howard's hardware store," Hazel said excitedly. "And over there is his house. Look, there's Aunt Vivian out on the porch."

She was out of the car and on her way up the sidewalk, almost before Ted could turn off the motor. Grandpa Bailey was at her side as Hazel hugged Vivian. They laughed with joy.

Grandpa Bailey was pleased to see his sister-in-law, Vivian's, smiling face. He hugged her with tears of love shimmering in his eyes. The travelers were invited to spend as much time as they could in her home, and there were wonderful aromas coming from her kitchen.

Joyce and Jane were pleased to see their mother and Grandpa so happy. Then they noticed their father standing alone with a look of profound sadness on his face. The contrast between the coldness of Ted's siblings and the warmth of Grandpa Bailey's family was startling.

Howard came into the house from work and Hazel flew into his big arms. He walked toward Grandpa Bailey with his hand stretched out and a huge smile on his face.

"Well, here they are," he said as he crossed the room to take the girl's hands. "Welcome to the family."

Jane and Joyce stood before him with stupid grins on their faces. They both instantly fell in love with Uncle Howard.

After lunch, Vivian and Howard took them on a guided tour of Sioux City. They saw where Grandpa Bailey was born and where he went to school. For the second time that day, there were tears in Grandpa's eyes as they walked up to the door of the church where he and Grandma Jennie were married.

It was a perfect afternoon. Jane and Joyce were elated when Grandpa Bailey treated them to an ice cream cone while they walked in the park.

Soon Vivian said, "It's time to go back and check on supper."

She had set the timer on the oven and didn't want the pot roast to burn to a crisp. The girls were happy to go back. The memory of the smells coming from the kitchen, earlier in the day, had their mouths watering.

The phone was ringing when the happy group returned to the house. Vivian excused herself and disappeared into the kitchen to answer it. Then she reappeared in the doorway looking ashen and stunned.

"Annie died," she sobbed.

Howard ran to her and wrapped his big arms around her. Then he led her to the nearest chair and helped her sit down.

Annie lived in Wisconsin and was Vivian's sister. Both Vivian and Annie were sisters to Grandpa Bailey's dead wife, Jennie. Jane and Joyce had come to live with the Bucks long after Jennie had passed away. They had never met Grandma Jennie, but they had often heard what a wonderful woman she had been.

Just the thought of Grandpa Bailey losing someone he loved made the girls cry. Annie's funeral would be in two days and the family needed to be there on time. Everybody went to bed right after supper so they could be on the road early in the morning.

So it was that the happiest part of the trip out west, was over in less than twenty-four hours. Ted was very quiet as Hazel and Grandpa Bailey talked about Aunt Annie and the family much of the way to Waupaca, Wisconsin, to attend the funeral.

Annie's body was laid out in the living room of her home. The funeral director stood at the door, looking very grim as he greeted the arriving guests. Grandpa Bailey and Hazel were grateful that Aunt Annie's death occurred at the end of the trip so they could attend the funeral. As sad as they were, they were happy to have the opportunity to see Annie's children and other relatives who would be there.

Once inside the house, it became clear why the funeral director looked so dismal. There was a ruckus going on amongst the dead woman's children. Not a civil word was spoken between them as they fought over the poor woman's belongings. Some of Annie's grown children were taking items out to their cars, while others were physically attempting to stop them from removing the things from the house.

The scene playing out before them was disgusting. Hazel and Grandpa Bailey stood watching with pure grief written on their faces. Jane began to sob uncontrollably, and Joyce put her head down to study her shoes. She tried to pretend she was invisible.

Ted suggested they find a motel and get out of there. Hazel agreed. When they finally got to their room, she was so upset that she sobbed all evening. The girls crawled into bed, covered their heads, and shivered until they fell asleep.

The funeral was held the next morning. Annie was laid to rest in a burial plot, among ancient headstones, in the cemetery behind the old brick church.

After the service, everyone gathered in the basement of the church. The reception was intended to be a time of sharing cherished memories and a celebration of her life. Instead, Annie's friends and family were forced to witness the snide remarks and awkward silences orchestrated by her children.

The guests waited in uncomfortable silence to be served ham, potato salad, baked beans, and cake. When the luncheon was finished, the Buck family sadly got into their car and drove home.

Chapter Twenty

The Newborn

One day a call came in from Ted's sister, Alice, who lived in Kemmerer, Wyoming. Their family had an emergency. Their daughter, Kim, had been raped a few months prior, and the doctor had confirmed the fact that she was pregnant.

Aunt Alice begged her brother to let Kim come to Cornell and live with him until the baby was born. Alice would tell all of their friends and relatives in Kemmerer that Kim wanted to spend some time with her Wisconsin relatives. She would also inform them that Kim would attend college there, for the fall semester.

Alice was sure no one would find out that Kim was to give birth to a baby out of wedlock. She assured Ted that Kim was eager to come to Cornell to see him.

"George will send a check every month for her keep," she promised. "Besides, Kim can help Hazel with the housework and keep 'those girls' occupied while she's there," Alice pleaded.

Ted decided that it would be all right for his niece to stay with them until the baby was born.

"We can talk about what to do with the baby later," he told his sister, and hung up.

"Alice and George are bringing Kim to live with us. They'll be driving out here next week," he told Hazel as he walked into the living room and turned on the TV.

Hazel stood in shocked silence. All she thought was, "More work and more ungrateful people to serve. Why me?"

Joyce and Jane, however, were elated. They remembered their cousin Kim and how nice she had been to them when they made their trip 'Out West' a few years ago. Wow! Things were looking up.

Two weeks later, the sisters were watching the street from their perch on the front porch. Joyce was elated for another reason. She was convinced that Ted would not touch her while Kim was living in the house. She remembered, *Daddy didn't touch me for the whole two weeks we were on our trip out west.*

At last, a car carrying Uncle George, Aunt Alice and Kim pulled up to the curb in front of the house. Joyce and Jane threw open the door and flew to the car, smiling and giggling.

Hazel wiped her tears and passed a smile across her face as she stepped through the door to wait on the top step. Ted walked to the car, patted his sister on the shoulder, and exchanged an uncomfortable handshake with his brother-in-law. Grandpa Bailey had gone to his bedroom earlier in the day, and did not join the greeting party.

Although she settled into the spare bedroom with little commotion, it was soon apparent that Kim was not eager to spend the rest of her pregnancy in exile. Especially galling to her was that she had been exiled, against her will, to Cornell, Wisconsin.

Once her mother and father left to go back home to Wyoming, Kim's true colors began to show. She expected to be waited on hand and foot, and she was mean and snide to her two adopted cousins. Hazel's complaints to Ted fell on deaf ears, which caused her to cry even more often than usual.

Ted had often expressed his interest in woodworking. With Kim in the house, and Hazel's constant bawling, he began going to the basement every night after supper. The first week he produced a couple of cute lawn ornaments. Soon he had several patterns cut out and asked Joyce and Jane to go to the basement with him to help him with his project.

Jane proved to be a disappointment to him with her careless use of sandpaper and paint. Joyce, on the other hand, was shown to be careful and talented. Ted grinned with glee. He had finally found the perfect method of operation in his quest to take the molestation of his oldest daughter to the next level.

From that day forward, he came home from work, ate supper, and called Joyce to accompany him to the basement. While they worked side by side at the table, sanding or painting lawn ornaments, Ted would touch her between the legs.

A few days after they started the nightly project, he began to insert his fingers into her vagina.

She squirmed around and told him, "That hurts, Daddy. What if Mama comes down?"

Ted told her, "Be quiet and keep working. Even if Mama comes to the door, she can't see nothing."

His fingers were too big for her body. She was in terrible pain and upset to the point that she became sick to her stomach. Joyce was so terrified of being caught that she began to wretch and hyperventilate. She ran up the steps to the kitchen and sought her mother.

Hazel followed her to the bedroom that she shared with her sister, and closed the door. There, Joyce told her mother what was going on in the basement. For a moment, the room was perfectly silent. Neither one of them even took a breath.

Then Hazel uttered the most devastating words a molested child could ever hear.

"If I believed that, I would have to kill myself."

Then with pure venom in her voice, she said, "If he has touched you in a bad way, it's your own fault. You must have asked for it."

The hatred in her mother's voice, and the sense that she would be guilty of her mother's death, shut Joyce off from seeking help from Hazel for the rest of her life.

Did Hazel confront Ted about the molestation? No one will ever know. Not another word was ever mentioned. Therefore, life with Ted went on without interruption. There was no freedom from abuse even with Kim in the house. If anything, the terror escalated for Joyce.

Hazel had made a decision. Kim's baby would be born right after Christmas, and she was going to adopt the baby herself. She always wished they had adopted a baby instead of the Colburn sisters, and now was her chance. All she had to do was convince Kim that she was the perfect choice. She could be as calculating and manipulative as her husband.

The next morning, the campaign toward motherhood began.

With the sweetest smile possible, Hazel asked Kim, "What would you like for breakfast this morning, dear?"

From that time on, Kim's slightest wish was Hazel's command. She treated the younger woman like a queen.

The two women soon became best friends. They were not related by blood, but their bond grew beyond that of blood relatives. Kim confessed to her favorite aunt that she had not been raped after all. She had been having sex with her boyfriend, Carl, and had become pregnant. She didn't want her parents to hate Carl, so they made up the story. Kim just knew Hazel would understand, and Hazel did. She smiled warmly and encouraged Kim to confide in her.

Disappointing was the word used by Hazel to describe her two adopted daughters. She explained to Kim that she had always wanted a baby to love, but Uncle Ted was sterile. She told her there was no hope for her to fill her arms with the baby she craved. Thus, Hazel planted the seed.

Nellie Cellars was Grandpa Bailey's sister. She and her husband, Harry, had adopted a little boy many years ago, and they named him Jim. Jim was now a grown man who lived and worked in Milwaukee. Often, Jim came home to Cornell on the weekends and holidays, to see his parents. That's also when he would go drinking with his high school friends.

Jim was home for Christmas. Aunt Nellie and Uncle Harry brought him over to the Buck's to see Hazel and Grandpa Bailey. Aunt Nellie lived only a few blocks away and she seemed to love Joyce and Jane. At least, she was civil to them and talked nicely to them when she was around.

When Ted spotted the Cellar family walking toward the house, he began his tirade.

"Son-of-a-bitch, here they come again," he ranted. "If Jim says anything to me, I'll throw him out on his ear."

Actually, Ted was more mouth than action. He said all of that before they came to the door. Once they were inside the house, he treated them as normally as he was capable of treating anyone.

The girls grew up with mixed feelings about Uncle Harry, Aunt Nellie, and their cousin, Jim.

They were told, "Smile and sit quietly," when they had company.

However, on the other hand, they were told how terrible the company was.

Cousin Jim swore and used profanities in every sentence. To make matters worse, Hazel said he was homosexual.

Hazel, such a very Christian lady, said, "Jim is a queer sinner. He is over thirty-five and doesn't have a girlfriend yet. Why, he's never even been on a date with a girl," she sneered.

Needless to say, the Christmas visit with Aunt Nellie and her family was always tense.

Kim was still living with the Bucks when the Christmas season arrived. The girls marveled at how large her stomach had become. They were jealous of the way their mother treated her, as if she were the long lost daughter she had always wanted.

Hazel's pandering was very noticeable, especially in the gift that she bestowed on Kim on Christmas Eve. Grandpa Bailey even raised his eyebrows in surprise and then lowered them in sadness as his daughter presented Kim with her prized handmade quilt. It was the last gift Hazel's mother had made for her before she died. The girls had been warned when they first arrived to live with the Bucks, to never ever touch the cherished quilt.

Christmas had always been a cheerless holiday for the sisters. They wished they could see their brother, Alan, more at Christmas than any other time of the year, except on his birthday. They wished that Grandpa Bailey could be happy as they gave him the presents they had spent so much time making and wrapping for him. They wished their father would leave them alone. This year, they wished their mother would love them as much as she loved Kim. Together, Jane and Joyce Buck wished for a better year to come.

Just before New Year's Eve, Kim went into labor. Ted and Hazel helped her into the car and drove the forty-five minutes to St. Joseph's Hospital in Chippewa Falls. Joyce and Jane stayed home with Grandpa Bailey and excitedly waited for news of the baby. Would it be a boy or a girl? How much would it change their lives? Would it have dark hair like Kim's?

They were fast asleep when Hazel and Ted returned home. In the morning, the girls rushed down the steps to find out if their parents were home, and if the baby had been born.

Hazel was sitting at the table crying and Ted looked as mad as a wet hen, as he fried an egg in a pan on top of the stove. Grandpa Bailey was in his bedroom, sensibly staying out of the way.

"I don't care what you say, Ted, I'm keeping that baby," Hazel sobbed and then blew her nose. "I will not let Kim put him up for adoption and give him to strangers."

Ted snorted and was about to say something when he noticed Jane and Joyce standing in the doorway. He looked at them and something changed in his face. His look of black anger turned into a half smile and then a smirk. Instinctively, Joyce knew what he was thinking.

If he said yes to the baby, Hazel would be preoccupied and he would not have to worry so much about being careful. She would have her hands full with the baby and be less apt to catch him with his daughters.

Just like Dr. Jekyll and Mr. Hyde, Ted turned toward Hazel and told her the baby was hers. She couldn't believe it was going to be that easy. It was obvious by her reaction that she didn't trust him. She smiled happily and then her jaw dropped.

"Do you mean it?" she asked with squinted eyes, as if she were trying to see something in front of her that wasn't there.

He nodded, and she went to the phone to call Kim at the hospital to tell her the news.

One week later, Hazel and Ted brought Kim and the baby home from the hospital. Hazel kept the baby away from Kim as much as she could. There was a problem, however. Kim wanted to take the baby home to Wyoming with her. She had decided to keep him.

Hazel was beside herself with worry. That afternoon, she sent Kim to her room to take a rest. When she was sure Kim was asleep, she called Aunt Alice in Kemmerer, Wyoming.

She explained, "Kim is being unreasonable and has decided to keep the baby!"

Alice let out a yell and screamed, "Over my dead body! George and I will be there to pick Kim up in two days."

The call ended with, "Kim will be going home without the baby."

Hazel and Ted named the baby Roger. They had him baptized at the Presbyterian church in Cornell, as soon as it could be arranged. Joyce and Jane thought he was the cutest baby they had ever seen. Hazel stopped crying all the time, and even hummed sometimes, as she took care of little Roger.

Chapter Twenty-One

School

Joyce hated school from the time she was five years old. Now, finally, it was nearly over. She would soon graduate and be free. Her high school years had been wrought with bullying from her classmates and sexual abuse from her father. She had not done well in most of her classes, because all of her life, she believed what people said about her. She had been told she was "Dumb and just plain stupid." So when Ted and Hazel told her the same thing, she believed them.

Office practice was the only class where Joyce felt really comfortable. She liked to work on the office machines. With an adding machine at her fingertips, she wasn't stupid about math. Joyce wasn't dumb when she worked in her office practice class. She caught glimpses of a bright future if she could just get her parents to let her go to vocational school in Eau Claire after graduation. She knew she would be successful working in an office.

Through the years, the girls had never been free to attend school activities. The only time they went to a ball game was with their father, but they were not allowed to cheer for the team. They had to sit quietly and watch the other kids have a good time.

The only school activities allowed were the ones held during school hours and properly supervised by school authorities. Ted ruled there would be no dancing, singing popular songs, or talking to boys. His motto, "If something is fun, it must be immoral."

Joyce and Jane were not allowed to wear fashionable clothing. They wore the dresses and skirts that Hazel sewed for them. Of course, there was no makeup or nail polish allowed, and that included also anything that would make them look pretty and attract boys.

Ted preached, “It is not Christian to be boy crazy and wear clothes sanctioned by the devil—not for my daughters. You will dress and act like good moral girls.”

The high point of Joyce’s senior year in high school had nothing to do with education. Her dear brother, Alan, had telephoned to say that he was on furlough and was coming to Cornell for a visit. He was bringing his new wife, Tina, to show her off to his sisters.

Joyce and Jane were beside themselves when Ted told him he could come. He was married now.

Three days was a long time to wait for the brother she missed so terribly. Alan said they would arrive on Saturday afternoon. Joyce wondered, “How am I going to make it through three days of school, without bursting?”

All morning, on the day of Alan’s arrival, Jane talked non-stop. Her excitement filled the big green house and even made Hazel smile. Joyce, on the other hand, was quiet. She worried that Ted would change his mind and not let them see their brother. Worse yet, she worried that he might kick Alan out and embarrass them in front of his new wife.

The girls were standing in front of the picture window in the living room, watching for Alan and Tina. When they drove up, Jane screeched with joy and Joyce let out a long sigh when they spotted the car.

Jane was the first out the door, with Joyce following on her heels. Both girls stopped dead in their tracks as Tina got out of the car and turned to greet them. She was beautiful with long black hair and sparkling dark brown eyes. The pink blouse and black skirt she wore looked as though they were especially made to fit her slim body perfectly.

Alan came around the front of the car and gathered his sisters into his strong arms. The three Colburn children laughed and hugged each other, tears streaming down their cheeks.

Alan was so handsome and Tina was so beautiful. It was apparent to Joyce that the newly married couple were very much in love. She felt her heart expand. Alan had finally found happiness. Silently she vowed that she would do everything in her power to find the same for herself and for her sister.

Alan said to Ted, "I am going to be transferred to Germany. Tina is going with me. I would like to stay in touch while we are over there. Can the girls write to me?"

Joyce and Jane smiled from ear to ear as Ted said, "Okay."

Finally, they would be part of their brother's life again and it made them feel complete.

The night before graduation, Joyce had a dream that she needed more credits to graduate. The superintendent, Mr. Perry, wouldn't let her walk down the aisle to get her diploma. She woke up panicked and crying in desperation until it finally dawned on her that it was only a bad dream.

For many years, Joyce looked back at her high school graduation as one of the happiest days of her life. She wished with all her might that her brother Alan could have been there to help celebrate, but he was in Germany. She knew it would do her no good to ask.

Joyce smiled to herself as she walked down the aisle of the Cornell High School gym. She had a wonderful secret that she would never divulge to anyone. The most popular boy in her class had wished her good luck and kissed her on the cheek, just before they went to get their diplomas.

To Joyce's surprise, Hazel and Ted invited a few of their friends and relatives to a graduation party in honor of Joyce Mary Buck. She was very happy to be finished with school.

Graduation, however, did not stop the production of lawn ornaments in the basement. Production actually increased once Roger came into the family, preoccupying Hazel with the chores of motherhood.

Before Ted would motion for Joyce to follow him to the basement, he would always go into the bathroom and gargle. The mint smell of mouthwash became the sickening smell of dread.

Roger was now six months old and Ted worried that he might scoot to the basement door and somehow push it open, and fall down the steps.

He told Hazel, "I'm going to lock the basement door so nothing happens to the baby."

So Ted began locking Joyce in the basement with him, while they worked on his projects. Now, safe to do whatever he wanted without fear of detection, he took the seduction to the next level.

He found a plank, laid it on the cement floor and ordered Joyce to lie down on the plank. As she lay there in terror, he lifted up her skirt and removed her panties. He stared down at her for a long time and then removed his overalls. It seemed like forever, as she concentrated on breathing slowly in and out, terrified that she might scream. If her mother heard her and committed suicide, it would be all her fault. She prayed lightning would strike him dead before he could do what he had in mind.

A gasp escaped from her lips as Ted removed his boxers and she saw his manhood hanging between his legs. She knew she was about to be raped, but she was trapped. Her body tightened in terror and became as rigid as the board she was lying on. Ted lay down on top of her and tried to penetrate her. He grunted and rutted for several minutes. Then, with both hands, he forced her legs open wide and tried again.

Joyce pressed her hands across her mouth to keep from making any noise. The pungent smell of after-shave, the cloyingly sweet smell of cologne, and the fetid stench of mouthwash filled her nostrils and caused her to wretch.

Ted swore, stood up, and pulled on his underwear and pants. He looked down at Joyce in disgust and motioned for her to get up. In a black rage, he picked up an unfinished ornament, slammed it to the floor, and stormed up the steps.

Joyce put on her panties and sat on a chair for a few minutes to get her breathing under control. Why hadn't her father raped her? She just couldn't understand what had happened. Her prayer must have been answered, but she heard no thunder.

For several days, Ted did not work on his project. One day, Hazel asked him to make a lawn ornament for one of her friends. The next night he motioned for Joyce to follow him to the basement and the seduction began…again.

Chapter Twenty-Two

Office Practice

The subject of Joyce attending vocational school in Eau Claire, and living on her own, was broached only once. The idea was banned immediately with no further discussion.

"I've looked into it and found out that Eau Claire does not offer the classes you need," Ted told her.

Then one night after supper, Hazel said to the girls, "Stop what you are doing and join Daddy and me in the living room. We have an announcement to make."

Hazel looked directly at Joyce, and said, "My cousin Theresa called today and invited you to go live with them in Milwaukee." She continued, "Theresa says Don asked around the vocational school and found out they offer everything you need for office practice classes. Besides," Hazel added with a grin, "Theresa and Don are only going to charge us ten dollars a month for your room and board."

Joyce didn't know anything about the arrangements until after they were made. Her parents had no idea how happy she would be going to vocational school. She really didn't care where she went. She just had to get away.

The problem facing her next was her clothing. All she had were the old-fashioned homemade dresses and skirts that she had worn in high school. Then, as if by magic, the fashion problem was solved. One day Hazel came home from a church meeting with a big bag of clothing for Joyce.

The Crawford girls had gone away to college a couple of years before. Their mother had finally cleaned out their closet and gave Hazel a bag of their cast-off clothing. Most of the clothes fit Joyce. She now had fashionable clothing to take with her to Milwaukee.

Registration for classes at the vocational school was scheduled for 8:00 a.m. on Monday. On that bright and early Saturday morning, Hazel, Ted, Joyce and baby Roger piled into the car for the long ride to Milwaukee. Grandpa Bailey and Jane stayed behind to take care of Smokey. Ted dwelled on the trip out west and refused to take the dog along.

Joyce had never been away from her sister for more than a day in her life. She was scared, but determined to break away by herself to find a better life for the two of them. It worried her deeply that Jane would be alone in the house with Ted, but she knew she had to escape.

They arrived at their destination mid-afternoon. Theresa and Don's children, Lanna and Mary, were waiting for them. The girls were looking forward to having a grown-up cousin move into their house.

While everyone sat around snacking and talking, they waited for Don to come home from work.

Hazel asked, "Theresa, will you be able to take Joyce to school and get her registered?"

Theresa nodded as Hazel handed her some money for books and school supplies.

Then Theresa said, "I'll ride the bus with her the first time, too, so she can learn all the stops."

Joyce was relieved. She had worried herself sick about how she would get to school and back without getting lost.

In the evening, they visited with several other relatives who also lived in Milwaukee. On Saturday night, they stayed with Theresa and Don. When Sunday morning arrived, Joyce felt slightly nervous as she watched her parents pack up the car and drive away without her.

Chapter Twenty-Three

Dear Diary

Once Joyce was in Milwaukee attending school, Jane became the target of Ted's lustful desires. He began whispering love words into her ear and became more aggressive as he washed her hair and helped her with her showers. His good night kisses became more passionate than before. Jane knew it would do no good to complain, so she gritted her teeth and tried to accept her life as it was.

On her birthday, her parents surprised her with a new red diary, complete with a little gold lock and key. From that day forward, she wrote, "Dear Diary," at the top of a new page every evening. Not one for introspection, Jane's diary was a log of daily activities rather than intimate thoughts. Usually her entries consisted of snippets about the weather and who had talked to her at school—until she fell in love with Jason.

Jane thought Jason was the most handsome boy in her class. All he had to do was walk past her in the hall and shivers began chasing each other up and down her spine. When he smiled at her, the shivers turned to heat and made her melt.

Greg was Jason's best friend and Jane was in several classes with Greg's girlfriend, Sheila.

Jane finally worked up the courage to ask, "Sheila, will you ask Jason if he likes me?"

Sheila worked her magic and arrangements were made to meet in an unused classroom right after lunch.

The morning of the tryst dragged on for Jane. She couldn't concentrate in class. All she could think about was that Jason had agreed to meet her. "Is it possible that he likes me, too?" she thought to herself.

As the bell rang for lunch, Jane grabbed her books and rushed out the door to get home as quickly as possible. She gulped her sandwich and made an excuse so her mother would let her go back to school early. A few minutes before the warning bell rang, she was running through the halls to meet up with Sheila and the guys.

Almost as soon as she entered the dark classroom, Greg came hustling in. He walked right up to her, dropped his books on the floor, grabbed her roughly by both arms and tried to kiss her.

Jane gasped and squirmed out of his arms just as Jason walked through the doorway. Jason told Greg to leave her alone. Then Jason walked over, took her face in his hands and kissed her tenderly on the lips.

That was it for Jane. She fell head over heels in love. Jason had protected her, like that fairy tale knight, and then he showed her that he loved her, too. She was walking on air.

That night after supper she disappeared into her room. With pen in hand, she began the nightly ritual, but this time her message was different.

"Dear Diary, I am in love. Today Jason came to my rescue. He loves me. He kissed me on the lips. He loves me. He loves me. He loves me."

The next evening she wrote, "Dear Diary, roses are red, violets are blue, Jason loves me and I love him, too.

Monday morning dawned cold and crisp. Jane didn't even notice the piles of snow as she ran through the alley on her way to school. She was eager to see Jason. It had been a long boring weekend and her heart skipped with anticipation just knowing they would be under the same roof.

She nearly fainted as she approached her locker and saw him waiting there for her. He walked her to class, and at the end of each period Jason would be standing outside the room waiting to walk with her. Jane was flushed and giddy with happiness.

At home that evening, it became apparent something was wrong. As Jane set the table for supper, Hazel began asking questions.

"What are you doing with boys?"

"NOTHING."

"You aren't doing anything you are not supposed to do, are you?"

"NO."

"Who is this boy. Jason?"

"NOBODY."

"You aren't kissing him, are you?"

"NO."

Minutes before Ted walked in the door from work, the lecture began.

"You have to be a good girl. You can't have anything to do with boys. We are trying to raise you to be a good moral girl. What will the neighbors think if you get pregnant? You'd better shape up, young lady, or I will tell your father."

Supper was a quiet affair that night. Jane knew her mother had read her diary. *So that's why you gave it to me,* she raged silently, as hate seeded itself further inside her heart. *Just so you could keep track of what I do.* Not a word was said about the confrontation in front of Ted.

Jane waited as long as she could to take out the trash after the supper dishes were done. Jason said he would meet her behind the garage around seven o'clock.

Hazel told her twice, "Take out the garbage," but she stalled as long as she could.

The plastic bag was full but Jane didn't feel its weight as she skittered down the back steps. She was fully anticipating a good night kiss from Jason. He was there just as he had promised. With the moon at his back, he looked like a Roman god surrounded by a halo of light.

Behind the garage, Jason held out his arms to her. She put her arms out to envelope him, but was stopped in her tracks by her mother's sharp voice.

"What are you doing out there? What's taking you so long?"

Hazel had followed Jane out of the house and was standing on the top step waiting for her. Jason ran for his life.

Slowly, Jane walked up the sidewalk in the moonlight wondering how things could have turned out so badly. Rejection lay heavy on her heart as she went up to her room and reread the latest entries in her diary. With tears in her eyes, she took a tiny piece of ribbon and slipped it between the cover and the first page of her little red book. If she found the ribbon on the floor she would know for certain that her mother was intruding on her privacy.

"Jane, come down here," Ted yelled up the stairs in a syrupy sweet voice. "I need your help in the basement."

Bile rose in her throat as she shut the diary and slid it under the bed in its usual hiding place.

"I can't stand to have him touch me tonight," she shuddered. "I want to kill him."

"What do you need?" she asked as she entered the kitchen to find Ted standing at the basement door.

"Your help," he snarled. "Is that too much to ask?"

Silently, she stepped in front of him and led the way down the steep steps. The sound of the lock sliding into place and the odor of mouthwash followed her as she descended into her private hell.

Ted grabbed her by the arms and roughly pushed her against the wall. He began by kissing her and telling her how much she would love what he was about to do to her. She tried to pretend she was with Jason standing in the dank basement with her back to the wall. She shut her eyes, and forced herself to remain calm and rigid as his shaking hands unbuttoned her blouse and raised her skirt.

The sound of his zipper made her open her eyes. She saw the demented look in his eyes and fully understood the danger she was in. He pried her legs apart with such force that she lost her breath. She feared that she might faint, as he rutted between her legs.

His knees were slightly bent and his pants had fallen around his ankles. His eyes looked wild and un-human, as he violently slammed her against the wall, in his attempt to penetrate her.

Just as violently, Jane pushed her father away from her. He was astounded and hadn't expected her to fight back. As she pushed, his legs got tangled up in his pants and he fell with a thud onto the cement floor. He lay there dazed. For the first time, she saw how vulnerable, pathetic, and cowardly he looked. She laughed out loud at him.

Quickly, he gathered his wits, pulled up his pants, and zipped them. He did all that while struggling to stand. Jane was no longer afraid.

She hissed at her father, "If you *ever* touch me or Joyce again, I'll tell mother, and then I'll kill you."

The look of determination on her face and lack of fear in her eyes told Ted it would be a big mistake to mess with Jane again. He promised to leave them alone.

Jane was shaking when she crawled into bed that night. Now more than at any time in her life, she needed her sister to confide in. She was very aware that her father could come to her room and kill her. She laid awake most of the night, listening for the footfalls on the stairs. Yet she felt strangely empowered as her newfound courage filled her chest.

The sound of Roger screaming for his breakfast brought Jane to sudden reality. She hopped out of bed, got dressed, and headed down the stairs before her mother could start yelling for her to "get up." She didn't want to face Hazel this morning. She was still reeling from the events of the night before and she didn't know what lay ahead.

Jane couldn't wait to get to school to see Jason, but each time she spotted him, he turned the other way and totally ignored her. Gone were the smiles and winks of yesterday. The school day lagged on with no end in sight.

To make matters even worse, Mr. Sanderson was not in the room when the bell rang to signal the start of English class. With no teacher to keep order, the kids became unruly, and soon everyone was out of control.

Mr. Sanderson was very disappointed with his class when he returned to find the students running around the room and making noise. Jane was one of the few kids sitting at her desk, but the outcome was mass punishment. Everyone in the class had to stay an hour after school to serve detention.

The Bucks had a rule for their daughters. No lollygagging after school. They were expected to be home ten minutes after the last bell.

For the first time since she came to live with the Bucks, Jane was not on time getting home from school. When she walked in the door an hour late, Hazel erupted like a livid red-hot volcano. She was not about to believe her daughter's story about the detention.

"Liar," Hazel screamed at her.

Ted smirked at them as he walked through the kitchen on his way to the Masonic Temple for a meeting. The look of satisfaction on her father's face caused Jane's skin to crawl.

"I have to get out of here," she thought. "They hate me." She began to mentally plan what her next move should be when the phone rang. With her father out of the house and her mother on the phone, she saw her opportunity to run.

She got her coat and silently let herself out through the front door. Once outside, she forgot the cold and ran with all her might through streets and alleys toward her love.

She reasoned that once she could talk to Jason and explain everything, he'd understand. After all, he loved her. In her innocence, she believed that they could make a plan to run away and be together forever.

Gasping for breath in the frigid night air, Jane finally saw his house. The lights were shining brightly through the windows and reflecting off the cold white snow. Her heart felt warm deep inside. She ran up the front walk and knocked at the door of her sanctuary.

The look of fear that crossed the face of her prince, when he saw who was at the door, was more than she could stand.

"You can't come here," he said as he started to shut the door in her face.

"Wait, wait," Jane pleaded. "I don't have anywhere else to go."

"Go to Sheila's house, just get out of here."

The door slammed shut, leaving her standing alone in the cold.

By then, snow was falling steadily. Unaware of the chaos caused by her disappearance, Jane headed toward the house of her friend, Sheila.

Hazel had heard the front door shut and realized that Jane had gone out without permission.

"She can't defy the rules around here," Hazel raged to herself as she hung up the phone.

Without missing a beat, she dialed the number of the Masonic Temple. The phone rang repeatedly. At length, a kindly voice answered and immediately went to summon her husband.

Ted was angry, times ten, with Hazel for daring to interrupt a lodge meeting.

He told her in no uncertain terms, "I am not going to go looking for that little slut. I don't care if she freezes to death."

"Then I am going to call the police," Hazel screamed into the phone.

That was all it took for Ted to decide it would not be good to get the police involved. He remembered last night very clearly. He didn't want Jane talking to the cops.

"All right, I'll go find her," he said menacingly, in a quiet voice that kept him out of earshot of the other lodge members. "Where should I look?"

"Get over to Carter's," Hazel yelled. "She's been messing around with Jason."

The phone went dead. Hazel sat down at the kitchen table with an evil gleam in her eyes and a satisfied grin on her face.

"Ted loves those girls more than he loves me," she thought. "Let him deal with the little slut."

Grandpa Bailey saw the whole show through the crack of his bedroom door. He felt powerless to protect his granddaughter from the woman who had once been his sweet little girl. The reality that Hazel had become almost as evil and conniving as her husband, settled hard on him. He offered up a prayer asking God to forgive him for his weakness.

Jane wished she had thought ahead and considered the possibility that Jason would not lovingly welcome her. She slugged through the snow with no boots on her feet or mittens on her hands. Tears of relief welled up in her eyes as she saw the streetlight shining ahead. She knew Sheila's house was on the corner, only a couple of blocks away.

Suddenly, from nowhere and heading in her direction, came the lights of a car. The driver was going very slowly, as if searching for something. Jane wasn't sure what she felt when she recognized the car as her father's. She wanted to hide but the drifts were too high to get away. Cold and fear were hers as she stopped walking and waited for the vehicle to come to a complete stop beside her.

Ted jumped out of the car and came menacingly toward her. Then, as if he had thought it over, he stopped and turned back toward the vehicle.

As he walked, he motioned for her to get in the front seat.

"We're going home and you will apologize to your mother for worrying her," he said as he revved up the engine and pulled slowly onto the street. "I should beat you within an inch of your life," he growled.

Jane slumped into the front seat. The dashboard lights cast an eerie green glow across Ted's pathetic face. With great sadness, Jane saw her dreams crushed, and along with them…her soul.

Chapter Twenty-Four

The End of the New Beginning

Life had been pretty bleak since her attempt to run away to Jason's. Now he wouldn't even look at her at school. Much worse, the time spent at home was even more desolate. Jane's mother and father barely spoke to her and it was clear that she was unwanted and barely tolerated in the house.

One bright spot in her otherwise dark gloomy life was the arrival of the Christmas season. The only part of the holiday Jane looked forward to was Joyce coming home. She had written to say she could stay for two whole weeks.

As the days grew shorter, Jane began to feel life stir in her soul again. The despair she felt those last few weeks began to lift and anticipation began to build.

Joyce came home four days before Christmas and the mood of the whole house visibly changed. Ted began to smile and talked as if nothing was wrong. Hazel decorated the tree and baked cookies. Much to Ted's chagrin, Aunt Nellie and cousin Jim even came for a visit. Jane had her sister back again. Life was good.

During the two weeks Joyce was home, Ted was a happy man. Every evening, he and Joyce went to the basement to make presents or help him catch up on his lawn ornaments. It did not dawn on Jane that her father had gone back on his promise to leave Joyce alone. She was just so glad to have happy days again.

In the basement, Ted threatened, "Don't be a problem now, Pumpkin. You know I'll kill your damn sister if you won't come to the basement with me whenever I want. After all, I only have two weeks to show you how much I love you," he added almost wistfully.

Joyce could hardly wait to return to Milwaukee to get back to the school she loved. She worried about her sister, but she had gotten Ted to promise that he would leave Jane alone while she was away.

"You are the only one I love," he told her. "I'm not interested in that troublemaker, Jane."

The train ride back to Milwaukee was a blessing for Joyce. She relaxed for the first time in two weeks, and she was happy to be going back to her classes. Yet she felt terrible leaving her sister in that house.

Without warning, the train derailed. Joyce was scared to death before realizing she was safe. The conductor announced that the people waiting for them in Milwaukee would be informed of their three-hour delay.

While she waited, she spent most of her time daydreaming about the cute young man she had met a couple of days before Christmas break. His name was Danny and he was from the little town of Stanley, Wisconsin.

Joyce and Danny had agreed to meet for a cup of coffee as soon as they were both back in Milwaukee. Danny was so nice that Joyce couldn't imagine why he wanted to spend time with her. She let out a happy sigh, pressed her forehead against the cool train window, and dreamed about her first real date.

She had not mentioned Danny's name to her family. Not even her beloved sister was aware that she was going back to Milwaukee with the hope of dating a boy. Joyce also kept her friendship with Danny a secret, from Theresa and everyone else she knew.

Her life was wonderful. This was truly the new beginning she had prayed for. Joyce loved school and she loved being far away from her father. She liked Danny.

The week before spring break, Joyce and Danny decided to meet at the Museum of Natural History. The exhibits were fabulous and the time got away from the happy couple. Suddenly, Joyce realized she would have to leave immediately. They ran, and arrived at the bus stop just in time to see it pull away from the curb.

Joyce understood that it was extremely important for her to catch the 5:15 bus back to Theresa's house every evening. If she missed the bus, she would have to wait for the 6:00, and Theresa was the worrying kind.

Joyce started to cry but Danny convinced her that everything would turn out all right. She knew that he meant well, but he didn't know her family. Missing the bus would more than likely turn into a disaster.

At 6:30, Joyce burst into the kitchen with a well-rehearsed excuse on her lips. Theresa informed her that she had called Ted and Hazel to tell them that their daughter had come up missing. Joyce was told to call home immediately.

"You boy-crazy little bitch," Ted yelled when he heard her voice. "I knew you couldn't be trusted. I knew you'd start messing around with boys as soon as my back was turned," he ranted.

"Let me talk to Theresa," he growled.

Joyce handed the phone to Theresa while wondering what the conversation was really about.

"Uh huh, uh huh, okay. Goodbye," was all she heard from Theresa's side of the conversation.

"Eat your supper and go to your room," Theresa told her. "You've caused enough trouble already tonight."

The next day Ted called and informed Theresa that Joyce was to finish out the week at school and then take the train home for spring break.

He told Theresa, "I've run out of money and can't afford that overpriced school. Joyce won't be coming back."

"Another open well," Joyce thought.

She cried all the way back to Cornell.

She had feared her beautiful new life would be over, and over it was. Upon Joyce's return, Ted tightened the screws on both of his daughters. He now had facts whirling around in his demented head. He had proof that neither Joyce nor Jane could be trusted, and they were both promiscuous.

Despair is the only word to describe how Joyce felt about the turn of events in her life. She decided the best way to spend her days was to be as far away from the house and her parents as possible.

She found a job as a baby sitter for a neighbor. Then she worked up the courage to apply for a job at a local restaurant, The N-Joy. In addition, her father and mother agreed that she could take a correspondence course in dental assisting. These activities successfully kept her out of Hazel's sight, most of the time.

Ted was a different matter. Now that Joyce was back where he wanted her, he dominated her time in the evenings. It seemed that he never tired of needing her help down in the basement. He complained that his projects were never done.

Hazel, Jane, and Grandpa Bailey spent many evenings in front of the TV in the living room while Joyce and Ted "labored" in the basement. Thus, the days and evenings marched on from spring to summer at the Buck household.

As summer neared, Jane began to get very excited about graduation. Secretly, she had been making big plans for her sister and her. With the help of Mrs. Haase, the school librarian, she wrote several letters of application to hospitals in the area who were looking for nursing assistants.

To her delight, graduation was a festive affair. Many of the activities were off limits to Jane, but she was allowed to attend a few. In fear of not making a good impression, Hazel lobbied Ted to give in a little where their daughter's graduation was concerned.

Jane was allowed to go to the Senior Tea because it was held across the street at Kathy's house. Many of the girls in the graduating class attended the tea, dressed in their best, and accessorized with picture window hats and white gloves.

The Sunday before graduation the whole Buck family attended Baccalaureate, a religious event for the senior class, held at the high school gymnasium. Grandpa Bailey was with them as they all walked down the aisle to find seats near the front. He searched the mass of navy robes and mortarboards until he found his granddaughter. The heaviness in his heart lifted a bit at the happiness he saw on her face.

Excitement ran high the night of graduation. In the minutes before the band began to play *Pomp and Circumstance*, heralding the start of the grand march, much hugging and best wishing went on amongst the graduates. Instinctively, they knew this would be the last time they would ever see some of their classmates. Tears glistened in many eyes as they, the apprehensive new adults launching into the unknown, found their places in line.

Chapter Twenty-Five

Free at Last

As she walked, the evening breeze swirled the gold and yellow leaves, scattering them up the street in front of her. Cool autumn air chilled Jane to the bone, making her realize that her heart was as cold as her body.

In the weeks before her graduation from high school, Jane had applied for the position of nurse's aide at three different hospitals. Since Joyce was now living at home, she had made application for her sister as well. She was told she would be notified by mail.

With great anticipation and excitement, the girls had made lofty plans. Many nighttime hours were spent whispering about earning money and what they would do with it. Once they were employed, they would be free of their father, and would be free to have friends!

Summer had passed and still they had not heard a word.

"What's wrong with us? Why haven't we been accepted?" they questioned. "All three hospitals had openings. You'd think we would have heard by now."

A deep yearning clutched Jane's heart, threatening to squeeze from it the last shreds of her soul. Jane raised her face toward the autumn sky for comfort. Suddenly, calm spread through her and it became crystal clear. *Before the basic human needs of clothing, food, and shelter stands the primal need for freedom.*

Jane quickened her pace as she walked the few blocks home from her babysitting job. At this time of the evening, her sister and father would be home from work, and her mother would be watching for her.

It was a rule that no one could eat until the whole family was seated at the table.

As usual, things were quiet at supper. Hazel and Ted seemed strained. "What was it this time?" Grandpa Bailey seemed to say, as he looked at Joyce and Jane, and gave them a hint of a smile.

After supper, the girls cleared the table, did the dishes, and reset the table again for Ted's breakfast the next morning. As soon as they were finished, they quietly tiptoed out of the kitchen and down the hall toward the stairs leading to their bedroom. All they wanted was a moment alone together, and to not draw Ted's attention.

Partly down the hallway, Joyce whispered, "We forgot to take out the garbage."

"It's your turn," Jane reminded her.

Joyce went back to the kitchen to finish the task.

As Jane stood there in the hall waiting for her sister to return, it struck her that anyone looking through the windows would think the Buck's were a regular "Leave it to Beaver" family. Ted was sitting in his recliner reading the newspaper. Grandpa was nodding off in front of the TV, and Hazel was knitting a pretty blue baby sweater for a friend.

Joyce came around the corner from the kitchen with a dazed look on her face. Jane did a double take and took a quick peek into the living room to see if Ted was still in there. He was. Jane had seen that look on Joyce's face before, and it was always after an encounter with Ted.

"Look what was in the garbage," Joyce whispered the minute their bedroom door was shut. "It's an acceptance letter from Lakeside Hospital."

"It was in the garbage?" Jane asked, "How did it get in there?"

"Look at the date," Joyce choked. "Almost two weeks ago."

"I bet they weren't going to tell us. They want to keep us here forever," Jane murmured, mostly to herself.

In that moment, desperation turned to courage. She grabbed the letter, swung open the bedroom door and stomped down the steps toward her despicable parents. Jane had had enough. *I need to be free and I don't care what happens. They are not going to stop me.*

"What's this?" she asked swinging into the living room with a belligerent snarl on her lips.

"What is it, darling?" Hazel said in her sweetest voice. "Bring it here. Let me see."

She studied the page for a long time and then said, "Congratulations, girls. It looks like your prayers have been answered."

Hazel gave Ted a questioning look, but he just stared her down, and she didn't say another word.

Hazel and Ted Buck.

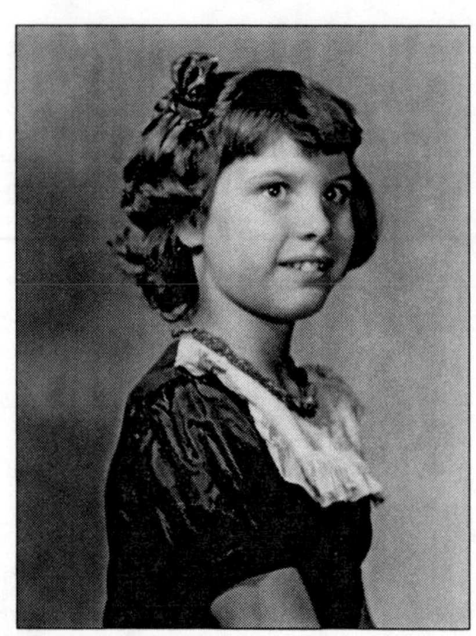

Sharon Ann Colburn."Desert Princess,"
age seven years, nine months.
Became Jane Alice Buck.

Shirley Maye Colburn
"Bright Meadow," age ten.
Became Joyce Mary Buck.

Sharon (left) and Shirley (right).
The day they arrived in Cornell, wearing the new dresses the social worker gave them. They brought nothing else with them, to their new home.

Shirley and Sharon with their new mother, Hazel.

 1

Finally, they have dolls.

First Christmas as Jane and Joyce,
with Grandpa Bailey.

The sisters with their black dog, Smokey.

Jane (left) and Joyce (right)
The day they were formally adopted, one year after arriving in Cornell. Their year in paradise is over.

Jane and Joyce with their little brother, Roger.

Alan Hale Colburn.
"Handsome and Peaceful"

Alan's foster mother helped him locate his sisters. She took this picture of the three Colburn children, together for the first time in many years. One look at this picture and you know how much they cared for each other, how much they had survived, and how strong they had become.

Book Three...

Life on Their Own.

Chapter Twenty-Six

The Beginning of the Fall

The beautiful, old, three-story house that would be their new home, stood across the street from the Lakeside Hospital in Rice Lake, Wisconsin. There were private rooms for ten girls in the house, and all the girls worked at the hospital.

Ted and Hazel helped the girls carry their belongings into the house. The housemother took the family on a tour. They all marveled at the beauty of the big living room and the practicality of the laundry room. The Buck's gave the impression of a happy family as they went to Jane's room on the main floor to deposit her things, and then up to the second floor to Joyce's new room.

Looking pleasant and happy, Hazel and Ted played their parts well. They asked all the right questions, and chatted casually with the housemother as they went from room to room.

That night, Jane slept by herself in her strange new bedroom. The room felt cold and foreign, especially without the warmth and security of her older sister sleeping beside her. For almost twenty years, except for the short time she had been in Milwaukee, Joyce's presence had helped Jane feel safe and cared for.

Training would begin on Monday morning. Joyce would start her training on the second floor of the hospital, which catered to maternity, surgery, and recovery. Jane thought the supervisors made the perfect choice for her sister, a true "angel of mercy."

On the first floor, Jane hoped she would learn quickly to care for outpatients' needs, broken bones, and the elderly. She was nervous and scared to finally start out on the "rest and best" of her life. Jane's dreams had come true. Se was actually going to work in a hospital!

For Jane and Joyce, fear was a real problem in the first few weeks at Lakeside. Their jobs were demanding and everything was new. Self-confidence was something the sisters horribly lacked, but fortunately, they weren't aware that self-confidence even existed.

Disbelief was the only word to describe how Joyce felt while living and working in Rice Lake. She had finally escaped the clutches of her father. She was beginning to feel grown up, ready to grab the world by the tail and soar. She truly cherished the two things that had eluded her before coming to Rice Lake—friends and freedom from her father's abuses.

Slowly, Jane and Joyce began making friends. One day, Joyce realized that she hadn't giggled and chatted so much with other girls in her entire life. She was not used to being accepted. She found it hard to believe that even though she hadn't started drinking and smoking like the others, she was becoming part of the gang.

Maxine and Dorothy lived in the house and became their first friends.

Sometimes they would yell, "Hey, you guys, do you want to cruise the gut?"

Then all the girls would jump into Maxine's old car and ride up and down Main Street.

Another friend, Janice, usually had a good idea.

"Let's run downtown," she'd yell across the hall.

"I'm coming over. Do ya want me to bring you a Coke?" Mary Ann would ask as they all walked back to the house, after their shift at the hospital.

Both girls relaxed and realized their dreams were being fulfilled. There was no longer a constantly crying mother, no more upsets and fighting parents, no more locked basement doors, and no more sex with the man they had grown to hate.

Joyce felt happy, but she still felt afraid, and very unsure of her future. From experience, she believed that joy was fleeting and would soon come to an end.

On days when they were feeling down, they would get off work, change into street clothes and walk downtown. They'd tell each other their troubles and then start talking about their dreams. The sisters would walk, talk, and window-shop until their hearts were filled with joy. Then they would go back to the hospital in time to eat supper.

On Sunday mornings, if they didn't have to work, Joyce and Jane went to church. When they both had the same weekend off, they were required to catch the bus and go home to Cornell.

Jane hated going home because Ted and Hazel would grill her about what she did and where she went. They'd want to know, "How much money did you spend? Are you drinking and smoking?"

The irony was that when they were children, Hazel had told the girls repeatedly that drinking and smoking were evil. Now all of a sudden, she seemed to expect her daughters to be doing evil things.

Besides that, Ted made Jane's skin crawl when they were in Cornell. He would look longingly at Joyce and spend his time trying to get close to her. It was as if he just couldn't get enough of her. At least he left Jane alone, and for that, she was grateful.

As the busy days at Lakeside turned into weeks, the training period ended. The sisters didn't have much chance to be alone, just to talk, any longer. They not only had separate rooms, they worked on different floors, had different schedules, and spent lots of time with their new friends.

Two months after moving to Rice Lake, Joyce began feeling sick at work. Every morning, when she took the breakfast trays to her patients, she would become ill. The smell of food proved to be too much for her. She soon began rushing to the bathroom to throw up.

The charge nurse noticed Joyce's distress and asked, "Are you feeling all right? Is it possible that you are pregnant?"

"No," Joyce answered with certainty. "I just had my period."

The nurse told Joyce, "Take a couple of days off and get better. I don't want you to bring the flu bug into the hospital."

Joyce was sure she had the flu or something worse. Even though she worked at the hospital, she was afraid to see any doctor besides Dr. Zenner, in Cadott. He had been her doctor since she came to live in Cornell.

On her supervisor's advice, she called her mother and arranged to go home.

Hazel told Joyce, "We're not coming all the way to Rice Lake to get you. Take the bus to Bloomer. Dad and I will pick you up at the bus station there. I'll have your dad call Dr. Zenner to make an appointment for tomorrow."

The tone of Hazel's voice told Joyce that her mother wasn't happy to have her coming home. She wasn't happy about it, either, as she sadly walked to the station to catch the bus.

Joyce spotted her parent's green sedan drive up, just as the bus came to a stop, in Bloomer. Hardly a word was spoken the whole way back to Cornell. Roger played peek-a-boo with his big sister from time to time, but he soon dozed off on Hazel's lap.

Silence roared in her ears as the car cruised down the highway. Joyce didn't know that she was racing toward another open well.

The sullen family arrived home at suppertime. Hazel hurried to warm some soup, and she instructed Joyce to make the sandwiches. As they sat down to eat their supper, Joyce noticed that Grandpa Bailey was not looking very well.

Joyce went to bed in her old room, this time without her sister. Fear that Ted would come up the stairs to see her, and worry of being terribly ill, kept her from falling into a peaceful sleep.

Suddenly, Joyce felt her lungs constrict. Her breathing became labored, as though someone was sitting on her chest. She sat straight up in bed, and in a panic, bolted toward the bedroom door. As she moved through the darkness, she found that she had to use her hands to break through the cobwebs that had formed in the stairway.

She heard someone behind her and instantly the hair stood up at the nape of her neck. The instinct for survival was strong and Joyce knew she had to get out of the house.

The faster she ran, the harder it was to breathe, and the slower her legs seemed to move, until she felt she was moving in slow motion. She looked down at herself and realized that her body had grown larger, which made it hard for her to run.

As Joyce stumbled through the kitchen, she saw that the door had been moved and it was locked. She tried to open it, but in her terror, she couldn't get the strange doorknob to work.

Again, she heard the footsteps and fast breathing of someone closing in on her. Wild eyed, Joyce looked around the kitchen until she saw the frying pan on the top of the stove. She grabbed it and swung several times, until the window beside the door was shattered.

In blind terror, she crawled through the opening and jumped into a strange world of darkness. Unexplainably, Joyce found herself running through the field at the old Colburn farm in Turtle Lake.

As she ran, she looked over her shoulder and saw what she was afraid to see. Ted Buck was chasing her and his eyes glowed green in the darkness. Her bulk made it hard for her to run fast enough.

She heard her brother, Alan shout, "STOP."

Rocks and dirt dislodged and fell out of sight as she skidded, bare feet first. Her grasping hands found clumps of dry grass in an effort to stop the forward motion of her pregnant body.

A sharp blade of terror ran through her, as she looked over her shoulder into the gaping mouth of the old open well. She lay there in the dirt, clinging to the grass. Her legs and feet dangled above the abyss.

The smell of mouthwash caused her to look upward, and into the eyes of her father. As she watched, Ted's face slowly morphed into the shape of a wolf. Joyce watched in complete horror as she saw his hand, with its long bright red fingernails, extending toward her. The snarling leer on his evil face, forced her to let go of the lifesaving grass. With a blood-curdling scream, she fell into the black hole.

Joyce heard the scream and sat upright in her bed, disoriented for a moment, until finally she understood that it was her own screaming that had awakened her. In complete panic, she realized that she was pregnant, and the real nightmare was about to begin.

While Joyce was in Cornell, Jane was having the time of her life in Rice Lake. Maxine and Dorothy had boyfriends named Tom and Art. Jane wanted very much to have a boyfriend, too, but she was tongue tied around boys. She even found it hard to talk to her friends' boyfriends.

Two of the girls who worked in the kitchen at the hospital had an apartment of their own. Often, Jane would go over there with Maxine and Dorothy to listen to music. That's where she learned to dance. Back home, she was never allowed to listen to popular music or dance. Ted believed it was sinful.

Some of the girls smoked, and there was always beer. Jane started smoking cigarettes. With a cigarette in her hand, she felt she was truly one of the gang.

Sometimes they would all pile into the old car and go cruising for guys. That's when they would end up at the Green Parrot Tavern. Jane learned how to dance and how to talk to guys at the Green Parrot.

One night when it was time to leave the bar, Dorothy and Jane realized their friends had already gone. They decided to accept a ride from some guys they had been talking to earlier in the evening. They were young and drinking heavily. It was all so exciting.

As they left town, the driver started "stepping on it" until they were driving down the highway very fast. Suddenly, Jane noticed they were drag racing with another car. It was totally black outside. As they came up over a hill, Jane saw headlights in the distance, coming directly toward their speeding car.

Her life literally flashed before her eyes and she realized if she didn't do something, she would die. In a panic, she looked at the speedometer, which read 125 miles per hour. With super human strength and courage, she hit the driver in the arm, and grabbed the steering wheel.

Her prayers were answered when the car was finally pulled over on the side of the road. Jane believed that God had saved her life that night. The car that was speeding toward them turned off the road and never passed them.

Jane would have asked God to save her sister that night, too, if she had known what was going on in Cornell.

Ted had surmised, by her symptoms, that his daughter was pregnant. He called Dr. Zenner and told him that Joyce had been raped and needed an appointment as soon as possible. Joyce was scheduled for an emergency appointment the next morning.

Ted drove Joyce to her doctor's appointment. On the way, she tried to prepare herself for the onslaught of questions the doctor might ask an unmarried pregnant girl. Joyce was worried sick because she didn't have the answers. She only knew she couldn't tell Dr. Zenner the truth.

To her surprise, Dr. Zenner didn't ask her any questions. The tests came back positive. The doctor informed her, in a professional tone, that she was indeed pregnant.

As soon as they returned home from the doctor's appointment, Ted nodded at Joyce to follow him to the basement. In the basement, they discussed how they were going to tell Hazel that Joyce was pregnant. They wondered what Hazel would do when she found out.

Ted had the story all planned out. He instructed Joyce to say that Jane and she had stopped at the Green Parrot, with some friends, after work. Joyce was to say that she didn't want to go into the tavern so she stayed out in the car. While Jane was in the tavern, drinking and picking up guys, Joyce was being raped.

Hazel read Joyce the riot act when she was told that she was pregnant.

"If you were raped, why didn't you go to the cops?" Hazel asked with disdain in her voice.

"Because I didn't know who it was that raped me and I was too scared," Joyce sobbed in answer.

One day, to Jane's surprise, Hazel and Ted brought Joyce back to Rice Lake to pick up her things. They were taking Joyce home, bag and baggage. The sisters cried together when Joyce told Jane that she was pregnant. Jane was not surprised, nor was she puzzled by the look on Ted's face. *See, I've won,* the look said.

That day, their lives took a drastic turn. That day was the beginning of the fall for the Colburn/Buck sisters.

Chapter Twenty-Seven

It's All Your Fault

Jane was getting very worried about her sister because Joyce hadn't written or answered any of her letters, since she had gone back home. Jane wondered if Ted or Hazel had thrown her letters away. She felt sure Ted had been responsible for keeping the hospital acceptance letter from them. *Mama read my diary so I know she is capable of reading Joyce's mail,* she reasoned.

Near Christmas, Jane became very ill at work. The head nurse let her go back to her room early to lie down. By evening, she was much worse. She crawled out of bed and managed to get back to the hospital before she fainted.

The emergency room doctor put her in a room and ran some tests. Jane was diagnosed with pneumonia and stayed in the hospital for a week.

"You'd better take another week off work to recuperate," the doctor told her.

The thought of spending a week alone in her small room without anybody to care for her was more than Jane could stand. She needed help, so she decided to catch the bus and go back to Cornell, where her sister was. Jane knew Joyce loved her and would take care of her.

When Jane arrived home, Hazel and Ted were all over her. They were wild with anger because Joyce had been raped.

"It happened when Joyce waited in the car, while you were drinking, smoking, and picking up boys at the Green Parrot Tavern," Hazel screamed. "It's your fault."

Her time in Cornell changed Jane's attitude about the relationship she shared with her sister. Jane didn't know that Ted had threatened Joyce to stay away from her. The sisters were even put in separate bedrooms during the visit.

Joyce was too afraid of her father to go against his will, and confess the truth to her sister.

She hates me now, Jane thought sadly. *Why would she lie? She didn't get pregnant in Rice Lake. We didn't go out with guys while she was living there,* Jane sobbed into her pillow.

Somehow, Jane had failed again. She had lost the love of her sister, which to her meant she had lost everything.

By the time she returned to work after New Years, she had decided never to go home again. Without the stabilizing influence of her beloved sister, Joyce, Jane's life began to reel out of control.

Jane started going out more often and she began drinking heavily. On one of those nights at the Green Parrot, a tall, dark, and handsome young man named Bill asked her out on her first real date. He worked on his parent's farm and she thought he was wonderful. They hit it off and began spending as much time together as they could. They went to the movies and for long walks in the park.

Snow was falling softly through the cold winter air, and Bill's bright blue eyes were warm and shining as he slid his high school class ring on Jane's finger. She couldn't believe they were actually going steady, and she finally had a boyfriend of her own. Jane Alice Buck was delirious with happiness.

Jane met another girl named Jane who was now working at the hospital, and they soon became good friends. On Valentine's Day weekend, both Jane's were invited to a house party. They laughed together and talked about the fun they were planning to have.

To her surprise, Jane learned that Art and Tom had been invited, too. She also realized they were the only other people she knew who were going to the party. When they arrived, everyone was dancing and the music was blaring. "Booze, beer, and bodacious broads," was the catch phrase of the evening.

The girls soon found their way upstairs, where it wasn't so crowded and the noise level was cut in half. On the desk was a stack of records and an old record player. They put on a record, and Jane's new friend went downstairs to tell Tom and Art where they were.

After she left, Jane sat on the bed listening to the music. She still found it hard to believe that she was one of the gang. It ran through her mind that her sister, Joyce, should be there, enjoying this moment with her.

Presently, the bedroom door opened and someone came into the room. Jane recognized him as a friend of her boyfriend Bill, and she smiled. He looked her in the eye and nodded his head.

Even though it was happening very fast, Jane saw it in slow motion. He switched off the light, came over to her, and pushed her back onto the bed. Before she could react to this sudden attack, he had her panties down and was unzipping his jeans.

Jane gathered a huge breath to let out a scream, but he hit her in the face with his fist. Only a squeak escaped from her lips. Her breath came out in a sputter, and she could taste blood in her mouth.

His face was inches from hers. She would always remember the wretched smell of his breath.

He snarled, "You scream, and I'll beat you to death."

Instinctively, she knew that he meant it.

The shear weight of his fat body kept her from moving. He was smothering her and she couldn't take a full breath. She knew she was going to die.

There are many sides to the pain of rape. Physically, the searing pain is unbearable. Mentally, the helplessness is overwhelming. Emotionally, the fear is debilitating.

The assailant jumped off the bed as the door opened and Jane heard her friends enter the room.

She screamed, "Don't turn on the light."

She didn't want her friends to see her humiliation and she was afraid the man would kill them all if he thought they could identify him.

Tom grabbed the guy and threw him out of the room. Her friend Jane helped her get dressed and then took her back to the house. The two Jane's stayed together and cried, while they used a cold washcloth to clean the blood off her face.

Jane didn't want to go to the police because she was so ashamed. But later that night, Tom came back and told them the police had raided the party and arrested a lot of people. She found out that her beloved Bill and his rapist friend were both in jail.

A few days later, Jane saw Bill and asked him about the party. He said he was sorry, but he looked for her and couldn't find her. After that night, Bill and Jane saw less and less of each other. She felt more distance between them each time they met, until one day, she took the ring off her finger and wore it on a chain around her neck.

The head nurse at the hospital began to notice her social behavior. She changed her hours so she would have to work nights. On the graveyard shift, Jane was expected to work all night, and that forced her to sleep most of the day. With this new schedule, her nightlife came to a screeching halt.

In the spring, Dorothy moved out of the house and the two Jane's became roommates. Her friend Jane had the kind of family she had always wished for herself. Whenever they visited the farm, her friend's mother cooked wonderful meals and everyone in the family had so much fun.

For a couple of days, Jane would lose herself in the love and happiness that filled every corner of the old farmhouse.

"When I get married, I want to have a family just like this," Jane vowed every time she visited.

As Jane dreamt about a happy home life, her sister Joyce was experiencing just the opposite. Hazel hated Joyce, and she hated having her around the house. She just couldn't stand to look at her daughter's pregnant body. She ignored her completely, and kept busy by engrossing herself in the care of her son, Roger.

Though he acted normal around other people, Joyce thought Ted looked rather smug, but seemed standoffish and distant in her presence. Joyce felt that her dad hated her. Since she was forced to tell the lie about her sister, she believed Jane hated her, too.

Joyce felt totally alone in the world. Grandpa Bailey was ill, and Roger was kept far away from her. The only relief she found was she didn't have to have sex with her father, during the time she was pregnant.

For six months, Joyce stayed around the house and helped Hazel. She kept out of sight as much as possible. She was not allowed to go to church, but she was allowed to visit Aunt Nellie and Stella Berg. Stella was one friend of Hazel's who was kind to Joyce.

For days, Joyce rehearsed what she would say to Hazel. She had finally decided to tell Hazel that Ted was the father of her unborn baby.

Monday afternoon, when Ted had gone back to work after lunch, and Roger was down for his nap, Joyce found her mother in the living room.

She asked, "Can we talk?"

Hazel looked up from her knitting, and said, "What kind of lies do you have for me this time?"

Joyce nearly lost her nerve, but cleared her throat and began, "Daddy is the father of this baby."

Before she had a chance to continue, Hazel screamed, "Your father is sterile, and you are a liar. If I believed you, I would have to kill myself."

Joyce looked at her mother and thought about the time Hazel had used those same words, when she had tried to ask for help years ago. Then she heard a sound and looked up to see Grandpa Bailey standing in the hall with tears running down his face.

She often wondered if Grandpa Bailey knew what was going on with her father. Now there was no question. He had just heard her tell Hazel. His tears were a comfort to her. They showed Joyce that he was sorry for what she had been forced to endure.

Joyce did not talk to anyone about her situation again. She decided it was best to wait until the baby was born and then find a way for them both to escape.

Chapter Twenty-Eight

The Military Man

One cold March evening, Art and her roommate, Jane took Jane out to the Green Parrot. That would prove to be the night that would change her life forever.

Shortly after the friends arrived at the Parrot, a tall handsome man sauntered over and asked Jane to dance with him. The jukebox was playing "Puff the Magic Dragon," and during the dance, he asked, "Will you marry me?"

She couldn't believe someone wanted to marry her. He said he had recently returned from Germany, and had been discharged from the army.

He introduced himself as John Botsford, and then he told her, "You are beautiful."

Jane truly believed that a military man wouldn't lie to her, and besides, they were having so much fun. They danced, talked, and laughed until she fell madly in love with the handsome military man.

Too soon, Jane's friend had to go back to the house. Jane didn't want to leave John, so she asked Art if he could give John a ride home, after he dropped them off. Art agreed and they all piled into his car and drove away.

Jane didn't have to go to work until the next night.

"Can I ride along with you when you take John home?" she asked Art.

Mostly, Jane wanted to spend more time with her new love, but she was also curious to see where he lived. John and Jane stayed in the back seat while Art walked her friend to the door. All the way to John's house, the lovers made out. Jane had never felt anything close to love before and thought, "This is wonderful."

They arrived at John's house in Dallas, Wisconsin, around one o'clock in the morning. They shared a long passionate kiss and then reluctantly said good night.

On the drive back to Rice Lake, Art began making suggestions. He thought Jane should "put out" for him the way she "put out" for John.

She told him, "NO! I am going to marry John, and besides, you are dating my best friend."

Art's anger began to grow until Jane was very afraid. She was alone with him in the car on a strange dark country road. Her fears were realized when he turned onto a side road and stopped the car.

He began pulling at her clothes, but she kept kicking and trying to keep him away. Finally, his anger got the better of him. He opened the door and roughly shoved Jane to the ground beside the car.

Gravel flew, pelting her with hundreds of small stones, as he took off in a rage. Jane lay there, on the side of the road, watching the red taillights grow smaller. Suddenly she realized the car was turning around. She knew Art was coming back after her.

In a panic, with shear adrenalin running through her veins, she clawed and dug her way to the top of the hill. Jane lay down, trying to hide in the tangled brush. She was on the bank high above the dirt road, where she had been deposited only seconds before.

As the lights of the car came nearer, she could hear Art yelling, "I'm going to kill you when I find you. Where are you?"

Many times, he drove past her hiding place that night—back and forth, back and forth, calling out threats each time he passed.

In the face of such fear, it took every thread of will she had to remain quiet and wait. With each pass, his threats grew wilder, until one time he didn't turn around and come back. Jane laid there in the dirt and blackberry bushes for a long time, just waiting for him to return. He never did.

In Wisconsin, the month of March can be a nasty, cold, and wet month. That night was no exception. Once Jane felt safe enough to move from her hiding spot, among the snow covered bushes, she found that she was so cold she had difficulty walking.

Blackberry brambles had scratched and cut her face until it was bleeding. Mud was caked in her hair and her nylons were in shreds. To top it off, she had lost her purse. Inch by inch, through the briers, she searched until her bleeding hands felt the smooth leather. Jane picked up her lifeline and clutched it to her breast. She stood there shivering and sobbing, but she knew she would survive.

Gingerly, Jane started down the bank toward the road. The distraught young woman thought she could remember the way to John's house. There were a few stars and only a sliver of a moon out that night. The sounds of the night made the hair stand up at the back of her neck. Hesitantly, she headed in the direction she thought was right.

The dark night held many terrors. She was certain Art was somewhere on the side of the road, with his lights turned off waiting to carry out his threat to kill her. To Jane, it seemed like hours of walking and straining to hear the slightest sound of a car. She jumped every time she heard a cow moo or an owl hoot.

At last, she saw lights burning brightly through the window of a barn. She saw a man herding some cows into the building through a wide door. She was freezing and exhausted. The sight of another human being made her begin to cry.

Jane trudged through the mucky cow yard to the barn. When the farmer noticed her, he nearly dropped the milk bucket he was carrying.

Apprehensively, she asked the man, "Do you know John Botsford?"

"Yes," the farmer said. "Why don't you follow me to the house?"

The man's wife was standing in the kitchen when they entered the farmhouse. She was very worried about Jane being so cold and scratched up.

"I'm fine," Jane told her. "I just need to get to John Botsford's house."

"He lives with his grandparents," the woman said. "Stay inside where it's warm. I'll go get the car and take you there."

"Thank you," Jane accepted gratefully.

That night, Jane decided to quit working at the hospital. She was afraid to come in contact with Art again. John and his grandparents gave her a home for the next three months.

John's Grandma Nora was very strict. She insisted Jane sleep upstairs in the guest room, and she demanded that she stay away from her grandson's bedroom. She was a very fastidious housekeeper, too. Nobody was allowed to walk in the house after Grandma Nora cleaned the floors. She also had distinct ideas about how people should act. Jane felt like an outsider most of the time, but she was truly in love with John, and happy to see him every day.

The young couple kept busy and out of Grandma Nora's way as much as possible. John worked across the street at a gristmill during the day, and at night, they would go to a neighboring town, drinking and partying.

One night they heard about a party at the local park. They actually didn't get a chance to go until around 10:00 p.m. There were cars all over, with little campfires all around. Several car radios were tuned to the same rock-and-roll station, and the kids were dancing, drinking, and setting off firecrackers. Everybody was having a ball.

John and Jane had a case of beer and were in the process of having a pretty good time when they heard sirens and saw flashing lights. She had never seen so many kids going in so many directions at the same time. Some of the guys didn't have shirts on, while others were pulling up their pants. Girls were screaming and trying their best to hide behind trees and under the picnic tables. Some were trying to drive away without their lights on.

Of course, John and Jane were caught. The police officer instructed them, along with the others, to go to the police station and wait. By the time John and Jane got to the station, there were already fifty or seventy-five people there. They joined the crowd in the small room and tried to act as innocently as possibly.

John was mad that they had been caught. They waited for the police to return. After a little while, one or two at a time started to sneak out of the station without the attendant noticing. Finally, Jane and John took their turn and walked out, got in their car, and left.

They went out of town just as fast as John could drive. Jane was afraid her parents would find out that she had gotten into trouble with the police. She hadn't seen them for several weeks and Joyce had not answered any of her letters. She decided she didn't really care what they thought.

Hazel, on the other hand, did care what people thought. She kept Joyce pretty well out of sight, now that she was hugely pregnant. Stella Berg, a friend of Hazel's, who had now become a friend to Joyce, invited the lonely pregnant girl to lunch. As they sat talking and eating, a sharp stab of pain shot through Joyce's side into her back.

The unsuspecting girl was terrified. Joyce was given no information on childbirth, and thus, she had no idea what to expect. This pregnancy was so embarrassing that no one mentioned it, or even seemed to notice for that matter.

Stella immediately phoned Hazel. Twenty long painful minutes later, Joyce was on the way to St. Joseph's Hospital in Chippewa Falls. Ted and Hazel left Roger in Stella's care as they sped down the highway, with Joyce moaning in the back seat.

Hazel stayed with Joyce through forty-eight hours of labor and a very difficult birth.

"You should have thought about the pain before you went and got yourself pregnant," Hazel smiled at her daughter. "You deserve it."

When Joyce saw her baby, it was a case of love at first sight. On May 19, 1963, Robert Edmund Buck was born. Joyce called him Robbie, for short. Everything she had gone through, in her entire life, was worth it when she looked at the face of her beautiful baby boy.

The day Joyce and Robbie came home from the hospital, she laid the baby in his bassinette, while her little brother looked on.

Roger said, "Hi, this is your old Uncle Roger."

Joyce laughed and gave him a grateful hug.

Things were getting serious for John and Jane, and they made the decision to get married. A week before the wedding, Jane went home to Cornell to see her sister and tell her parents about her plans. It was a mistake. Her parents threw a conniption fit and opposed the marriage.

Ted yelled, "I don't like John, and I am not going to help you ruin your life."

Jane asked Hazel, "Will you go with me to buy a wedding gown?"

Hazel said, "You didn't ask me to go with you while you lived in sin. Why would I go with you to buy a dress?"

The pain of it went deep. Jane decided to skip the ordeal of buying a gown. She'd have to get married in her graduation dress. Joyce pitched in and helped her make a veil. She also put some artificial flowers together for a wedding bouquet.

Jane pleaded with her sister, "Joyce, I know you just had a baby, but you have to stand up for me at my wedding. It is going to be the most wonderful day of my life. I need you there."

"We have to find a best man, too," Jane added.

"Maybe Jim would do that," Joyce suggested.

So Jane asked her cousin Jim Cellars to be John's best man and he agreed. Arrangements were made for Jim to drive Joyce and Jane back to Grandma Nora's house, the morning of the wedding.

That night, Jane called John to tell him of their plans, and to say they would be there in the morning. Grandma Nora answered the phone and said that John was at a party. She gave Jane the phone number where he could be reached.

"John, honey, someone wants to talk to you," a girl yelled into the noise, when Jane asked for her fiancé.

When John came to the phone and found out Jane was on the other end, he started laughing.

"Don't be upset," he chuckled. "Some friends are throwing me a bachelor party."

He sounded so drunk that Jane reminded him to be home in time for the wedding, the next day. She told him that her cousin Jim was going to be his best man, but he wasn't very interested in what she had to say. It was clear he was busy having fun at his bachelor party.

Early the next morning, Jim and the two sisters headed for John's house in Dallas. The trip took over an hour. By the time they arrived, Jane couldn't wait to see John. The week she had spent with her parents had all but killed her. Jane needed to feel John's love.

John wasn't home from his bachelor party when the trio arrived, so they sat with Grandma Nora in the kitchen and waited. Jim was upset and ready to go back to Cornell, but Jane begged him to stay.

The groom came staggering home one hour late for the wedding. Jane was so relieved to see him. All she wanted to do was be with the man she loved.

He wasn't dressed for the wedding.

"Wait a minute," John slurred. "I'll be ready in a minute."

He changed into his suit and the four of them left for the church together.

Neither Ted and Hazel nor John's grandparents had agreed to attend the wedding. Jane was angry that John was drunk, and hurt that no one came to celebrate her marriage to the man she so dearly loved. Besides that, the minister was in such a hurry that he almost married the groom to the maid of honor.

A wiser, more worldly, woman may have been able to see what lay ahead for her, but Jane was young and blinded by love.

So it was on June 15, 1963, in a little Methodist church in Dallas, Wisconsin, witnessed by Joyce Buck and James Cellars, that John Wayne Botsford and Jane Alice Buck became husband and wife.

One afternoon, a month or so after the wedding, Grandpa Bailey was in the living room. Joyce asked him if he wanted to hold the baby.

"Could I?" the old man asked.

Joyce put her son in his great grandfather's arms. She smiled as Grandpa Bailey looked at Robbie with sheer love in his eyes.

Hazel was not amused, and yelled at her father, "Give me that baby before you drop him, you old fool."

With that, Hazel grabbed Robbie from her father's arms and made it clear that she would be taking over the care of the child.

"You're obviously not smart enough to take care of a baby," she sneered at Joyce.

Hazel insisted, "Joyce, find a job so you can pay off your hospital bill. Your father and I have paid enough to get you released from the hospital. There's still a big bill left, and it's up to you," she snarled at her daughter.

Joyce felt lucky to find a position as a nanny and house girl at the Beyer's. The hours were long and she had to clean the house and make the meals. Since her mother proclaimed herself the caregiver for Robbie, Joyce had little contact with her own baby. She filled her empty arms by taking care of the two little Beyer girls.

On August 25, 1963, just three months after Robbie was born, Grandpa Bailey died at St. Joseph's Hospital in Chippewa Falls.

Just before bedtime, Grandpa Bailey had gone to take a bath.

When he came out of the bathroom, he said, "Hazel, I have a terrible headache."

In a few minutes, he began throwing up. Joyce and Hazel got him to the bed and tucked him in.

"I'm going to call the ambulance," Hazel said, and she went to dial the phone.

Joyce was beside herself with worry. She loved him and felt that Grandpa Bailey was the only person in the house who treated her with kindness and respect.

"Here they come," said a very relieved Joyce, as she opened the door to the paramedics.

Dale Bailey died of a cerebral aneurysm.

Jane came for the funeral. She and Joyce talked about how strange it seemed that Hazel acted cold and unmoved by the death of her father. Aside from a few tears when guests were present, it was as if nothing had happened. The sisters grieved their grandpa's death, and believed it would change their lives forever.

Chapter Twenty-Nine

Confusion

Jane Botsford was happy to be married, and happy to have found someone to love her. She could see a long and prosperous life stretching out before her.

The day Jane told her husband she was pregnant, however, was a big disappointment. She had expected him to be as elated as she was.

"What do you expect me to do about that?" John growled. "You've got good timing, that's for sure. I got laid off today," he yelled, as if it was all her fault.

The next few weeks were hard on Jane. The excitement over starting a family was tempered by the unsettled state of her marriage and future.

Every day, John would go to the tavern. When he came home, he was sure to be roaring drunk. Filthy language, that Jane had not heard since she had lived with her biological parents, Esther and Hale Colburn, spewed from his mouth.

For the first time, Jane was afraid of her husband. When he came into the room, she had the urge to crawl under the bed for protection.

One day he came home earlier than usual and said, "You'd better start packing. I got a job at the Stanley Corporation."

She was pleased that they would be moving to Stanley, Wisconsin. *That's only a few miles from Cornell. I might be able to see Joyce a little more often,* Jane thought wistfully.

Jane was worried about Joyce living in that unhappy and potentially dangerous environment. She would have been more worried had she been aware of the changes developing in the big green house on Main Street.

Though Joyce had often felt hatred for Ted, since the birth of her baby, she had begun to feel a connection to him that she couldn't understand. She knew it was crazy, but she felt as though she might be falling in love with her father.

Joyce was confused by the jealousy she felt toward Hazel. Hazel was Ted's wife, but Ted was the father of her child. She wanted Hazel out of the way, and she wanted Ted for herself.

To make matters even more confusing, Ted had begun to treat Joyce like a wife. Right in front of Hazel, he would greet his daughter with a passionate kiss as he walked through the door from work.

Gradually, he had begun making less of an attempt to hide his actions from his wife. It was as if he was saying, "Hazel, you are helpless now that your father is dead. I have a son, and this young girl loves me. I have nothing to fear from you."

Joyce began to go to the basement more willingly and didn't mind when Ted locked the door behind them. She began cooking his meals, washing and ironing his clothes. All the tasks a good wife performs were tasks that Joyce willingly performed for Ted. In time, she began to feel like a newlywed.

The hatred Joyce once felt toward Ted now became the hatred she felt toward Hazel. In her mind, Hazel stood between her and the happiness she so desired.

In 1963, it was hard to understand the relationship between Joyce and her father. Ten years later, the confusion of their relationship would finally be given a name—Stockholm Syndrome.

Stockholm Syndrome recognizes that emotionally bonding with an abuser is actually a strategy for survival, for the victims of abuse and intimidation.

According to Counseling Resource, it has been found that four conditions are present that serve as a foundation for the development of Stockholm Syndrome.

Joyce exhibited all of the conditions. The first condition was the presence of a perceived threat to her physical being, or to the physical being of her loved ones. In the beginning of the molestation, Ted threatened to kill Joyce, and later he added a threat to her sister Jane's life as well. Joyce was well aware that someone would die, if she told what he was doing to her.

The second condition was the presence of a perceived small kindness from the abuser. Ted often called Joyce "Pumpkin," and told her she was the one he loved. He also made it very clear that she would have nothing to wear and nothing to eat, if it were not for him. She was brainwashed to believe she needed Ted to survive.

The third condition was the isolation from perspectives other than those of the abuser. Ted was a dictator who took control of the family; no one was allowed to disagree or question his motives. Joyce and Jane were made to believe he was truly important to the town, and to the world, for that matter. Ted kept Joyce isolated from other people, from her sister, and from education. He had frequent outbursts of anger, so she began to feel the need to fix things that might prompt an outburst. She also began doing things that a wife would normally do, in an attempt to please him.

The last condition was the perceived inability to escape. Over the years, Ted had made sure that she had no self-confidence or self-esteem. Total dependency was created when Joyce became pregnant, and then gave birth to his baby. She had no money, and no place else to live. Joyce was made to fully understand that she and Robbie had no way to escape.

In the meantime, her sister Jane, along with her new husband, John, had settled into a new life in Stanley. They moved into a small upstairs apartment, and John began his job at the factory. Jane spent her time making baby clothes in anticipation of the birth of her baby.

"I'm going to build a crib for my son," John told her.

"How do you know it's a boy?" Jane asked, in a teasing voice.

Once John's project was finished, Jane used her sewing talents to cut and remake a mattress to fit the baby's new bed. They worked together to prepare for the birth of their child.

Many of the people who worked with John frequented the hotel bar. He took Jane to the bar on weekends, and soon the Botsfords had new friends. Dave and Marie invited John and Jane to their house to play cards and drink beer. After that, they got together a few times a week.

Drinking became even more important to them as they began to build friendships in Stanley. Jane loved to party. She drank right along with John, even though she was pregnant.

About once a month, they would drive to Dallas to visit Grandma Nora. The drive was not complete unless they stopped at a couple of bars on the way, and a couple of bars coming home. The Last Chance Bar was one of his favorites, and John took the name seriously. The last chance for a drink would have him falling down drunk, by the time they reached home.

On a rare occasion, they would drive to Cornell to see her sister, but Ted and Hazel didn't want them around Jane's little brother Roger. They drank beer and Ted didn't want Roger influenced by such evil behavior.

Jane's once slim body grew heavy with her pregnancy. As the cold Wisconsin winter turned the colorful autumn trees into rigid frost covered skeletons, she became gloomy. She decided she needed a lift.

I am going to get a new look, she decided. So, one day she walked downtown to the Beauty Nook Salon to get a haircut.

"Oh, my gosh. It's Jeannie Laird," Jane laughed in surprise as the beauty operator turned around.

Jane recognized her as a classmate from Cornell High School. Jeannie cut Jane's hair and bleached it to a beautiful champagne blonde.

"Do not come to this house again until that hair is gone," Ted screamed the next time he saw his daughter. "Get out of this house. You have always been an embarrassment to us."

Their first Christmas together was disappointing to the new Mrs. Botsford. Even though they had fun making caramel apples and they laughed together when the peanut brittle boiled over the sides of the pan, the holiday made Jane sad.

Her dreams of a gloriously happy Christmas, with loving words from her husband and nice gifts under the tree were crushed, when John failed to come home from work on Christmas Eve. Jane knew where he would be, so she trudged through the snow and ice to the hotel bar to find him. He had already been drinking heavily when he spotted her come through the door.

"Merry Christmas, sweetheart," he said in a sloppy voice. "Come on, I'll get you a drink."

Time flew as the couple partied with their friends. At closing time, they staggered home to a dark and cheerless apartment.

John and Jane both woke on Christmas day feeling ill. Jane went to the tree and picked up the gift she had wrapped for her husband.

"I don't want that damned thing," John said gruffly, still suffering from a massive hangover.

She began to cry as she realized her husband had not gotten a gift for her on their first Christmas together.

"You selfish bastard," Jane yelled, and the fight was on.

Later in the morning, Jane spoke a truth she had almost forgotten. As she looked in the bathroom mirror, she scolded herself, "What did you expect? You know every time you want something, you get disappointed. Grow up. You know you can't trust anybody but Joyce."

The hurt didn't go away easily, but Jane couldn't help being happy. Strength and hope were growing steadily inside her pregnant belly.

The morning of St. Patrick's Day dawned cold and gray. A strong wind blasted through the town leaving huge snowdrifts in its wake. Jane hadn't felt well most of the day, but John wanted to go to the bar for corned beef and cabbage after work.

"Come on, honey," he pleaded, "They're going to have green beer."

"Maybe it's the green beer," John moaned when Jane woke him at 5:00 the next morning to say she was in labor.

As Jane got her things together, John swilled down a beer in an effort to clear his head. He grabbed another for the road, and they walked gingerly down the snow piled steps. John drank the second beer as he drove the car toward St. Joseph's Hospital in Chippewa Falls, at a high rate of speed.

While Jane was being prepped for delivery, John went to a bar across from the hospital on Elm Street, to call Hazel and Ted. He went to that bar often in the next couple of days, always returning with a swagger and foolish talk. John felt no pain through the delivery of his child.

Ted and Hazel arrived before the baby was born.

"Where is John?" Jane asked her mother.

"He's probably at the bar," Hazel answered.

Then she stayed with her daughter until the doctor came to deliver the baby.

Ronald Wayne Botsford was born on March 19, 1964. Ronnie was the prettiest baby Jane had ever seen.

Once mother and baby were out of delivery and settled back in the hospital room, the nurse went to find John to usher him in to see his new son. Jane was proud and eager to show her beautiful baby to his father.

John came staggering into the room, smiling from ear to ear.

"I can't believe it," he told his wife. "My baby in Germany was born exactly two years ago today."

Jane stared at her husband, open-mouthed.

"What did you say?" she asked.

"You heard me. I have two sons born on the same day," he grinned with pride.

Jane felt her heart thump in her ears as she struggled to get her breath. She looked up at her husband hoping to find that he was joking. John looked down at her with an unwavering stare. Despair claimed her as she realized this was no joke. Things changed for the Botsford's that day.

Joyce went to the hospital to visit her sister.

Jane asked, "Can you and Robbie come to Stanley and stay with me for a few days when I get home?"

She was crushed and she needed her sister more than ever.

"She can stay one week," Ted decreed, and Jane was grateful.

Once they were home from the hospital, John started drinking more heavily than ever. Each night after work, he'd go down to the bar for a couple of beers. Jane tried not to care. She was having a wonderful time with her new baby and her sister.

Six days into Joyce's stay, John came home from the bar with his hands burned and his face bloody from a fight. He was terribly drunk and ranting about how tough he was.

"What happened to you?" Jane cried in terror when she saw him.

"I showed them," he bragged. "I poured lighter fluid in my hands and lit a match," he crowed. "It didn't even hurt me. Those bastards are done messing with me. I showed them."

The truth was John had burned his hands badly. Joyce was so frightened that she panicked and called her father. Ted came to the rescue, picked up Joyce and Robbie in the middle of the night and took them back to Cornell.

Chapter Thirty

The Liberation

One day, John announced, "We are moving to the country."

With that, he drove Jane and Ronnie to Thorp, Wisconsin, to look at the house they were to live in.

It was a two-story farmhouse with stained glass windows at the front and an acid etched front door that was simply gorgeous. That's where the beauty of the house began and ended.

There was no indoor plumbing.

"I'm not using an outhouse," Jane stated emphatically.

There was only a wood stove for cooking.

"I'm not chopping wood for that old stove, either," Jane went on.

"We have to live here," John said. "I lost my job at the factory and I start working on this farm on Monday."

Jane's mind flashed back to her life as a young child, with Esther and Hale Colburn. She and her brother and sister were jockeyed from place to place, following a series of her father's failed jobs, and living in one hovel after another.

"Is this all I have to look forward to in my life?" Jane asked herself mournfully.

With a heavy heart, she packed their meager belongings and made the move to the desolate old farmhouse in Thorp. Once the move was made, Jane seldom had a chance to go to town, so she didn't do much drinking. With a clear head, she found that she was angry with John on many levels. The hatred she was beginning to feel toward her husband scared her. It made her want the only person who always loved her—her sister, Joyce.

The next weekend was their first anniversary and Jane asked John, "Will you take me to Cornell to visit Joyce?"

"Hell no," John refused belligerently.

In defiance, Jane called Ted and asked him to come and get her. She knew John would be wild when he found out she had gone behind his back. In her heart, she knew she had to leave him, and she was angry enough to do it.

The first days in Cornell were terrible for Jane. She was upset and felt sick. So sick, in fact, that she could hardly get out of bed in the mornings.

"Get a divorce from that drunken bastard," Ted told her. "You're so damn dumb. Do you want to stay with him until you have a dozen kids?"

That's when it struck Jane that she was pregnant again. Suddenly, she realized she was going to have another sweet little baby like Ronnie. Hope loomed large in her heart. She was sure John would be proud to have another baby. She felt the child would save her marriage.

Jane went to the phone to call the farmer, "Would you just tell John that Ronnie and I are ready to come home?"

Ted and Hazel both stopped talking to her when they found out she was going back to her husband.

The phone rang and Joyce said, "It's for you. It's John."

Jane smiled as her husband said, "I'll be there before lunch tomorrow to pick you up. Be ready. I don't want to have to come in the house."

"I will," Jane said. "I love you."

"I love you, too," John replied before he hung up the phone.

With those words of love, the burden she carried rose lightly from her shoulders and vanished into a mist. They would have a happy family after all.

That evening, Aunt Nellie and cousin Jim arrived at Hazel and Ted's for a visit. Ted fumed under his breath. He just couldn't stand Jim.

Jim, however, seemed very happy to see Jane.

"Where are you living now?" he asked.

He was surprised to hear they were living nearby, in Thorp.

"Do you think John will mind if I drop in sometime, when I come up this way again?" he asked. "I'd like to buy that old guy a drink."

"We'd love that," Jane answered with enthusiasm.

Therefore, Jim Cellars made the transition from reluctant best man at their wedding, to good friend and drinking buddy. Whenever he came to visit his mother in Cornell, he would make a side trip to Thorp where he would party hardy with his friend, John.

On those visits, after John passed out drunk on the bed, Jim and Jane would sit up and talk for hours. Together, the cousins would attempt to solve the problems of the world. One problem Jane was unaware of was that her sister Joyce was running off track, at a high rate of speed.

Hazel was very aware of the changes in her home and had begun keeping score. She hated Joyce, wanted her gone, and she always got what she wanted.

Joyce felt the increasing sense of hostility from her mother as each day moved into the next. She began to fear, *if I don't get away from her, something terrible is going to happen. Maybe she's planning to kill me so she can have Robbie to herself.*

Since she had lived with looming violence her entire life, Joyce really was afraid for her life and for the life of her little boy. She didn't know where to turn. *I wish I could find a man to marry me,* she thought in jest.

Ted kept her isolated from men and the only one she was ever allowed to see was her cousin Jim. *The next time Jim and Aunt Nellie come to visit, I should ask Jim to marry me and get us away from here.* Joyce smiled at her own joke.

He seems to like me, she reasoned. *He usually talks to me and we get along pretty well.* She let her fantasy take wings.

He lives in Milwaukee, which would get us far away from mama, and maybe I could be free like I was in Rice Lake, Joyce let herself dream as she talked herself into the idea of asking Jim to marry her, and take her away from Cornell.

Meanwhile, Hazel was biding her time. For months, she watched and kept track until she was satisfied with the evidence, and then she struck!

One afternoon, she ordered Joyce to take care of Robbie and Roger. Then she waited by the garage until Ted drove in from work. She opened the passenger door of the car and got inside.

"Let's go for a ride through the park," Hazel said in a tone that broached no argument.

Ted saw the determination in her face. Without a question, he backed the car out and slowly drove away. The couple smiled and waved at several of their neighbors as they drove down Main Street. They turned right toward Brunet Island State Park.

"I know you are the father of that slut's baby," Hazel said. "Don't bother to deny it. He looks just like you."

"Where do you get those crazy ideas?" Ted began.

"Oh, please, do you think I am deaf, dumb, and blind?" she countered. "All these years I haven't said a word, but now Dad is gone and the house is mine. I own it all and you have nothing."

"If you don't get rid of Joyce and her bastard, I'm going to spread the word all over town. Just think what the Masons will say about you then."

Hazel smiled as she played her trump card. She knew Ted was proud to be a Mason and would do anything to keep his reputation with them.

"What do you want from me?" he asked, with a shrug of his shoulder and a scowl on his face.

"I want you to arrange a marriage between Joyce and Jim Cellars. He is thirty-five years old and not married yet," she said. "I think he is a homosexual. If he doesn't want to marry her, tell him you're going to tell the family that he's queer," Hazel added, with venom in her voice. "He won't want Aunt Nellie to hear that."

So, on a Wednesday evening, sitting in their car in a parking area on Brunet Island State park, Hazel and Ted developed another plan that would control Joyce's life.

Ted was happy with Hazel's idea. He was happy to give Joyce to a homosexual man who would not want to have sex with her. He knew Joyce loved him and would still have sex with him on weekends, especially if she wasn't getting any love from her husband. Perfect!

The next time Jim Cellars came home to visit his mother, Ted telephoned and asked him for help with something in the garage. Once in the privacy of the building, Ted blackmailed Jim.

"I know you are queer, and unless you marry Joyce and take her to Milwaukee, I'm going to spread the word to all the relatives. Hell," he added, "I'll just put it in the paper so nobody misses it."

Jim began to breathe hard, as he stuttered, "Y-y-you, you wouldn't do that. It'd ruin me."

Then Ted threatened him, saying, "If you don't do it, I'll write a letter to your boss, and fill him in, too."

Suddenly Jim began to smile, and said, "You just gave me the solution to my problem in Milwaukee. If I have a wife and a kid, nobody will know. It's the perfect cover," he said, sticking out his hand to the older man.

"Just so we understand each other, I will not be paying for any child support or giving you money for anything," Ted said, as he shook hands with Jim.

The men went their separate ways.

As usual, Jim made the trip to Thorp to party with John and Jane.

Once John was sleeping soundly, Jim asked Jane, "Do you think Joyce would marry me if I asked her?"

"Yes," Jane responded.

"Then I'm going to ask her tomorrow. Can I bring her over to visit so we can celebrate?" he asked the surprised woman sitting across from him.

"Absolutely," said Jane, "She has to get away from there or she'll die. She needs to be liberated," she added, as she smiled broadly at her cousin.

Late the next morning, Jim knocked on the front door of the Buck house and walked in. He ignored Ted and Hazel and walked straight to Joyce.

"Do you want to go for a ride with me?" he asked.

"Well, I don't know," Joyce stammered as she looked toward her father for the answer.

"If you're not gone too long," said Ted with a strange look on his face.

Joyce couldn't believe what was happening. Her father was letting her go for a ride in a car with a man and he seemed okay with it. Something must be wrong.

"Will you watch Robbie while I'm gone?" she asked.

Her parents only smiled and nodded.

"Where are we going?" she asked Jim as they left the house.

"I thought we'd take a ride to Thorp and visit Jane and John," Jim answered, matter-of-factly.

About a mile out of Cornell, Jim glanced at Joyce and said, "Would you marry me?"

Taken aback, Joyce was speechless for a second.

"Yes, I would," she said with an incredulous look on her face. "I was going to ask you the same thing, but you beat me to it," she added in surprise. "I need to get out of there and I have to take Robbie with me. If you marry me, you have to marry Robbie, too," she said, almost afraid to voice the words.

"That's great," Jim laughed. "I need a kid and he'll do just fine."

Joyce couldn't wait to get to Thorp and tell her sister that she was going to be married. They no sooner entered the house and the sisters were hugging each other and making wedding plans. Jim wanted to get married right away. He told Joyce he wanted to marry her in two weeks, when he planned to come to Cornell again.

"Two weeks?" the sisters giggled. "We have lots to do in only two weeks."

"I think we should go to Chippewa today and apply for our wedding license," Jim said sensibly. "I want to be sure everything is all right, since we are cousins."

"We aren't blood cousins though," Joyce said. "We are adopted so we are cousins in name only."

Joyce quietly watched Jim as he talked to the lady who would issue the marriage license. She really saw, for the first time, the tall thin man with dark hair and blue eyes who she would soon call her husband. She noticed how he held his cigarette and the way he fluttered his hands as he talked. She didn't know what to feel about the man she would soon marry.

On the way back to Cornell, it was decided that Joyce would wear her blue suit and Jim would wear the suit he had worn at Jane and John's wedding. Though Jane was hugely pregnant with her second child, and the wedding was planned only two weeks before her due date, she eagerly said yes when Joyce asked her to be matron of honor. John agreed to be best man for his drinking buddy, as well.

"How are we going to tell mother and daddy?" Joyce worried. "They said I could go for a ride, and I'm coming back engaged."

"Don't worry about anything," Jim comforted her. "If they say no, they will have me to deal with. Besides, they probably want to get rid of you," he joked.

Happiness and apprehension weighed heavily on Joyce as she lay silently in her bed waiting for the alarm clock to signal the arrival of her wedding day. *This is the day I've dreamed of my whole life,* she thought.

So far, most of her dreams had become nightmares. Could this be the first to come true? She dared herself to believe that her one and only chance for happiness would not be spoiled.

Two big questions ran through her mind and she just couldn't find the answers. *Why did mama and daddy agree to this marriage? It's obvious daddy doesn't like Jim. He's always complaining because he swears so much, and mama says Jim is a queer.*

Why is Jim Cellars interested in marrying me? Why would a handsome, charming, successful man like Jim settle for a wife like me? I have nothing to give him but another man's baby. It just doesn't add up.

Joyce had learned years before that Ted Buck didn't agree to anything unless it served his own purpose. He was letting Joyce marry another man and take Robbie away from him, without a fight. *I sure hope daddy doesn't do something to stop the wedding.*

The buzzing sound of the old alarm clock broke through her reverie, leaving her feeling disoriented and dazed for a second. As the fog cleared, she began to hear noises filtering up the stairs from the main floor of the house. *Today, I leave this house forever,* she smiled.

Neither Ted and Hazel nor Jim's mother agreed to attend the wedding. Occasionally glancing over her shoulder to make sure her father was not there to stop them, Joyce walked with Jim to the front of the church, to stand before Reverend Koch.

A wiser, more worldly, woman may have been able to see what lay ahead for her, but Joyce was young and blinded by need.

So it was on March 6, 1965, in a little Presbyterian church in Cornell, Wisconsin, witnessed by Jane and John Botsford, James John Cellars and Joyce Mary Buck became husband and wife.

Joyce had always dreamed she would wear a white flowing dress, with flowers and a diamond tiara, on her wedding day. Part of that dream was a tall, dark, handsome man who would marry her and then wine and dine her on their wedding night. In her mind, she could visualize a beautiful hotel room with flowers and candlelight.

Her dreams of a white wedding dress had been dashed when she and Jim decided to get married on a two-week notice. As the newlyweds drove toward Ladysmith, Joyce let her dreams of a perfect wedding night take over. She again visualized the flowers and candlelight.

They arrived at the Evergreen Motel and were ushered to room number nine. Joyce waited at the door for Jim to carry her over the threshold or take her hand to lead her into their new life together. Instead, Jim opened the door and walked through, leaving Joyce standing alone outside the motel.

By the time Joyce entered the room and put her overnight bag on the bed, Jim had tuned the radio to the Cornell/Barron high school basketball game, and was totally engrossed in the action.

When the game was over, Joyce went to the bathroom to get ready for bed. She put on her new nightgown and brushed her hair carefully. She wanted to look nice for her new husband. Shyly, she opened the door, only to find the room light off and Jim apparently asleep.

Mrs. James Cellars laid in the darkness beside her new husband and cried.

"I can't make love to you," came the voice from the other side of the bed. "Every time I think about it, I see Ted's face."

Robbie was staying with his grandparents while his mother and his new dad were in Ladysmith. The next day, the newlyweds stopped at Hazel and Ted's to pick him up. Joyce took their clothes and their few treasures. Then she said goodbye to her parents.

"Come on, Robbie, let's get going," she said. "We're going to our new home."

"I've rented a nice mobile home and it's all furnished," Jim told his mother when they stopped at Nellie's to say goodbye.

Jim had been living in the same boarding house for years, but he knew he had to find a place for his new family to live. Joyce was excited to be moving into her own home.

"I can't wait to see it," she told her new mother-in-law, as she hugged Aunt Nellie goodbye.

Quiet is the word to describe the long trip from Cornell to Milwaukee. Jim didn't have much to say. He only grunted answers if Joyce asked him a question.

A few times, Robbie made a noise, which prompted Jim to say, "Shut that kid up. I can't concentrate on the road with all that noise."

The trailer house was nice and cozy. Joyce was happy with her new home. She spent the next few days putting things away and rearranging her house to suit her needs.

Payday for Appleton Electric was always on Thursday. The first week they were married, Jim gave Joyce his check and told her to cash it and get groceries.

"Make sure to get two cartons of cigarettes," was all he asked for.

Joyce had no idea how to buy groceries. In the past, Hazel had always made a list and given her the correct amount of money.

At the grocery store, Joyce put Robbie in the shopping cart and began tossing all the things she thought they needed into the basket. She had no idea what the cost of the groceries would be. When she went through the check-out she found that she had used all of the money.

"Are you that stupid?" Jim asked. "What do you think we are going to live on for the rest of the week?"

"You goddamn dumb broad," he screamed. "Now I have to call ma for some money, or I can't pay the rent. Don't you know anything?"

"Don't be mad. I'll do better next time," Joyce said sheepishly.

"You are so stupid. Don't you even know how to add?" he continued.

Joyce said, "I'm sorry, I swear I'll be very careful from now on."

Jim's outburst of anger subsided just as quickly as it had come, and all seemed to be forgiven. Joyce was terribly insulted by her husband's words, but she knew if he said she was stupid, it must be true.

In anger, he pushed past her and went into the living room to turn on the TV. To her surprise, the matter was never spoken of again.

Chapter Thirty-One

Rejection

Exactly six days after her sister's wedding, Jane woke up early, in full labor. Fortunately, John had come home from his nightly outing, though he was barely able to function.

"Hurry, this is different," Jane said in a scared voice. "We've got to go now!"

Jane bundled Ronnie into his snowsuit and grabbed her bag as John stumbled out to start the car. Chaos went with them as the car careened through the blowing snow, toward Stanley Hospital.

Ronnie screamed all the way, which put John over the edge. In his intense anger, he drove erratically and added his yelling to the child's screams. Jane cried loudly and moaned in pain.

"You are going to get us all killed before we get there," she screeched.

She was afraid the baby would be born in the car.

The baby was in such a hurry to be born, there was no time for the nurses to prep Jane for delivery. John stayed with her until the nurse shut the delivery room doors in his face.

Jane was very upset from the terrifying ride to the hospital, and the trauma of giving birth. On March 12, 1965, when the nurse put John Dale Botsford into his mother's arms, she looked down at her beautiful baby boy and felt her heart swell with love for him.

She had told John she felt this baby would be a boy, so they did not have a girl's name picked out. Jane wanted little Jonnie to be named in honor of her deceased grandpa, Dale Bailey.

"That ain't my kid," John stated matter-of-factly, when he saw the baby for the first time. "He don't look nothin' like me," he began raising his voice. "Who's is it? Who you been sleeping with?" he wanted to know loudly.

John stormed out of the hospital, in a black rage. He didn't come back until a few days later when it was time to take Jane and the baby home.

When she returned to the farmhouse with her new baby, she couldn't believe her eyes. Joyce had come from Milwaukee, and was ready to take care of her. The sisters stood just inside the door with their arms around each other and cried.

That's when John dropped the bomb.

"We have to move outta here," he said in a controlled voice. "That bastard didn't like it that I had to stay home with Ronnie while you was in the hospital and he canned me," he added. "That kid ain't even mine and I got fired cause of him."

John pointed a finger at the new baby and stomped out of the house.

That night, John came home drunk and raging mad, ready to do damage.

He began waving a shotgun around and ranting, "I'm going to kill you and that bastard kid. He ain't my child and I don't have no place to go," John raved and paced, back and forth, totally out of his head.

Joyce was able to slip out and run to the farmer's house to call the police. Once she was sure the police were on the way, she called Jim to explain the situation. She asked her new husband to come and get her.

"I don't know how soon I can be there," he said. "Give me the phone number and I'll call you back in the morning," Jim promised.

The police parked their cars on the road and silently came toward the house. John was standing in the kitchen with his back to the door. The first officer grabbed the gun, while the others dragged him out to the porch and forced him to the floor. He was fighting and swearing. It took all four officers to subdue him and get the handcuffs on.

Spending one night in jail, however, sobered him up and helped to straighten things out between them. John told Jane he loved her and he was sorry for what he did.

"I'm going to change," he told her. "Things are going to be different from now on."

Later that morning, Jim called Joyce to say, "There's a job open where I work. I called my boss and he is willing to give it to John if he wants it. The Jackson's moved and their trailer is empty, so there is a place for them to live if they come," he added.

"I'll tell them," Joyce said in a relieved voice. "I'll let you know."

"Yes, absolutely," John said when he heard Joyce's news. "Get your things packed. We're on our way to Milwaukee."

The next morning they all crammed into the old car. Along with their meager belongings, they drove off to Milwaukee. Jane was exhausted, but she felt she was on her way to the "Promised Land."

The Botsford's rented a trailer at the College Trailer Park on Sixth Street in Milwaukee, and John began working with Jim at Appleton Electric. For a month or so, things seemed to be going very well. One day, John came home and told Jane that he had quit Appleton Electric and found a job at the Brach's Candy Company. Jane really didn't care where he worked, as long as he had a job.

The Botsford's lived in the same trailer park as the Cellar's. Jane and Joyce were able to see each other every day. Joyce had no friends in Milwaukee, and since Jim frowned on her getting to know other people, she was very happy to have her sister living so near.

Joyce had learned a month or two earlier that she was pregnant again. She knew Ted was the father because she and Jim had never had sex. Ted was the only man she had ever been with.

Jim was angry when he found out his wife was pregnant. He felt deceived because Ted did not pay child support, and he hadn't known there would be two babies to feed when he had agreed to marry Joyce.

Joyce's baby was due at the end of October, but Jim decided that Joyce and Robbie should go back to Cornell the beginning of August to live with his mother. Aunt Nellie agreed to have her daughter-in-law and grandson stay at her house until the baby was born.

"It's all set," Jim said. "You will have to have the baby in Cornell, anyway, if you want Dr. Zenner to deliver it," he reasoned.

Joyce didn't want to leave Milwaukee and go to Cornell.

"What if Dad starts coming around again?" she worried aloud to Jim.

"Just tell him to stay away from you. What's the matter with you, anyway?" Jim said. "Are you too dumb to figure that out? I guess what they say about you is true. You are stupid," he said scornfully.

Dutifully, Joyce packed up all of the things she and Robbie would need to spend several months away from home. As usual, she gave in and obeyed her husband. With a heavy heart, she did her best to be pleasant as Jim drove the long road to Cornell.

Aunt Nellie, who was also her mother-in-law, treated her very well. Joyce began to enjoy Nellie's company and soon felt more relaxed with her than she felt back in Milwaukee, with her husband.

Joyce stayed away from Ted and Hazel's as much as possible, even though they were now living only a few blocks away.

"Nellie, will you go with me to Ma and Dad's?" Joyce asked.

Nellie thought Robbie should see his grandparents and his uncle Roger once in awhile. On those visits, she proved to be a good buffer. Her presence helped ensure that Ted would leave Joyce alone.

Hazel resented Joyce and Aunt Nellie for keeping their distance. She wanted the neighbors to think she was the important mother and grandmother. Hazel hung onto the fantasy world she and Ted had concocted years before.

Jim came to see his mother and his wife only twice in the three and one-half months Joyce and Robbie stayed in Cornell. On his first visit, he told her what was going on with her sister Jane, in Milwaukee. Joyce was horrified, but powerless to help in any way.

Chapter Thirty-Two

Desperate Days

After spending the night in jail, while they were living in Thorp, John promised things would change. All of John's good intentions soon spiraled into a destructive pattern. Whenever he thought he had crossed the line, he would start treating Jane better. But soon he'd be out drinking again. She'd threaten to leave and he'd swear to change. Their life became a roller coaster of emotion. Love—hate, love—hate. Up and down.

Another familiar pattern was developing. Jane had begun to walk in the footsteps of her biological mother, Esther Colburn. She dragged her family from one dilapidated house to another, screaming and fighting with her drunken husband, as she followed him from job to job.

Jane felt depressed and desperate. The new start she had hoped for was slipping away. John was drinking again and they fought constantly. She had two babies, no friends, and her sister was miles away.

Her cousin Jim had deserted her as well. In the past, the two of them had spent many nights sitting up late and talking. Now, with his wife in Cornell, Jim was nowhere around. Jane would see him drive by on his way home from work. He would stay long enough to change his clothes and he'd be gone again.

He's seeing another woman, Jane thought. *That's why he wanted Joyce and Robbie out of the way.*

Jane wanted to do something to help her sister, but she couldn't even help herself just then. She was not aware of the deal Jim had made with her father, or she would have realized that he was probably seeing another man.

One afternoon, John showed up early.

"Oh no," Jane thought. "He's lost his job."

But instead, John said, "I think we should go to the bank and see if they will give us a loan. Then we can pay off our bills and start fresh," he smiled confidently.

John went next door to ask the neighbor, "Can you help us out in a pinch and come over to watch the kids so we can run to the bank?"

"I'd be glad to," she replied. "I'll be over in a few minutes."

The banker agreed to loan them $500.00 on a ninety-day note. It didn't cross their minds to consider how they were going to pay the money back. They left the building with the money tucked inside John's pocket, and high hopes tucked into Jane's heart.

"Let's celebrate," John said as they drove up to the Blue Canary Tavern.

The bar was located at one end of the trailer park, and was a constant temptation to him.

Jane was happy to follow him into the bar. It had been awhile since she had been out drinking with her husband, and she was ready to have some fun.

Just like old times, Jane thought happily.

An hour into the party, John said, "Why don't you go on over and get the kids from the babysitter? I'll be home in a few minutes."

"No, you come with me," Jane pleaded.

"Come on, baby, I'll be home in a minute. We'll have a nice supper and when the kids are in bed, we'll figure out how to use this money," he wheedled, patting his pocket for good measure.

Reluctantly, Jane walked toward home, got the boys and then began cooking supper. It got late and John had not come home yet. She fed the little ones, put them to bed, and waited.

It's midnight and that bastard isn't home yet, she raged silently, as she placed a call.

"He went home four or five hours ago," said the bartender lamely before he slammed the receiver in her ear.

Jane's heart fell to the pit of her stomach. She knew her husband was gone, the money was gone, and so was her dream for a better future.

She fell into a fitful sleep and woke the next morning with a start. *That son-of-a-bitch didn't come home,* she stormed.

In desperation and anger, she called the police.

"How long has he been missing?" the woman on the phone asked.

"Since last night," Jane answered.

"I'm sorry, we can't do anything until he has been missing twenty-four hours," the lady replied.

When Jane insisted they do something to help her, the dispatcher said, "I'm sorry, ma'am, that's our policy. I'll make a note that you called. If he isn't back within twenty-four hours, give us another call. Is there anything else I can help you with?" she added sweetly.

Almost two weeks had passed, without a word from her husband, and Jane had nowhere to turn. The police were no help, since John had obviously taken the car, and there didn't seem to be foul play involved.

There was no money, no car, no food, and no outside contact. With two little boys who were starving and constantly crying from hunger, Jane fell apart. She put the boys in their cribs, went to the bathroom and took every pill she could find. A razor blade was in the cabinet next to the pills. She slit her wrist.

When she saw the blood spurting from her arm, Jane snapped out of it and realized what she had done.

She didn't want her little boys to wake up and see all the blood, so she stumbled next door and asked the lady, "Can you come over and be with my boys?"

The woman screamed at her husband when she saw blood dripping on the porch, "Harold, call the police."

Jane was taken to the psychiatric ward at the hospital.

"Who should we contact?" asked the social worker. "You can't go home yet. You are in no condition to take care of your little boys," she added.

"I don't have anybody," she sobbed.

"Then we will have to put your kids in foster care until you are better," the social worker reasoned.

"NO!" said Jane firmly. "I will call my parents and see if they will take them."

The hardest thing Jane had to do, in her life, was to call her parent's house and admit to them what she had almost done to herself. She asked if they would come and get the boys until she was discharged from the hospital. Hazel and Ted drove the five hours to Milwaukee to rescue the children.

"I told you to divorce that no good bastard," were the first words out of her father's mouth when he entered her hospital room.

She was so grateful to him that she didn't care what he said or how mad he was. Her children needed care and she had nowhere else to turn. Ironically, Ted was telling the truth. Jane agreed with her father and finally made the decision to file for divorce.

She was in the hospital for three weeks, and when she was about to be released, she called her cousin Theresa.

"I'm in the hospital and I was wondering if I could come and stay at your place for a few days before I catch the bus to Cornell?" she asked hesitantly.

"That would be okay," Theresa answered. "Your parents told me what happened. Are you sure you're all right?" she asked.

"I'll be fine, but I have to get our stuff out of the trailer before I go back to Cornell," Jane answered.

Theresa came to pick her up the morning she was released from the hospital.

"I don't know what's wrong with me," Jane confided to her. "I feel so sick to my stomach."

"Are you sure you're not pregnant again?" Theresa replied. "It sounds like morning sickness to me."

"Oh, no," Jane began to cry. "If I'm pregnant, what am I going to do?" she asked herself.

She was desperately lonely for her little boys, and terrified for her unborn child.

Chapter Thirty-Three

On the Move Again

Alan Colburn had been keeping in touch with his sisters since he joined the army. He, along with his wife Tina, were stationed at Fort Hood in Killeen, Texas. Joyce knew her sister Jane was in trouble, so she called Alan to ask if he had any ideas that might help.

"I think they should move down here with us for awhile," he said. "I can send airline tickets and we can get her and the kids as far away from that place as possible," he added. "That should give her time to figure things out."

"She's staying with Theresa in Milwaukee for a few days," Joyce told Alan. "Is it possible for you to send the tickets there?"

"What's the address?" Alan asked. "I'll have the airlines get the tickets to her by Monday," he promised.

Jane couldn't thank her brother Alan and sister Joyce enough when she found out what they had done for her. Ted and Hazel were overjoyed, as well, and offered to drive the boys back to Milwaukee in time for the flight to Texas.

The little boys had proven to be a handful for their grandparents. They cried often for their mother, and they had the Buck household in chaos. Joyce spent as much time caring for them as she could, but she was pregnant and had her own little boy to care for. Everyone was eager to get the boys back with their mother and on the plane to Texas.

Jane, Ronnie and little Jonnie loved it in Texas. Alan and Tina were good to them and they seemed to love the little boys dearly. Alan was back in Jane's life and she loved him very much. He had saved her life many times as a child, and it felt heavenly to be safely in his care again.

As summer turned into autumn, Jane and the boys flourished in Texas. Joyce, however, was not doing quite as well in Cornell. As her belly grew, so did her longing that Jim would love her enough and come to get her. Even though she was having a pleasant time with his mother, she was a lonely young wife, aching for a normal family life.

Joyce was again visiting with Hazel's friend Stella Berg, when she went into labor. This time when the pain began, she knew what was happening. She excused herself and walked the couple of blocks to Nellie's house.

Nellie called Hazel, and said, "Joyce is in labor," she said excitedly. "Can you come and get her? I'll stay with Robbie while you take her to the hospital."

Ted and Hazel took Joyce to St. Joseph's Hospital in Chippewa Falls. On October 29, 1965, Randy Lee Cellars was born. Joyce called Jim in the morning to tell him.

"It's a boy and everything is fine."

Jim was uninterested and cool.

"I can't come up for a couple of weeks," he said. "You'll just have to stay with ma until I can get there."

Joyce hung up the phone and cried her eyes out.

Then she called the only people she knew would care about her.

Tina answered the phone and let out a yell, "It's a boy."

Alan and Jane laughed at her excitement and Joyce smiled in gratitude.

On the second day in the hospital, the nurse came into Joyce's room to say, "You have a visitor. Do you want to see him?"

"Sure, send him in," Joyce answered with enthusiasm. *Jim did come after all*, she thought.

The door opened and in walked Reverend Koch, the Presbyterian minister who had performed her wedding to Jim.

"If I had known you were pregnant when I married you, I would never have performed the ceremony," he said with a hateful glare. "Your father told me about you sleeping around," he said through clenched teeth. "How can you do this to your parents, after they've been so good to you?" he said angrily.

Joyce was squeezing the nurse call button without knowing it. The nurse came into the room, just in time to hear his final words.

"You will go to hell."

The nurse was a true angel when she said, "I'm sorry, sir, you will have to leave. We can't have the patient getting upset now, can we?"

On Saturday, two weeks after Randy was born, Jim drove from Milwaukee to pick up his family. Joyce was eager to see her husband and show off her new baby boy. Jim was unimpressed and his attitude made her sad.

"Come on, Jim, take a look at this little fellow," Nellie said, trying to get her son to show more interest in the baby.

"Babies make me nervous," was his response.

All of her efforts fell on deaf ears. Nellie had come to love Joyce, and her heart broke to see the lovely young woman so dejected. She had a hunch that these two sweet little boys would be the only grandchildren she would ever have.

Hazel had invited them all to her house for Sunday dinner. Jim informed Nellie that they would be leaving for Milwaukee at three o'clock.

"Fine," she said. "That will give us plenty of time to eat and visit a bit before you leave."

Exactly at 3:00, the Cellar's pulled out of the driveway. They began the long arduous trip home. Hardly a word was spoken between them. Joyce busied herself by watching out the window and tried to enjoy the scenery. Robbie was fidgety and found it hard to sit still in the back seat.

"Shut that damn kid up," Jim yelled. "He's getting on my nerves."

Joyce was exhausted by the time they drove past the Blue Canary and into the trailer park. A strong sense of loneliness washed over her, as they passed the trailer her sister no longer lived in.

Life quickly took on a routine. Jim's job was to go to work and bring home the money. Joyce learned immediately that she was to do everything else.

Jim told Joyce, "I want you to stay home, and I want supper on the table when I get in from work."

Jim rarely talked to Joyce and spent his time at home, lying on the couch, smoking, and watching television.

"Tell those fucking kids to shut up," he'd yell if they made too much noise. "If you don't shut those dumb bastards up, I will," he'd threaten.

One morning, Robbie woke with a high fever and a bad cough.

"I have to get him to the doctor. What am I supposed to do?" Joyce asked her husband.

"Take me to work and get him there yourself," Jim said with a sneer, as if he couldn't believe how dumb she was.

That morning, Joyce loaded the kids in the car and drove Jim to Appleton Electric.

"Be here at 5:00 to pick me up and I want my supper on the table when we get home," he ordered.

That afternoon, Joyce took Robbie to see the doctor. After the appointment, she hurried home to put supper in the oven and set the table. When that task was finished, she put the kids in the back seat of the car and went to pick up her husband. They made it by the skin of their teeth. It was only ten minutes before he came sauntering out of the building and got into the car. Supper was ready when they walked in the door, and that seemed to make him happy.

The doctor told Joyce that Robbie just had a cold, but the real good news was that from that day on, Jim let Joyce keep the car during the day. She drove him to work in the morning and picked him up in the evening. Having the car at her disposal was very helpful with two young children at home.

One evening, a woman named Lori was waiting for her husband Tom. He and Jim walked out of the building at the same time and Jim introduced Lori to Joyce. After that, the two couples became friends and visited each other once in awhile. Joyce finally had a friend in Milwaukee.

Jim talked often about his friend Donny, another guy he worked with. Joyce had always been curious because Jim spoke of his friend with such fondness. The two men had been friends for many years and were obviously very important to each other.

One Saturday, Jim announced that he was taking Joyce and the kids to Donny's house to meet him. Even though Donny was in his early forties, he still lived at home with his mother and disabled sister.

Joyce was surprised at how handsome Donny was. He dressed very nicely and spoke pleasantly to his mother and sister. She wondered why he wasn't married. *I wonder why some woman hasn't caught him yet,* Joyce thought to herself.

Donny had a grace about him that Joyce had never seen before. His hips swayed from side to side and when he talked, his hands fluttered and his speech was peppered with sighs.

His mother was very sweet to Joyce and the children, but Donny acted as if none of them existed. Jim had lots to say and seemed very animated while he talked to Donny. Joyce found this interesting, since he seldom even spoke to her and the boys.

Chapter Thirty-Four

Back With John

When they were first married, Tina and Alan had decided not to have children. Alan's upbringing had been so abusive that he worried he would not be a good father. He liked his beer, too, and was afraid he might abuse or neglect his own children.

Jane knew Alan and Tina were only trying to help her out when Alan asked, "Tina and I have been talking. What would you think if we adopted your baby when it's born?"

"I'm sorry, I know you'd be great parents, but I just can't give up one of my babies."

Jane believed that until a person had a child of their own, it was not possible to understand the special love they felt for them.

All too soon, their time in paradise was over. Alan received his transfer orders to Germany and would be stationed there for at least two years. Jane and the boys would not be able to go overseas with him.

They stayed in Texas as long as they could, and then Jane and her children took the train back to Milwaukee. Theresa met them at the train station. Once they were settled in the car, Theresa told Jane that John had come around looking for her.

"I didn't tell him that I knew where you were, but he left an address, in case you were interested in contacting him."

After sleepless nights and much soul searching, Jane decided to get in touch with John. They met for a cup of coffee and talked things out.

"The kids need a father," Jane said.

"Yup," added John. "I'm going to change, and we can have a good life. I love you and I can't live without you," he said with a very serious look on his face.

Deep down in her heart, she knew better, but he had spoken the words she was so hungry to hear. Jane still clung to the hope that they could be one big happy, loving family.

John had lost his job at the Brach's Candy Company. One evening, Jim and Joyce went to Theresa's house to visit with Jane and John was there.

Jim said, "Ma said they are hiring at the sanitation department in Cornell. If you are interested, give them a call."

The Botsford family was on the move again. They found an apartment above Prentiss Brothers Hardware on Main Street in Cornell and settled in.

Hazel and Ted had been talking to Jane again, ever since she had to ask for help while she was in the hospital in Milwaukee. She knew her parents would be worried about what the people of the town would think. Since she felt indebted to them, she bent over backwards to treat them with respect.

For awhile, things went very smoothly between Jane and her parents. Ted and Hazel visited often and seemed to dote on their little grandsons. It was a dream to have them act like loving parents.

The Better Business Bureau of Cornell held a promotion called "Cornell Pay Day." Each week, anyone who purchased something in participating stores had their name put into a box. At noon on Mondays, there would be a drawing. The catch was that the winner had to be present at the drawing, in order to win the money. If the winner was not present to claim their winnings, the money would stay in the pot for the next week.

The drawing was always held at Prentiss Brothers Hardware. Jane and her family lived in the apartment upstairs, so every Monday she went downstairs in hopes of being the winner.

The second week in May, 1966, Jane took her two boys and ran downstairs to be present at the drawing.

Just as she burst through the door, she heard, "Jane Botsford," called by Jerry Prentiss.

All of the merchants present were excited. Jane had won the largest pot ever in the history of the contest. The newspaper was there to take her picture. She stood in front of the camera, grinning from ear to ear, holding onto the $175.00 prize money.

Thank you, God, she thought. *Now I can feed the boys and buy some things for the new baby."*

With her winnings in hand, Jane took Ronnie and Jonnie over to the Ben Franklin store. There was a small children's clothing department, at the back of the store. She did something that she had always hoped she would have the money to do, someday. She bought her two little boys each a brand new shirt and a brand new pair of pants. Each boy was allowed to choose a toy as well.

Ronnie and Jonnie were so excited when they got home and put on their new clothes. The two little boys spun in circles and giggled until they were dizzy. Jane was filled with happiness watching her sons enjoy their new things.

With a smile on her face, she went to the kitchen and put the rest of her prize money into its hiding place in the sugar canister. She thanked God again for the good fortune of winning the $175.00.

To the outside world, the Botsford family looked pretty good, but in their private life, things had hit the skids. John was drinking heavily again, and he and Jane fought constantly. The fighting had escalated into physical violence.

Jane didn't let anyone know what was happening. She was living in her hometown, and she knew so many people. She was too ashamed.

One night, John came home drunk and started pushing Jane.

"Get out of my way, bitch," he yelled.

"You can't do this to me anymore," she yelled back.

"I'll do anything I want," John screamed. "I work my ass off and you squander it all on new clothes for those damned kids," he ranted. "At least that won't happen again," he glared at her.

Jane looked at him and something clicked in her brain.

"You've taken my money, haven't you?" she shrieked and ran to the sugar canister and tore off the lid. "It's gone! What have you done with it?" she yelled.

"It's not yours. It's mine. It was my money that you spent on the groceries in the first place," John hollered back with blood vessels bulging in his neck.

"You ugly, fucking bastard," Jane screamed as she slapped him in the face.

A terrible fight ensued. Every time John hit Jane, she hit him back. She matched him swear word for swear word. She had never fought him like this before. She was so angry that she totally lost control.

John was out of his head in a black rage. He grabbed his wife by the neck and pushed her head through a window. Broken glass and blood flew in every direction. Jane realized he was determined to kill her. In an attempt to stay alive, she stopped struggling and played dead. John took one look at her bloody face and limp body, and ran out of the apartment.

Two days later, John walked through the door of the apartment, with a smile on his face, as though he had never left.

"What are you doin' here?" Jane growled.

"I figured since your obituary wasn't in the paper, I didn't have to worry about the cops coming after me for killin' ya," John laughed at her.

One look at his mother's face told Ronnie there would be a fight. He was only two years old but he helped his little brother get into the bedroom and together they crawled under the bed. The screaming and crashing of dishes always terrified the little boys.

Before Jane could respond to John, she heard a loud knock on the door. She opened it to find two policemen standing in the hall. John made a move as though he was about to run, and the officers drew their guns.

"John Botsford, you are under arrest for robbery and car theft," the officer said.

Ronnie and Jonnie started screaming and crying, "Don't take my daddy."

"You have to come with us," the first policeman said forcefully.

Then they put handcuffs on him and took him down the stairs to the squad car waiting outside.

Ted and Hazel were elated that John was in jail. They brought over some food for the grandchildren and Ted gloated.

"I hope they throw away the key this time."

Later that night, sharp pain pierced through Jane's body. Labor had begun. She was frantic. John was in jail and the only thing she could do was call her mother and father.

"I'm in labor. Can you get me to the hospital?" she cried when Ted answered the phone.

Ted and Hazel drove Jane to St. Joseph's Hospital, and this time, they seemed happy to help her. Hazel stayed with her until she was wheeled into the delivery room.

On May 27, 1966, Tammy Lynne Botsford was born. Jane had given birth to a beautiful baby girl, and she was so proud.

There was a surprise waiting for Jane in her hospital room. Her roommate was Jeannie Laird Gygi. She was the classmate from Cornell High School who had worked at the beauty salon in Stanley. She had colored and cut Jane's hair just before Ronnie was born. Jane was elated.

"What a small world," she smiled.

Jane and her friend talked and laughed. They enjoyed their time together, but she didn't tell Jeannie about the life she was living. In a few days, Jane was released from the hospital. Her parents came to take her and Tammy Lynne home.

Another surprise was waiting for Jane when she got back to the apartment in Cornell.

The landlord came and told her, "Your husband has not paid the rent, and you've broken a window," he said. "It's rather difficult for me to say, but we can't have the police coming to our building again. You have to be out by Friday," he added.

Jane had no idea what to do. She just sat in a daze, holding her baby and wishing she were somewhere safe.

That damn John, she raged. *He's such an ass. He doesn't have a care in the world. He's always out drinking and running around with other women. And now he's in jail and I'm here all by myself. He has three kids, too, but he leaves all the responsibility to me. I hate the ground he walks on,* Jane stewed.

The door opened and in walked John.

"How'd you get out of jail?"

Jane was so mad she couldn't stand the look of him.

"Good old Grandma Nora came down and bailed me out," John said mockingly.

"How much did she give you this time?" Jane wanted to know.

"Bail was $800.00 and she gave me a little extra."

John sounded disappointed, as if his grandmother hadn't given him as much as he wanted.

"Well, she's probably damn sick of giving you money. It's like dumping it down a rat hole," Jane tried to be as nasty as she could. "We just got evicted a few minutes ago," Jane's voice was rising. "It's because you drank up the rent money and you broke the goddamn window," she raved. "Plus, the cops came and hauled you away like a fucking criminal. Oh, I forgot, YOU ARE A CRIMINAL!" she screamed.

"What're you worried about?" John said, unfazed. "I've got money. We'll just move."

John looked at Tammy still sleeping in her mother's arms.

"That one's mine," he stated. "Looks just like me. I got an in," John told her. "I seen Dave and Marie," he added. "Dave says he lost his job in Stanley and they moved to Chippewa. Got himself a job drivin' a garbage truck. Makin' good money, too. Says they got some openings and I can have a job if I want it."

He stood looking down at her with a vulnerable look on his face, and said, "I love you. I'm sorry for all the stuff I put you through. I don't know why you stay with a good for nothin' like me. I drink too much and I'm a terrible husband."

He was crying now and he knelt beside her and took her hand in his. "I'm going to change. I can't live without you and the kids. I promise you if you come with me, it'll be good this time."

In spite of her best intentions, Jane melted.

"You're not a loser," she said, looking into his sad eyes. "I love you, too."

"How long do we have?" he asked.

"We have to be out by Friday," she answered.

"Let me hold my pretty little girl."

John picked up Tammy and nuzzled her little neck.

Jane loved how she felt when John was kind. For the time being, she chose to forget the fear she felt when he was drunk and crazy.

The Botsford's moved into a decent duplex in Chippewa Falls. It was the nicest house Jane had lived in since her marriage. John took a job as a garbage man, and their life straightened out.

Jane was kept very busy taking care of the three children. She was happy for the first time in years.

"I won't be home right after work tonight," John said one morning. "I'm going out with Dave. He has some stuff he needs my help with."

That was the beginning of the end of her contentment. One drink with his friend Dave, and John was off and running again. He was rarely sober, and he was gone most of the time. He seldom saw his family, and the money became scarce.

One day the landlord knocked on the door. Jane answered with a friendly word and a big smile.

"You haven't paid the rent for two months. I've come to collect it," the man said.

"I don't have any money. You'll have to get it from my husband," she answered with fear in her heart.

"If I don't get it by tomorrow, you have to leave," he said sternly.

John was not one bit worried when Jane told him they would have to pay up or leave.

"I saw a house for rent yesterday, out by the Wissota Mug Root Beer stand," he said. "I'll run out there and see if we can have it," he smiled.

They crammed their belongings and three little children into a one-bedroom house that was much too small. Jane thought back to her childhood with Esther and Hale Colburn. This was exactly how she had lived back then.

Again, she vowed to change things, but she just didn't know how. She decided that she would do what she could to be a good mother, and she would try to be happy, for the children's sake.

The Sunbeam Tavern was just down the road. John took Ronnie with him one Sunday afternoon. From then on, he would take his little boy to the tavern with him. Jane hated it when he took her son, but she didn't seem to have enough strength to stop him. It was just easier to let John take him then to fight for what she knew was right.

One afternoon, Grandma Nora brought John's mother, Vivian, to see them. Jane was happy to have the company and she wanted the women to get to know her children.

John came home drunk while his grandma and mother were there. Somehow it made him mad to see them. He became belligerent with Jane and started pushing her around. When he turned his rage on his mother, Jane slipped away and ran to the neighbor's house to call the police.

When he saw the police, John screamed, "Who called the cops? I'm going to kill you," he yelled, pointing a menacing finger at his wife.

John fought with the police until they had to call for backup. In the end, it took five cops to hold him down and put him in the squad car.

"I can't believe he's so mean," Vivian said in surprise. "He's so strong when he's drunk. I think you should get the kids away from him. He's apt to hurt them."

Grandma Nora was not surprised. She confessed, "John and his grandpa have treated me like this for years," she said crying.

John spent a couple of days in jail, just long enough to get sobered up. Word got around that he was in jail. When he went back to work, he was told to go home. They didn't want a jailbird working there.

With no money to pay the rent and no food for the kids, they were forced to apply for welfare. They moved to another "dump" in town. To make things even more hopeless, Jane found herself pregnant with her fourth child.

One day, while she was in one of her most desperate moods, she heard a knock at the door. She opened it and saw Aunt Lydia and her Uncle Tony standing there. For some reason, Jane knew who they were the minute she saw them.

She hadn't seen them since she was a little girl living with Esther and Hale at Grandpa Colburn's farm in Turtle Lake. Lydia was Esther's half-sister. She and her husband had been looking for Jane ever since they saw her picture in the paper—the day she had won the $175.00 prize money in Cornell.

Jane had the most wonderful visit with her relatives.

"We'd love to have you and the kids come to our house for a visit," Aunt Lydia said. "If you want to do that, we could come one day next week and pick you up."

"I'd love that," gushed Jane.

She still couldn't believe her aunt and uncle were standing there in the flesh.

Jane decided that she and the kids would spend the weekend with her newfound family. Saturday morning, right on time, Uncle Tony arrived to pick them up.

They had a wonderful time together. Jane felt whole while she was with them. They treated her the way she had always dreamed a mother and father would treat their child.

On another visit, Aunt Lydia asked Jane if she wanted to go with her to see her biological mother, Esther Colburn. At first, Jane said no. All she could remember was the way Esther had treated her when she was a tiny child. Though, after much thought, she decided to see her mother after all.

It had been twenty years with no contact from her mother. Jane was scared to death. Hesitantly, she followed Lydia into the living room. What she saw made her cringe. Esther looked drunk and smelled bad. It was evident that she hadn't bathed or washed her long greasy hair in quite sometime.

They spoke a few words and Jane again saw the mean look Esther had about her. After seeing her and talking to her, Jane realized that she really didn't like her mother at all. For a reason she couldn't understand, seeing her mother released her from the childhood dream that she still carried—the wish that Esther would love her and someday come to rescue her.

Chapter Thirty-Five

Out of Control

Jane knew the signs of labor well. When the first stab of pain pierced her side, she called the neighbor girl to come over to watch the kids. She knew John could not be trusted, so she had made other arrangements for the care of her children.

Once everything was under control at home, she called a cab, and took herself to the hospital. On July 13, 1967, the hottest, most humid day of the summer, Jane gave birth to her fourth child, Todd Alan Botsford.

Fear for the well-being of this beautiful baby boy made her heart pound, and she began to hyperventilate. She was in a desperate situation. She didn't have anybody to talk to, and she was totally alone.

After three days in the hospital, Jane called a cab and took her baby boy home. John was lying on the couch and the kids were in the bedroom when she walked in the door. Without as much as a word, she walked passed her husband and into the bedroom to see her children.

"Mommy, you're home," Ronnie yelled when he saw her.

"Mommy, Mommy," little Jonnie screeched, "Whet me see baby."

Tammy waddled over to see her little brother and cooed, "Babeeeee."

Jane's tears had many sources—pride in her children as well as fear for them, and an intense disappointment in her husband. Life, in general, scared her to death.

While she was in the bedroom with the children, someone knocked at the front door. John did not bother to get up to answer it.

When Ronnie ran to open the door, he immediately started screaming, "Don't take my daddy away."

John jumped up from the couch and Jane went to the bedroom door. She saw policemen in their living room.

"John Botsford, you are under arrest. Come with us peacefully."

"What did I do?" he mumbled, as they led him out of the house.

Jane didn't hear the answer the policeman gave. She only knew this had to stop.

This time, John was arrested for rape. The neighbor girl, Jane, hired to watch the kids while she was in the hospital, had called the police, and filed a complaint.

While John was in jail, Jane sought help. She started going to counseling. The counselor, Dr. Jones, thought the children should go to Head Start. It was extremely hard with four little kids and very little money, but she did her best.

The kids had a terrible time with the other children. They had never been taught to share, and they ran around like crazy. Jane didn't know how to control them in public, so she yelled and threatened. Finally, she gave up and didn't take them anymore. She was just so worn out and depressed, she could hardly function.

Her whole life had turned into a disaster that she was powerless to stop. She didn't know she was the only one who actually had the power to change things. She kept waiting for a miracle to happen.

One morning, Jane ran to the next-door neighbors for just a minute. She told Ronnie and Jonnie to stay in the house with Tammy and Todd. She barely got in the neighbor's door when Ronnie came running across the lawn.

He screamed, "Fire, fire."

In a panic, she hurried back to the house. Ronnie had turned on the front burner of the kitchen stove, had lit a piece of paper, and had thrown it in the wastebasket.

"What did you do that for? You know you're not supposed to touch nothing, you little bastard," she yelled at him.

"I'm sorry, Mama. I didn't mean it," cried the terrified little boy.

"I know you didn't," Jane said as she hugged her son. "You scared me to death. I'm glad you came and got me right away. Don't you ever do anything like that again!"

Jane didn't want to be a bad mother who couldn't control herself, but she didn't know how to be any different. It hurt her to think that she had called Ronnie a "little bastard," but she couldn't seem to find a better way to behave toward her children.

In 1967, intoxication while committing a crime seemed to be an acceptable defense. John was sentenced to only three months in jail for the crime of rape. As part of his sentence, he was required to go to Alcoholics Anonymous. In addition, a doctor prescribed medication to help him stop drinking.

"I'm going to AA," John said when he finally got out of jail. "I'm going to stop drinking and get a job. Things are going to get better around here."

Jane was having none of it.

"Yeah, right," she said rolling her eyes. "I've heard that before."

John left the house and was gone for an hour or so. He came back with a little wading pool.

"Here you go. Let's put some water in this thing and have some fun," he said to the surprised little kids.

Ronnie, Jonnie, and Tammy jumped up and down, clapped their hands and talked excitedly as John filled the pool with water. The three little kids splashed around in the sun all afternoon. By the time they went into the house, they were totally sunburned.

Jane felt terrible that she hadn't taken better care of her children than to let them get burned so badly.

"I'm such a bad mother," she thought as she covered their little bodies with salve.

The kids were miserable. Their crying got under John's skin.

He yelled, "Shut the fuck up," and then he stormed out of the house.

He went to his old haven with the intention of just hanging out with his buddies. He felt strong, healthy, and he knew he could resist temptation, especially with the medication the doctor had given him to help him stop drinking. He was told not to drink while he was on it, for fear of getting deathly ill.

"I'm clean and sober," he thought to himself. "I haven't had a drink in over three months. I don't have to drink to be in a bar with my friends."

His good intentions were short-lived.

"Have a beer on me," one of his buddies said, raising his bottle in a toast.

John began to explain that he wasn't drinking anymore, but the lure of the open bottle got the better of him. He nodded, and the bartender plunked a bottle of Leinenkugel's on the bar in front of him.

The devil wafted out of the open bottle and crooked his finger at John, bidding him to take a sip. *You're strong enough to have one beer and stop there*, the devil seemed to say. John believed the devil and took that one drink.

Doris was a neighbor who lived in the house across the street. She had five nice children, and Jane was very happy to have a friend to sit and talk with, while the children played.

One morning, while Jane and Doris were chatting over a cup of coffee, they heard a horrible scream. Then all the kids started crying. The women ran outside to find Doris's youngest daughter lying on the ground. She had fallen off the upstairs porch.

"Call the ambulance," Doris screamed as she cradled her baby in her arms.

Blood was pouring from a bad cut above the little girl's left eye. Jane knew with one look that the little girl's arm was broken.

"Where is Tammy?" she screamed.

Only a few minutes earlier, she had checked on the girls and they were playing quietly together. In a panic, Jane ran up the steps to search for her daughter.

Tammy and her little friend had been playing upstairs and had crawled through an open window, onto the roof of the porch. When Doris's little girl fell, Tammy crawled back through the window into the bedroom. Jane found her sitting by herself sobbing. She gathered Tammy in her arms and they cried together.

Jane was at the end of her rope with her children's behavior. She realized that it was totally out of control. They were loud, sassy, and daring to the point of danger. They didn't listen to their mother. Jane loved them so much that she couldn't bring herself to discipline them. The real problem was that she mistook discipline for abuse, and mistook yelling for discipline.

The abuse she had suffered at the hands of Esther Colburn and the strict discipline she had suffered at the hands of Ted Buck had made her too soft on her own children. This lack of discipline was a major source of confusion to the children, since she yelled at them, hit them, and belittled them when she was in a fit of rage.

John had stopped going to AA and was drinking steadily again. He found the combination of beer and the medication actually to his liking. Jane often did not see him for days at a time. One night, he came home drunk and passed out on the living room floor. While he was unconscious, he gagged and began to throw up. Jane rolled him over and wiped away the foul smelling vomit to keep him from choking to death.

That was the turning point. She finally realized she didn't have the skills to control her own life. She didn't know how to take care of herself, and she didn't know how to take care of her kids. She understood that her precious children needed protection from both their father and their mother.

"I have to talk to Dr. Jones," she thought in defeat.

Though it was late in the evening, she decided to go to the doctor's house. She had no telephone or car, so she put the kids to bed, slipped a butcher knife in her sleeve for protection, locked the door, and started walking across town.

Her breath disappeared in puffs of steam as she walked downtown past the courthouse and then up the hill toward Irvine Park, in the stinging cold. She looked over her shoulder every few steps. In her state of mind, there was danger everywhere, and she was glad that she had the butcher knife to protect her.

When she reached the fairgrounds, she saw a light on in the house, and she knew Dr. Jones was home. She was nearly frozen with cold and fear.

The doctor was surprised when she answered the door, to find Jane Botsford standing there.

"Come in," she said with a question in her voice. "Please, take off your coat. You look frozen. Can I get you a hot drink?" Dr. Jones asked in concern.

Jane nodded and began taking off her coat. That's when the doctor saw the butcher knife she had concealed in her sleeve. The knife terrified

Dr. Jones, who immediately concluded that Jane had come there to hurt her. Jane did not realize the effect the butcher knife would have on her doctor.

"I'm sorry," said Dr. Jones. "I'll call Dr. Christianson for you, but you can't stay here," she added fearfully as she picked up the phone and dialed.

"I have a special case for you," she said into the receiver. "Jane Botsford is here at my house and she needs to see a counselor right away. Can you see her if I send her over?" the doctor questioned.

She hung up, and then called a cab.

Dr. Christianson was a man, and Jane did not trust any man. She didn't like the way he talked to her, either. She felt that he made judgments, and nothing she said seemed to be the right thing. He explained to her that John wasn't the real problem.

"It's how you deal with him. That's the problem," he said.

Jane became more depressed than ever. They made an appointment for the next afternoon and she walked home and went to bed.

The next day John was actually home to watch the kids when she left for her appointment with Dr. Christianson. John told her to stop and get him some beer when she finished with her appointment. By the time she was ushered into the doctor's office, she was so mad she could hardly say a word.

During the session, she blurted, "I am not going home. I can't go back to that life. I don't know what to do."

With that, she picked up her purse and walked out on the counselor. Her heart was so heavy that she could hardly breathe. She knew she would die if she didn't change her life. Her children were her life. She had to rescue them and get away. She didn't want to go back home, but she had to.

On the way, she stopped and picked up the six-pack John wanted. The resentment toward her husband made her physically ill, and she was sick by the time she walked into the house carrying the beer.

An hour or so after Jane arrived home from her appointment, they heard a knock at the door. She opened the door to find Dr. Jones standing there.

"Dr. Christianson called and asked me to check on you," she said. "He is worried about you."

"I think you are probably suffering from depression. I want you to check yourself into the hospital," the doctor said, and looked very concerned.

"I'm just fine," Jane said defensively.

"You have tried to commit suicide before. I think it would be the right thing to do," Dr. Jones tried to convince Jane that she was in trouble and needed help.

"You can't go," John growled. "I won't let you."

John's words triggered rage from deep inside her. She looked him square in the eye.

"You can't tell me what to do any more," she said.

Just to show him he had lost his control over her, she walked into the bedroom and kissed her sleeping children goodbye, and then followed Dr. Jones out of the house.

That was the last time she saw her children.

Two weeks into her stay in the psychiatric ward at the hospital, Dr. Christianson announced, "Your husband signed your children away to the state. They will be put into foster care."

"No! He can't do that. They're my children, too," Jane cried.

"I'm sorry, but we have to think of the welfare of the children," the doctor said.

Jane was so worried about her children that she made little progress in the hospital. Within the week, she signed herself out and went home. What she found there brought her to stark reality. John had been evicted, and her children were gone.

Since she and John were living on welfare, the agency found them another place to live. They moved into a little house on the west side of town. It was a riding stable, and the house had been used for the owner's hunting dogs. The house was filthy, and there was a dead horse carcass on the porch that the dogs had been chewing on.

The owners of the stable had placed an ad in the paper for someone to live in the house, rent free, if they would take care of the horses, pigs, and dogs. Welfare helped John get his job back at the sanitation department, and Jane went to work with the animals.

"We cannot tell you where your children are at this time," the social worker told Jane.

"If you straighten out your marriage and get your life in order, you will have a chance to get your children back," she promised.

Jane was heartbroken. She missed her children so much that she burst into tears at the slightest thought of them. She felt as though part of her had died.

"I know they are scared and homesick. Let me just talk to them on the phone so they know their mama loves them," she begged.

In her head, she heard them crying out in the night, "I want my mommy."

Jane was beside herself with worry.

She realized the only way to get the children back was to clean up her act. John was working again. He had promised to stop drinking and help get the kids out of foster care.

Jane worked like a mad woman cleaning up the dirty little house. She fixed the broken door and polished the floors until they shined. She fed the animals and mucked out the barn. Each day, she welcomed the sore muscles that she knew brought her closer to holding her children in her arms again.

The welfare agency made surprise visits to see how things were progressing, and everyone had high hopes that the four little Botsford children would be brought back to their parents.

Just when things were going smoothly, John started coming home from work late with the smell of beer on his breath.

On one of the home visits, the social worker asked Jane, "Are either of you drinking?"

"I'm not, but John is," Jane answered truthfully.

"We know your husband is still drinking and I need to document that you are not, for the agency," the social worker stated. "Because of your husband's drinking, we will not be bringing the children back," she informed Jane.

"I am going to go crazy without my children," Jane screamed.

Jane could not stand the sight of her husband. She screamed for him to get out and never come back. One day John just left. Jane decided to stop the foolishness and file for divorce. Logic told her that she would have to be free of John Botsford if she ever hoped to get the kids back.

One night, out of the blue, John walked into the house with his drinking buddy, Bob. They both were stumbling drunk. John told Jane that Bob was going to have sex with her so he could watch.

Jane was so scared she almost threw up. Then anger took over. She was livid with rage. She knew the only way to escape being raped was to somehow get the two drunks fighting mad at each other.

"Whoa, John, how did you like sex the other night with Bob's wife?" Jane leered at him. "She said you're no bigger than a pencil," Jane laughed in his face. "Hey, Bob," she continued. "I bet you didn't know John was screwing your wife, did you? He told me she was a nasty smelling whore."

"You bastard," Bob lunged at John.

That's all it took, and the two drunks were rolling around on the kitchen floor threatening to kill each other. Jane ran out the door and didn't look back. She crawled up into the haymow of the stable and stayed until she saw them leave the next morning.

Once they were gone, she went into the house and put some of her things in a bag. John's tax return had come the week before, and now she took the check out of its hiding place and put it in her purse. She walked to the farmer's house and asked if she could use the phone.

"Hello, Mama?" she asked hesitantly, into the receiver. "They took the kids away and I am filing for divorce. Can you and Daddy come and get me?" she pleaded.

"No!" came the answer. "We've done everything we can to help you, and you don't appreciate a thing we've done. We're not going to help you, ever again. You made your bed, now lie in it."

Jane looked at the receiver and listened to the drone of the dial tone.

She walked to the field where the farm hand was working. She had gotten to know him quite well, in the past few weeks, and found him to be kind.

"Can you take me to the bus station in Eau Claire?" Jane asked.

"When do you want to go?" was the reply.

"As soon as possible," she said.

The kind man said, "Give me a few minutes, and I'll pick you up at the house."

Jane left a note on the table saying, "I'm filing for divorce, and I've gone to visit Grandma Nora."

She lied to John because she wanted to make sure he would never find her.

The bus took her to Fort Gordon, Georgia. Her brother, Alan, was back from Germany, waiting to welcome her with open arms.

Ronnie, Jonnie, Tammy and Todd were gone. In their void, stood a hollow broken woman grieving for the family she could never have. The depth of her pain could not be measured, but could be felt by anyone in her presence.

Thursday, May 19, 1966 - The Cornell Courier - 3

Mrs. John Botsford, Cornell, was last week's Cornell Pay Day winner of $175. This is the largest amount won by any individual since Pay Day was started.

Jane wins $175.00.

Joyce Cellars with Robbie and Randy.

Todd, Tammy, Jonnie and Ronnie
Botsford, in foster care.

Book Four...

Women of Influence

Chapter Thirty-Six

Mothers

It has been said that the hand that rocks the cradle rules the world. Generally, the mother's hand is the hand rocking the cradle. The influence of the mother is felt throughout the family, the community, and the world.

Strong, ethical, faithful women set forth a positive influence. Good behaviors, demonstrated by these women, become the standard by which others learn to deal with the ups and downs of life.

Women of strength were not present in the lives of the Colburn/Buck sisters. The negative influences of the women who were their role models, set them up for failure and heartache.

The letter she received from her Aunt Lydia surprised Joyce. *I am so happy to have found Jane and she has given me your address. I would love to see you again after all of these years,* she wrote. *If you would like to see us, please write back or phone me. If you can't come here, Uncle Tony and I will drive to Milwaukee for a long overdue visit,* she added.

Joyce had mixed feelings as she read the letter. Her early childhood memories of Aunt Lydia were filled with gifts of food and toys, but along with those gifts came the cousins. She remembered how the cousins had hurt her, and Aunt Lydia, along with the others, had paid no attention.

I can't believe they want to see me, Joyce thought. *They must not have forgotten about me, after all.*

Her imagination began to run wild and she began to think about Esther. *Maybe Mama remembers me, too. Maybe Mama loves me after all.*

Maybe she didn't really mean to give me up. Joyce's heart was full of hope as she went next door to Bernie's house to use the phone.

The heavy feeling that was her daily companion lifted after speaking with her aunt. Lightheartedly, she skipped across the lawn back to the house.

"They're coming a week from Saturday," she told Jim excitedly.

"Why don't we go to Cornell to see them?" Jim's decision was posed as a question. "That way we can stay with Ma and it won't cost us anything to feed them. Plus, we won't be stuck entertaining them."

Two weeks later, Joyce and her family made the trip to Cornell for the eagerly anticipated reunion. To Joyce's delight, Aunt Lydia's half sister, Sylvia, who was actually Esther's full sister, was there and was dying to see Joyce again.

They all had a wonderful visit. From that time on, Joyce and Jim visited the aunts whenever they traveled back to Cornell for holidays.

Nellie and Harry Cellars had adopted Jim when he was just a baby. On one of their visits, Aunt Sylvia's husband, Harold, told them that he was actually related to Jim's biological family.

"Your family name is Huff, and your grandfather was a police officer in Eau Claire for many years," he told Jim.

"It's such a small world," Uncle Harold said. "Jim, you are related to me, and Joyce is related to Sylvia. We see your real mother once in awhile. Would you like to meet up with her?" he asked Jim cautiously.

"I don't know," Jim answered. "I guess it would be okay."

Some months after that conversation, Harold contacted Jim.

"I have made arrangements for you to see your mother, if you still want to."

"We're coming up next weekend," Jim answered. "I guess we can see her then."

Joyce looked forward to meeting Jim's real mother all week. Yet when she saw her, she couldn't believe her eyes. Jim's biological mother was a thin, dirty, homeless, and broken woman.

She felt so sorry for the ragged old lady that she asked, "Can we take her with us? She can live with us, can't she?"

Jim was having none of that.

"She's not my mother. She's nothing but a goddamn drunk. My mother lives in Cornell," he added firmly.

"I know Nellie adopted you, but look at her. She needs us," Joyce pleaded.

"What about when I needed her?"

With that, Jim strode toward the door.

Joyce followed her husband obediently out of the tavern. The subject of Jim's mother was never broached between them again.

Sadness and pity invaded Joyce every time she thought of the vulnerable old woman who had given birth to her husband.

Uncle Harold had said, "She was raped, and her father made her give up the baby. She's never been right in the head since."

Joyce said a silent prayer. She was grateful that nobody had forced her to give up her boys.

Robbie had started kindergarten and he just loved school.

"I'm a big boy now," he told his mother proudly, and Joyce shared his pride.

Her main concern was that Jim didn't have any time for the children. Either he was gone from the house, or he was on the couch smoking cigarettes and watching television. When he was home, the kids had to be quiet.

Generally his words to the boys were, "Shut the fuck up," or "Why did you do that, you dumb bastard?"

One good thing about Jim was that he loved his mother, Nellie, and made sure she got to see her two grandsons fairly often. Joyce loved Nellie and understood that she was the only strong, kind and loving woman in her life.

On one weekend trip to visit the grandparents, Joyce and Jim took the boys with them when they went to Eau Claire to see Sylvia and Harold.

Aunt Sylvia asked Joyce, "Would you like to see your mother, Esther?"

"I don't know for sure," Joyce answered.

"She's in town," she said hesitantly. "You could see her without driving to St. Paul."

Joyce finally nodded, and Jim agreed to drive them all downtown. He parked the car in front of the tavern where Esther and her husband, Tony Memkin, were drinking.

Sylvia and Harold went into the bar while Joyce told Robbie and Randy, "We won't be long. Stay in the car and be good. We'll be back in a minute."

Jim and Joyce walked hesitantly into the dimly lit tavern to see Aunt Sylvia speaking to a fat, greasy, very drunk, woman. As Joyce cautiously approached her aunt, Sylvia turned and introduced her to her mother.

One question had burned in Joyce's heart for over twenty years. She finally had the opportunity and the courage to ask.

"Why did you let the welfare people take us away?"

"I didn't want you anymore," Esther slurred. "I kept drinking for three days and decided I liked having fun more than I liked having you," she finished with a grotesque smile on her lips.

Joyce was hurt and very sad.

"Your two little grandsons, Robbie and Randy, are in the car," she told her mother.

"Bartender," Esther yelled hoarsely. "Get me two Babe Ruth candy bars."

"Here, give these to the kids," she said.

Esther handed the candy bars to Joyce and turned back to her beer.

The shock and disappointment of seeing Esther made Joyce feel lonely for her brother and sister, but she had no idea where Jane was. Hazel told her that John was in jail and the kids had been put in foster care.

Joyce was extremely worried about her sister, but Hazel was no help.

"Your father and I are not helping Jane anymore. We've had it with her."

One day Joyce wrote a letter to her sister and sent it to Hazel.

"Would you please forward this letter to Jane?" she asked.

Hazel responded quickly, "Jane doesn't want anything to do with you. She doesn't love you anymore," she wrote.

Joyce believed her mother and didn't try to communicate with Jane for quite some time.

In the meantime, Hazel told Jane, "Joyce is washing her hands of you because she doesn't want you to influence the boys with your lifestyle and low morals."

Jane was grieving for her children and was terribly hurt that her sister had abandoned her, too. She decided *I don't love Joyce anymore and I don't care if she hates me. I can live without her just fine.*

One day Joyce made a decision. *I'm not going to give up without a fight. I don't care what mother says, I have to know if Jane is all right.* With great determination, she strode across the lawn to her neighbor Bernie's, and telephoned her brother in Georgia.

"Do you know where Jane is?" she asked. "Mother won't tell me and I'm scared to death for her."

To Joyce's great relief, Alan said, "Jane is living here with us. I'm going to be sent to Vietnam for a year, and Tina and Jane are moving to Killeen, Texas. They are going to get the house we own, at Fort Hood, ready for sale."

"How is she doing?" Joyce asked.

"Good, I think," answered Alan. "She's not here or you could ask her yourself."

Joyce was cheered by the knowledge that Jane was in the protective care of their big brother.

Alan shipped out to Vietnam. Within the week, Tina and Jane were on their way to Killeen, Texas.

"I found a job at the hospital," Jane told Tina excitedly one day. "Now I can make some money and get my kids back," she added joyfully.

Jane had found herself an apartment and a job as a nurse's aid. Even though things seemed to be looking upward for her, she found that she was still terribly empty.

Ironically, there were two conflicting ways Jane chose to try to fill the void in her gut. She felt the need to be loved, so she went out and found a variety of men to sleep with. She felt the need for spiritual guidance, so she joined the local Baptist church.

Chapter Thirty-seven

Surprise

Jim had finally agreed to have a telephone installed in their trailer house in Milwaukee. Joyce was relieved that she wouldn't have to trouble the neighbors any longer when she needed to make a phone call.

One day, Joyce was outside when she heard her new telephone ring. It rang several times before she could answer

Aunt Lydia said on the other end, "I'm calling to let you know Esther is in Ramsey County Hospital. The doctors say she is dying."

"Oh," was Joyce's response.

"Esther is asking for you kids. She knows she's dying and she wants to see you all," Lydia continued.

"I have to talk to Jim," Joyce answered. "I'm not sure if we can get there before she dies."

"I have to contact Jane and Alan yet," Aunt Lydia was saying. "She wants to see them, too."

"Alan is in Vietnam and I think Jane is still in Killeen, Texas, but I don't have her phone number or address," Joyce said with regret.

"I'll call Hazel," said Aunt Lydia. "I'm sure she knows how to get in touch with Jane."

The next day, Lydia called with Jane's phone number. Joyce thanked her aunt. Nervously, she dialed her sister's number.

Jane picked up after the first ring, "Hello?"

"Jane, this is Joyce," she began. "Aunt Lydia called and said that Esther is very sick and the doctors say she is dying. She wants to see us before she dies," Joyce said before she could lose her nerve.

"Oh, my God," Jane answered. "I wonder if we contacted the Red Cross if they could help Alan get home from Vietnam for the funeral."

Jane was so happy to hear from her sister that she began to rattle on, "Wouldn't it be wonderful for the three of us to be together again? I don't know if I can get off work," Jane went on. "I don't have money for the plane tickets, but let me see what I can do."

Joyce gave Jane her new telephone number and the sisters both hung up smiling.

The next morning, Jane phoned Joyce with her news.

"The hospital is giving me time off and the church is buying my airline tickets. I arrive in Minneapolis at 2:30 on Thursday afternoon," she added. "Can somebody pick me up? I hope I can make it before she dies."

"Uncle Harold said he will meet you at the baggage claim area," Joyce told her.

Jim could not get off work, so Joyce took the boys and rode the bus to Cornell. Robbie and Randy would stay with Grandma Nellie while she went to St. Paul to see Esther at the hospital.

Esther was still alive when Joyce entered the darkened hospital room.

Slowly she approached her mother's death bed, leaned over her, and said, "Mama, this is Shirley, and Sharon is on her way."

Esther died before Jane could get there, and the funeral arrangements were made around her flight plans. Uncle Harold picked Jane up at the airport, and they drove directly to the church where the funeral was waiting to begin.

At the church, Joyce and Jane stood before the coffin of their dead mother and cried. They wished with heart and soul that their brother Alan could be standing beside them.

In that moment, they again were the little Colburn sisters, Shirley Maye and Sharon Ann, standing at the edge of the open well. Together they stood, surrounded by the ghosts of all their sorrows. They shed no tears for the loss of Esther Colburn, the woman who had given them life. They cried for what might have been.

Following the interment, the girls met relatives they had not known existed. Their cousin, Gary Tomnia and his wife Irene lived in

Milwaukee, very near Joyce and Jim. Irene and Joyce hit it off right from the start and made plans to meet once they were back home again.

The long ride back to Cornell gave the sisters an opportunity to chit-chat, but they didn't get into any deep personal conversation. They realized something had changed and they both felt the distrust and coldness that had grown between them.

Jane stayed with Hazel and Ted for a week. One day she noticed a card sitting on the buffet. It was obviously written by a young child. She picked it up and saw that her son Ronnie had signed it. It was a birthday card to his grandmother.

Quite by accident, she found out that her children were in foster care in Stanley, Wisconsin, only a few miles from her parent's home.

Jane was surprised when she was told that the foster parents were relatives of Ted and Hazel, and they had gone to see the children often. Another surprise was that the Marionkowitz's had brought the kids to Cornell to visit their grandparents a few times, too.

Jane didn't know her parents were spending time with her children. Even though she was worried about them being around Ted, she was relieved to find out the kids were not growing up isolated from their family.

Visiting with Joyce, Robbie, and Randy at Aunt Nellie's made Jane's heart ache for her own children.

"Ask Mama and Daddy to take you to Stanley to see the kids," Joyce suggested.

"I'm going to, but I'm waiting until you go back to Milwaukee before I do," Jane said. "I want to see them just before I go home to Killeen. Once I see them, I won't be able to stand it. I'll need to leave town," she sobbed.

At the end of the week, Jane went to Stanley with Hazel and Ted to see the kids. She hadn't seen them since the day she kissed them goodbye and checked herself into the psychiatric ward at the hospital in Eau Claire.

Two long years had passed. Her children had grown and looked healthy and happy. Ronnie and Jonnie recognized Jane right away and called her Mommy. Her heart broke into a million little pieces with the sheer joy of being with her children again. Yet, she experienced the unbelievable agony of knowing she would have to leave them behind.

Ronnie was six years old, and in the first grade. Jonnie was five, and told his mother he loved her. Tammy and Todd had changed the most. Todd had been a baby and now he was almost three. Tammy was a two-year-old toddler when Jane had kissed her goodbye, and now she was a beautiful, blonde, four-year-old girl.

Too soon it was time to leave and Jane didn't know how she would manage to say goodbye to her babies. Ronnie and Jonnie wanted to go with their mother. The boys put up a fuss and soon Jane and all of her children were crying.

Ted stepped in and said, "You can't go with your mother. She has no money to take care of you, and she lives far away from here."

Jane told her children, "You have a good home here, and they can take better care of you than I can. Just remember, no matter where you are, I love you very much."

She hugged each one and then walked toward the car.

The heavy burden of worry eased a bit, once she saw the children with her own eyes. They were well fed and well dressed. They had a beautiful home to live in, which was nothing like the dinky apartment she called home in Texas.

Yes, she had done the best thing by leaving them with the Marionkowitz's. *They have a chance to grow up and have a normal life if I leave them where they are,* she thought. Jane flew back to Killeen, with relief in her heart.

Chapter Thirty-Eight

The Wedge

One morning the phone rang and Irene Tomnia was on the other end. Joyce had met her cousin Gary and his wife, Irene, at Esther's funeral.

"Joyce, I have to run a couple of errands. When I'm done, how about I come over for a cup of coffee?" she asked cheerfully.

Joyce was overjoyed. She was lonely in Milwaukee and eager to know someone who would just drop by for a cup of coffee once in awhile.

After that first visit, the two women became good friends. Their husbands, Jim and Gary, liked each other well enough for the two families to spend time together. Irene and Gary's children loved Joyce.

"Aunta Joyca is here," they would squeal, using their childish pronunciation when they saw her drive up to the house.

"Why don't you go to Weight Watchers with me?" Irene questioned one day.

"I don't think so," Joyce answered. "I don't have the money, and Jim wants me to stay at home."

"Oh, come on," Irene pleaded. "We'll go while he's at work and the boys are at school. You can squirrel a little grocery money each week. It doesn't cost that much," she pleaded.

Joyce decided she was going to live on the wild side for a change and agreed to join her.

"I have a family membership at the gym and I can bring a guest," Irene added. "You can be my guest and we'll work out together. It's no fun going there by myself."

Every Monday afternoon, Joyce and Irene went to the Weight Watchers meeting. On Tuesday and Friday mornings, the friends worked out at the gym. Joyce began losing weight.

"You're gettin' to look pretty foxy there girl," Irene told her, one day.

For the first time in her life, Joyce began to have some threads of self-confidence. The problem was, Jim didn't like it that she was looking good.

"What have you been doing while I've been at work?" he questioned her.

"Irene and I have been on a diet and working out," was her truthful answer.

It was obvious by his behavior at the Appleton Electric Christmas party, that Jim didn't want Joyce to look good. The more he drank, the angrier he became. He acted like a bantam rooster protecting his hen.

"The guys are all lookin' at you," he huffed. "I'm goin' to kill um all."

For the first time in her life, Joyce felt proud of the way she looked. She felt rather like a princess that night, and had a wonderful time. Joyce began to believe that Jim cared about her with his puffed up display.

Pride in her new look came to a screeching halt on the way home. In the privacy of the car, Jim began ranting.

"You're so stupid. Don't you think I know you are spending my money just to look good for other men? That's it! No more Irene. She put you up to this nonsense."

"It's not Irene's fault," Joyce began.

"Are you deaf?" Jim yelled. "I said, no more!"

A lifetime of surrender prevailed, and it didn't occur to Joyce to disobey her husband. Without Irene, life went back to its usual bleak existence. The profound loss of her best friend left her smothered in defeat, sadness, and confusion.

She had grown to love Irene for the upbeat way she looked at life, and the wise advice she had often given. Joyce found that she truly needed Irene's advice once Randy started kindergarten.

Robbie was born when Joyce was single. Therefore, his last name was Buck. Since she was married to Jim when Randy was born, his last name was Cellars.

"The kids at school say that Randy isn't my real brother," Robbie said, looking very serious. "They told me it was a lie and I was making it up, 'cause we have different names."

Tears were welling up in his eyes.

"Them kids teasing you about it?" Jim asked.

Robbie nodded.

"Then I'll just adopt you and your name will be Cellars, too," Jim decided.

Joyce was so elated that Robbie would have the same name as the rest of the family that she felt something stir in her heart for Jim.

"Robbie, if you are adopted, your name will be Robert Edmund Cellars. How about that?" she asked.

"Great!" was all the eight-year-old said.

Just as one of Joyce's problems was solved, another reared its ugly head. Quite unexpectedly, Joyce received a letter from her mother, Hazel. In the envelope were clippings from the Chippewa Herald Telegram, a local newspaper. She had no way of knowing that her sister, Jane, had received the exact same letter.

The first article was dated Monday, August 9, 1971. It told of a fight at the Water's Edge Supper Club in Chippewa Falls that had occurred on Saturday, August 7, at around 11:45 p.m. The death of Darrel J. Konerik was chronicled in the article as the third drowning victim of the year.

According to the article, there had been a party going on and everyone was drinking heavily. Witnesses said that Konerik was on the dock holding his fiancée, Sandra Werlund, and they fell into the water. Sandra could swim, but Konerik apparently could not. Bystanders pulled Sandra from the water and then called the Chippewa Falls firefighters. Konerik's body was recovered in less than an hour in about eleven feet of water.

Both girls read the article and had the same reaction. *What's this all about?* they wondered.

The second clipping was dated Tuesday, August 10, 1971. It was the obituary of Darrell J. Konerik, aged twenty-seven. He was born July

9, 1944 in Chippewa Falls. He graduated from Cadott High School and served in the U.S. Army from May 15, 1963, until May 14, 1969. The obituary stated that funeral services would be held at the Jim Falls Methodist Church and interment would be at Union Cemetery in the Town of Goetz.

Neither sister had any understanding of why Hazel would bother to send them all of this information about someone they had never met.

The third clipping gave the answer. Dated August 19, 1971, the article read, "According to Chief Investigator Cardinal, a summons to appear in County Court on Thursday, August 26, was issued to John W. Botsford, 30, of rural Chippewa Falls, on a charge of homicide by reckless conduct. The charge stems from the drowning death of Darrel J. Konerik, 27, of Chippewa Falls in Lake Wissota on August 7.

Jane gasped, "Oh, my god! John killed somebody."

The fourth paper in the envelope, was a short note from Hazel.

Dear Joyce, This is the reason I worry about Robbie and Randy being around your sister. Jane lives a bad lifestyle and these clippings prove that she was married to a killer. The reason she doesn't want anything to do with you is because she doesn't love you. If she loved you, she wouldn't live the way she does. Mother.

Dear Jane, No wonder Joyce doesn't want her children to have anything to do with you. This is the kind of scum you always associated with. Mother.

The sisters never knew if anything came of the allegations against John. Hazel was careful not to share that part of the story with her daughters. Her obvious goal was to use the information to drive a wedge between Joyce and Jane.

Chapter Thirty-Nine

Broken Hearts

Robbie and Randy Cellars loved their grandma Nellie. She had no other grandchildren and she loved them back, with all her heart. As Nellie grew older, she found it hard to live alone, especially during the frigid Wisconsin winters.

"Ma, how about coming to Milwaukee to live with us for the winter?" Jim offered.

Nellie wanted to make sure she wasn't going to burden her daughter-in-law, so she talked with Joyce before she made her decision. Together, they decided that Nellie would spend the winters in Milwaukee with them, and the summers at her own home in Cornell.

Joyce was lonely and hoped that Nellie would prove to be good company. She was not disappointed. Nellie taught Joyce to knit and crochet, and she helped with the boys. The two women spent many hours working and laughing together. In the spring, Joyce begged her to stay longer, but Nellie didn't want to wear out her welcome.

When fall came again, Joyce eagerly awaited her mother-in-law's return. She had grown to trust Nellie in a way that she trusted no other woman. In time, Nellie became the mother Joyce had never really had.

One morning around 6:00 a.m., Nellie woke up and said, "Joyce, I don't feel very well. If I could just get rid of this cough, I'd be fine."

She coughed deeply and when she was finished, she said, "It's just wearing me out."

"Try to go back to sleep," Joyce suggested. "I'll take the boys to school and when I get back, we'll have breakfast."

Joyce was extremely concerned over the way Nellie looked, and that cough sounded bad. *I'm going to insist she let me take her to the doctor,* Joyce thought as she returned home a half hour later. She hurried in to check on Nellie and found the older woman sound asleep in her bed.

Around 8:00 a.m., Joyce went back to check on the sleeping woman and saw that she didn't seem to be breathing.

"Oh, no," she panicked. "I think she's dead."

Joyce ran across the street screaming, "Betty, come over right away. I think Jim's mom is dead."

"She's gone," Betty confirmed, as she put her hand up to Nellie's face. "I'll call the police. You'd better call Jim."

Joyce was crying and talking almost incoherently by the time Jim finally came to the phone.

"What did you say?" Jim asked. "Slow down. What's wrong?"

"Your mother's dead. You need to come home right away," repeated Joyce, more calmly.

Betty stood quietly as Joyce sat beside the bed of the dead woman, waiting for the police to arrive. In shock, Joyce rocked back and forth in her chair, trying desperately to grasp what had happened.

When the authorities finally arrived, Betty let them in and helped Joyce answer their questions. Both women watched helplessly as the men put Nellie on the gurney.

The coroner was removing Nellie's body from the trailer house when Jim wheeled in.

"We have to get her to the funeral home in Cornell," Jim told one of the men.

"Follow us back to the office and we'll get those arrangements made," the man replied.

On his way to the car, Jim stopped long enough to ask Betty if she could take Joyce to get the boys. She nodded.

"Go to school and pick up the kids," Jim ordered Joyce. "Then get packed so we can leave for Cornell, as soon as I get back."

Joyce was distraught and couldn't think of what to do next. *I have to tell Jane,* she thought. *I need her.*

"Jane, Nellie is dead," Joyce said into the phone. "She died an hour ago and Jim is making funeral arrangements. Can you come?"

"I'll do my best," Jane said.

The sisters talked a couple of minutes and then Joyce and Betty went to get Robbie and Randy from school.

The ride home was traumatic for them all.

"Why did she have to die?" Robbie asked, and started to cry.

"I don't want to go to Grandma Nellie's funeral," Randy sobbed in the back seat. "I don't want her to be dead."

Joyce, Jim and the boys stayed at Nellie's house in Cornell, while they made funeral arrangements and grieved. Joyce picked out Nellie's favorite dress for her to wear in the coffin. She hid her face in the pretty garment and cried for the woman she truly loved.

Jane was torn. She had been working at the hospital in Killeen, and had been putting her money away. She hoped, someday, to have enough saved to get her children back. Jane wavered emotionally as she agonized over her dilemma. Should she deplete her savings to go to Wisconsin to support her sister, or keep her money where it was and work toward her ultimate goal?

It's been almost two years since I've seen the kids, she thought. *I'll get to see them again, if I go back for the funeral.* For Jane, the emptiness and heartbreak had never gone away, but the anticipation of seeing her children again revitalized her. Once the travel arrangements were made, she couldn't wait to get back to Wisconsin.

When she arrived in Cornell, she was given her old room in the big green house on Main Street. Jane was very uncomfortable with so many ghosts floating around. To make matters worse, Ted and Hazel said very little and were cool toward her. Her brother, Roger, was the only one who acted a little bit glad to see her.

"I don't know why you came," Hazel said. "Joyce doesn't want you around the boys."

"I came because she called me and asked me to come," Jane answered sassily. "Besides, Aunt Nellie is my relative and I can come if I want to!"

The Buck family did seem a little closer to each other, though, as they stood together at the cemetery mourning the loss of Nellie Cellars. She was mother, grandmother, aunt, mother-in-law and friend. Jane thought she sensed the presence of Grandpa Bailey standing with them beside his sister-in-law's grave.

Hazel and Ted agreed to drive Jane to see the children. The day after Nellie's funeral, Jane awoke to find that nervousness had replaced her excitement. She was nearly jumping out of her skin by the time she and her parents left for Stanley. *I wonder if they will remember me*, she worried.

Jane's oldest children, Ronnie and Jonnie, had often told their younger brother and sister about their mother. Their memories had turned into a fairy tale filled with hugs, kisses, love, and fun times.

The older children believed that someday their mother would come to get them, and take them away to that wonderful life again. By the virtue of those repeated tales, the younger children truly believed they remembered, too. They longed for the love of their mother, as much as the older children did.

And so, to Jane's surprise, the four kids came squealing and running toward the car as it rolled to a stop in the driveway.

"Mama," they screeched.

"Come on in. They've been driving me crazy like this ever since you called," Mrs. Marionkowitz said to Hazel.

Even little Todd called her Mama. He was five years old now, and Jane thought he was very handsome.

"Look at my homework," Ronnie said as he slid his eight-year-old body onto her lap.

"Mine, too," said Jonnie, as he climbed up to sit on her lap, too.

Tammy had drawn a picture for her mother.

"I'm good at making pictures," Tammy said seriously and crawled up with her brothers.

Jane sat there with all four children on her lap, at the same time. *This is what heaven is all about,* she thought as her heart nearly burst.

She put her arms around all of them and held on.

Ted and Hazel gushed at how clean the children were.

"Quite a difference, huh mother?" Ted said to Hazel. "Remember how dirty they all were before they came here to live?"

"You kids have a good home here," Hazel said, as she turned her attention toward the scene before her. "Mrs. Marionkowitz is a good mother," she scolded her grandchildren.

Abruptly, Ted stood up and announced, "It's time to go."

In unison, a cry went up from the children.

"I want to go with you." "Take me, too." "I'm coming." "I don't care if I have enough food." "I won't eat much." "Please let me come with you."

Jane cried along with her children as they all hung on her and begged her to take them along.

Ted drew the line.

"Get in the car," he yelled at Jane. "It's time for us to go."

He was angry now.

"Behave yourselves," he said to the kids. "I knew it was a mistake to bring her here."

The ride back to Cornell was miserable. Her heart was breaking and Jane couldn't wait to get back to Texas.

Chapter Forty

Short and Not So Sweet

Sometimes life is just not what you thought it would be. Jane was distraught with hers. She loved her kids and missed them with every breath she took. She had a job at the hospital but didn't earn enough money to support them. On her salary, it was impossible to afford a big enough apartment to house four children. Aside from that, she didn't have enough money for airline tickets to bring the kids to Texas.

She had no one to help her.

Hazel had told her often, "You're a terrible mother," and Jane believed her.

She was totally miserable without her children, but she felt helpless in her efforts to get them back.

One day while she was having a sandwich at the Brown Derby Restaurant, a cute, short, red-haired man walked in and sat next to her at the counter. Jane had a big hole in her heart and she was looking to fill it.

"Is this seat taken?" Larry asked in a soft voice.

"It's all yours," Jane answered with a flirty smile.

"That looks good," he said as he looked at her plate. "The lady eating it looks good, too."

Jane giggled and offered him a taste of her lunch.

"See if it tastes as good as it looks," she smiled coyly.

"Ummmmm," he said as he slowly and provocatively licked his lips.

"Are you busy tonight?" Larry asked, raising his eyebrow and giving her his famous crooked grin.

"What do you have in mind?" Jane questioned.

"How about a movie?"

They met after Jane was finished with her shift at the hospital, and that night, Larry introduced her to the "Wonderful World of the Cinema." Larry was a projectionist at one of the local movie theaters. He took Jane with him while he ran the movie reels. He told her jokes and was a regular cut up. Needless to say, Jane enjoyed her first date with Larry very much.

For the next couple of weeks, Larry and Jane spent every spare moment together. Jane told him about her children and her desire to have them with her. He was very understanding.

"Let's get married and I'll help you get them back," he promised.

Jane was astonished that he asked and she was even more astonished when she said, "Yes."

"How about right away?" Larry wanted to know. "I can't get you out of my head. All I want is to have you for my wife and have a family."

Jane bought a wedding dress off the rack at a local department store. One of the cooks at the hospital was happy to bake and decorate a four-tiered wedding cake for her. The pastor at the Baptist church agreed to perform the ceremony.

Alan was back from Vietnam and living with Tina, in Georgia.

"Alan, guess what?" Jane asked, in a breathless voice. "I'm getting married next week. Oh, please, can you and Tina come?" she begged. "I want you to give me away, and I want Tina to be my matron of honor. I'm getting married on Saturday and he is going to help me bring the kids to Texas."

About thirty people attended the wedding of Larry Miller and Jane Botsford. Larry's brother was the best man and his little sister was the flower girl. It was almost the perfect day for Jane Miller. The only people missing were the bride's children and her sister, Joyce.

Once they were married, Larry moved his things into Jane's apartment and life went smoothly for the happy couple. Jane was in love with her new husband, and very happy that he proved to be cheerful, kind and understanding. *He'll be so good for my kids,* she thought happily.

Two weeks after the wedding, Jane hurt her back at work. The doctor told her to quit her job at the hospital, because he didn't want her lifting patients any longer. He also instructed her to stay in bed for several weeks. During this time, Larry continued to be upbeat and his attitude helped her stay optimistic. Even though she was in tremendous pain, her husband made her smile.

With Larry, there were always surprises. Some surprises were a bit shocking. Jane was still at home, recuperating from her back injury, when the telephone bill came. She opened the envelope, and couldn't believe her eyes. *Five hundred dollars,* she screamed. *There must be some mistake.*

When she looked more closely, she noticed that all of the calls were billed to the same telephone number, 555-5771, in California.

"Don't worry, babe. I had some loose ends to take care of. I'll pay the bill," Larry soothed her, when she confronted him.

Soon, Jane was feeling better and was able to be up and around. She began thinking of jobs that would not require lifting. A friend told her about an opening at a nearby restaurant. When she picked up the phone book to look for the number, she noticed that Larry had written, *Butch, 555-5771,* in the margin on the back page.

That's the number on our phone bill, she said to herself. *I wonder what this is all about.*

The answer to her question came a few days later. Larry brought his friend Butch to the apartment.

"Butch is going to live here with us," he announced to his bride. "Now, Jane, I know you will understand what I'm going to tell you," he smiled and spoke softly to her. "That's one thing I love about you. You are so understanding."

"What am I supposed to understand?" Jane asked warily.

"I love Butch and I can't leave him," Larry announced to her.

"Then what do you want with me?" Jane was nearly hysterical.

"I want to have us all live together. I want to have children with you," was his response.

In a daze, Jane walked over to the door, opened it, and gestured outside with her thumb. She stood staring through the open door, long after Larry and Butch were out of sight.

"I had a suspicion that he might be bi-sexual," Larry's brother said, when Jane called to ask him to pick up Larry's things.

The thought of seeing her husband again made her feel ill, so Jane filed for divorce immediately.

"I think I've set a record," she told Joyce on the phone. "Married and divorced in just three months."

Once again, the sisters cried together.

Chapter Forty-One

Another Military Man

Blackness crept in like a thief in the night, and sucker punched Jane as she struggled to put the pieces of her life back together. Her career as a nurse was over. Her savings account was depleted. Her marriage, and the promises of being a mother to her children, had vanished. *It's hopeless*, she cried into her pillow.

Eventually, she found a job and a friend at the Brown Derby Restaurant, but her life continued its spiral into a destructive pattern. After each shift, Jane and her new friend, Judy, would hit the bars. The raucous sounds of the jukebox beckoned as she walked toward the *medication* for despair.

In her search for numbness, Jane developed a personal relationship with alcohol. Her mind, body, and spirit, were at war. She was quickly losing the battle. Her mind was fogged over in its effort to forget. Her body was suffering from too much liquor and injury, and not enough food and rest. Her spirit was shattered and racked with depression.

That's how it was for Jane when the landlord came for the past due rent.

"I don't have the money to pay you," she sobbed.

"I'll give you the rest of the week. If you don't pay me, you're out," he threatened.

Judy knew of a seedy little one-bedroom place for rent, a few blocks from the café, for only twenty dollars a month.

One afternoon, Jane was finished with her shift, and it was raining "cats and dogs." She didn't have a coat or umbrella with her.

"My cab is outside. I have to pick someone up in six minutes. I'll drop you off on my way," Nick told her.

Nick was a cab driver, and a regular lunch customer at the Brown Derby. Jane was very grateful.

"I'll give you an extra cup of coffee tomorrow," she joked.

"This is it?" Nick clucked his tongue when he saw the dive she lived in.

"Yup, this is my castle."

Jane tried to make light of her situation.

"I've got a two-bedroom duplex and I've been looking for a roommate to share the rent. Would you be interested?" he asked.

"This place only costs me twenty dollars a month and I can't afford more," Jane answered.

"Twenty a month would help me out a lot. Besides, the place is right next to the Brown Derby," Nick coaxed.

Jane saw Nick as an angel sent by God. They became roommates and platonic friends. The duplex was nice. She did her best to keep it clean and make it her home.

Living next to the place she worked fit right in with her new lifestyle. She and Judy could get to the bars more quickly now that she didn't have to go so far to change her clothes.

On one particularly busy morning at the Derby, Jane had a hangover and an unusually bad case of the shakes. The guys who were regulars at the counter were laughing and kidding her about it. She enjoyed the camaraderie and exaggerated her condition, to play her part to the hilt.

Jane saw a tall G.I. walk in wearing green fatigues and jungle boots. *He must be new at the base,* she thought. *I've never seen him in here before.*

"He's mine, Judy. I'll wait on him," she told her friend.

Mac McDaniel had a mustache, wore glasses, and had an earring in his ear.

"I'll just have a coffee," he ordered.

Jane's hands were shaking so badly that by the time she got the coffee to his table, most of it had spilled into the saucer.

"Do you have time to talk for a minute?" Mac asked.

She looked around and saw that everyone was taken care of.

"Sure."

"I noticed your earrings and necklace," he told her. "Are they really made out of safety pins?"

"Yup, they are. My sister made them and sent them to me. Aren't they cool?" she asked.

"What do you think? Can I borrow one of them?" Mac asked. "I promise I'll give it back to you next week."

"I suppose that would be okay," Jane said as she began removing one of the safety pins from her ear.

"How about having dinner with me tonight? Have you ever eaten at the Rainbow Café?"

Jane looked at the man beside her and thought, "There is something about him I like."

Jane had a head start on the drinks by the time Mac walked into the Rainbow Café to meet her. Their coffee came first and Jane decided to put a creamer in hers. White liquid squirted all over Mac's shirt when she squeezed the container.

"I'm sorry," she gushed.

"I guess you know how to make a good first impression," he laughed, as he wiped himself off with his napkin.

From experience, Jane knew what would happen next. He would get mad, call her a stupid bitch, and she'd never see him again. But he didn't. Instead, he smiled at her. When they were finished eating, he asked her to go with him to a bar.

Jane was having a wonderful time with Mac. All too soon he called a cab. The windshield wipers kept time with the beating of her heart, as they rode through the rain back to Jane's place. Usually a night out with a man meant he would be coming in and spending the night.

To Jane's surprise, Mac opened the door for her and said, "Good night, I had fun. Can we do this again sometime?"

He left her standing at the door feeling angry, dejected and confused, as he rode away in the cab. Mac was the first man who had not touched her, or even kissed her on the first date, and she didn't know how to react. *I'll never see him again.*

One week later, Mac came into the Brown Derby to return her safety pin earrings.

"I have to get back to the base, but how about getting together later this evening?" he asked. "We could go for dinner again."

This time, Mac and Jane talked for hours and he stayed. Mac found out about Jane's children and he felt her pain.

He wished he could do something to help her, but he had troubles of his own. He had been flown back from Vietnam on the drug plane. The first day Jane saw him at the Brown Derby, he had just been released from the drug detention center where he had been held while he went through detoxification.

It felt good to him to be free of the chains the drugs had on his life. He had gone cold turkey and he was proud of himself. He was now ready to start his life over and do things right.

Soon, Mac moved in with Jane and they began building a life together. The problem was Jane didn't want to quit drinking. Mac would come home from the military base and she would be in the bar. He always knew where to find her.

One night Mac went to the bar to find Jane.

"Come home with me," he pleaded.

"No, I'm not ready yet," she resisted.

Mac left with his head hanging and a dejected look on his face.

Suddenly, as if by God's intervention, Jane had a strong feeling that she needed to go home.

Mac's best friend was at the bar and Jane said to him, "Grier, take me home quick! Something is wrong with Mac."

They reached the house to find the doors locked. Mac did not respond to their banging and yelling. Grier finally broke down the door and they both rushed in. What they saw sobered Jane up, fast. Mac had shoved rags in all the cracks around the doors and windows, and turned on the gas in the oven. He planned to kill himself and he almost succeeded.

"Mac," Jane cried. "I'm sorry, I'm sorry."

His body was limp. They opened the door and windows. Between the two of them, they got him up on his feet. With Jane on one side and Grier on the other, they walked him around in the fresh air, and then gave him coffee until he recovered.

"I love you and I can't live without you," Mac said, smiling weakly.

That was the first time in Jane's life that she realized someone could love her enough to die for her.

"Mac, I am sorry for what I put you through. I'll get better," Jane sobbed. "I'll stop drinking. I love you and I don't want to live without you, either."

A year passed with no drinking or drugs. They decided they were ready to get married. They chose not to have a big wedding, so they went to Waco and got married in the courthouse. Neither Joyce nor Alan could be there to help her celebrate. The judge's assistant was Jane's witness and Mac's best friend, James Grier, was his best man. The wedding wasn't fancy, but they were happy

Mac was honorably discharged from the Army on April 3, 1974.

"I want to take a month off before I look for a job. I was thinking that we should go to Wisconsin," Mac said to his surprised wife. "I've never been there, and I want to see where you grew up. It's time I met your parents. Then I'll know who you are talking about."

Jane agreed and called Hazel.

"Mama, Mac and I would like to come to Cornell on our vacation," Jane said into the telephone. "He wants to meet you."

"Well, I suppose that will be all right," Hazel answered.

"She must be curious to see you. She sounded fine with us coming," Jane told Mac when she hung up.

The newlyweds drove from Texas to Wisconsin. When they arrived, they were wearing their cowboy hats, jeans, boots, and buckskin jackets.

"You look like real Texans," Hazel giggled when they walked in the kitchen door.

Ted and Hazel seemed genuinely happy to see their daughter and her new husband. There were smiles and hugs all around.

"Howdy pardner," Jane's brother Roger said, with an exaggerated Texas drawl.

Doubt began to rise in Mac's head. He didn't want to distrust his wife but he was beginning to get a different picture of Ted and Hazel, than the one Jane had painted for him. The first impression he had of them was that they were warm, friendly and loving people who loved their daughter very much.

Mac was impressed with the meals and the amount of time Hazel and Ted spent taking them around to see the sights. However, the longer they stayed, the more the veneer of kindness began to crack. Hazel began making snide comments to Jane when she thought Mac was out of earshot.

Ted spent lots of time trying to convince Mac that he was very important in the community, and that he knew very important people. Roger was often rude to Hazel, and Mac noticed that Ted did nothing to stop it. Soon, he began to see through the façade, and understood that Jane had been telling the truth.

Ted and Hazel both liked Mac very much.

"You finally did something right," Hazel said.

"Now if you can only keep from being stupid and screwing this up," Ted sneered. "You'd better hope and pray you can keep him."

The day before they were to go back to Texas, Jane asked her father, "Daddy, will you and mama take Mac and me to Stanley to see the kids?"

"No! Are you crazy? Do you want to scare Mac away?" he yelled. "Besides, the Marionkowitz's do not want you to see the kids. It took a week to settle them down after you were there two years ago."

Jane began to cry.

"I have to see my children when I am this close."

"Tears won't get you anywhere. I'm not taking you, and I don't want to hear about this again," Ted said through gritted teeth.

Jane was defeated. She went to bed with a headache and an unbearable pressure in her chest. She prayed that their departure would come quickly.

On the drive back to Texas, Mac admitted to Jane, "I don't like your parents and I don't like Wisconsin. I couldn't live in a place where people are so mean. Besides, it snows there in April."

Now that they were back in Texas, Mac took a job in the oil fields where he would work on an oil derrick. They rented a two-bedroom house in Odessa, and settled in. Mac made pretty good money, but their accumulated debts proved to be overwhelming. The huge debt prompted Jane to start looking for a job.

"No, I don't want you to work," Mac told her. "You are my wife. I'll support you."

Jane was touched by his words and proud to have married a man with pride. She made a silent vow to always be true to him.

Chapter Forty-two

The Queen of Empty Threats

Though the years had passed, life in Milwaukee had not changed much. The only real difference was that Grandma Nellie wasn't around in the winters anymore, and Robbie and Randy were nearly grown up.

As a mother, Joyce had proven to be weak. Due to her confused understanding of discipline, abuse, and love, Joyce had become the *queen of empty threats.*

She found that she didn't know how to be a disciplinarian, and as her children grew older, their lives spiraled out of control. Joyce thought the boys would hate her if she punished them, or told them NO! Occasionally, out of frustration, she would lose it, and hit the kids in the head to knock some sense into them. They would laugh at her and she'd end up with a sore hand.

However, the boys bothered Jim more as they grew older. Part of the problem was that the Blue Canary bar served minors, and Jim always accused them of drinking.

"Those kids are hanging with a bad crowd," he would rave. "When are you going to do something about it?"

Joyce continued to drive Robbie and Randy to school in the morning. Then she picked them up in the afternoon. She didn't know that they often skipped school during the day. There were many things Joyce did not know about her son's activities, and she turned a blind eye to the things she did know. She resisted Jim's accusations against them because she was too depressed to confront him or the problems with the boys.

Pain was controlling Joyce's life—the emotional pain an abused child suffers, and physical pain.

"Oh," Joyce moaned. "I can't stand it," she cried to Jim, as he drove her to the hospital.

Jim deposited her in the emergency room and left.

"I'm not staying in here with you," he told her. "I can't stand to be around sick people."

She was admitted to the hospital and surgery was scheduled immediately, to remove her gall bladder. Joyce was shaking violently with fear and the sense of being totally alone. The nurses began to prep her for the procedure. *What if I die*? She thought. *Who will take care of my boys*?

The next thing Joyce knew, she was again Shirley Colburn, asleep under the bed in grandpa Colburn's house at Turtle Lake.

She could hear her sister Sharon and her brother Alan calling to her, "Wake up now. Open your eyes. It's time to wake up."

She came slowly awake with the feeling of calm in her heart. She was not alone. Her sister and brother had come to be with her. She watched them wave goodbye and then fade away through the wall of her hospital room, as the nurses brought her out of the anesthetic.

I'll never really be alone, she told herself. *Sharon and Alan will always be with me.*

After the surgery, when Joyce was finally settled comfortably in her hospital bed, the nurse introduced her to Germaine Lorbicki, her roommate. Germaine was about twenty years older than she was, and Joyce liked her at first sight.

Germaine had a daughter, Rosie, who visited her mother every day. In no time, Rosie and Joyce became friends.

"How about we go out for lunch as soon as you break out of this joint?" Rosie said to Joyce.

"I'd love that," she answered.

Joyce had found her first real, best friend. It wasn't long before she began to think of Rosie as a second sister. Rosie had a garden and flowers. Joyce found that she loved to spend time digging in the dirt. Soon, her routine included spending part of almost every day with Rosie.

She made the mistake of telling Jim, "Rosie and I worked in the flower garden today. The flowers are getting just beautiful." Or, "Rosie and I went to the museum today. Did you know they have dinosaurs there?"

One day Jim decreed, "I don't want you to see that bitch again. I want you home where you belong. She's stupid. I guess if you like spending time with that moron, you must be a stupid moron, too."

Joyce almost quit seeing Rosie. *He made me quit being friends with Irene just like this,* she thought to herself. *I'm not going to give up my best friend. We're not doing anything wrong.*

With that, Joyce defied her husband for the first time, and decided to stay best friends with Rosie.

"We'll have to keep it a secret," she told her friend.

"That's okay," Rosie said. "It won't change anything with us. We never see each other when he's around anyway."

Now that Robbie was a teenager, he had taken a job washing dishes at a local restaurant. When he worked, Joyce would drive over around midnight to give him a ride home. One night, shortly before she was to go pick Robbie up, Bernie, the next-door neighbor, started banging on the door, screaming and calling for help.

"Don't get involved," Jim ordered her.

Joyce couldn't stand it, so she ran to the window and looked out. What she saw scarred her for the rest of her life. A young man was plunging a knife into Bernie.

"He's stabbing him," Joyce screamed to Jim.

Suddenly, the man stood up, looked around and then ran away.

"The police are here," she yelled. "I see the flashing lights coming this way."

Bernie Toycen had been stabbed nine times. His lifeless body lay beside his trailer house in a spattered pool of blood.

Joyce talked to the police and gave them a detailed description of the young man who had committed the murder. She replayed the murder in her head many times, and was glad that she had paid attention to the details.

Bernie's death brought back bad memories, and the memories triggered nightmares of the times Esther and Hale had tried to kill her.

She saw how truly fragile life was, and she realized she was pretty lucky to still be alive.

The next day the detective came back to the scene of the crime.

"We found the killer and he has confessed," he told Joyce. "Thank you for helping us."

"Bernie wouldn't hurt a fly," Joyce said. "Why would someone kill him?"

"He was over at the Blue Canary bragging about the money he had on him," the investigator said. "I guess he sold some land in Bloomer, Wisconsin, and had $7,000.00 in his wallet, but the killer didn't get the money."

"Did you find the money?" Joyce asked.

"The wallet must have slipped out of his pocket during the attack. We found it under the trailer with the money still in it," he answered.

"Just think, that guy will go to jail for the rest of his life and spend eternity in hell, and he didn't even get the money," Joyce mused.

Chapter Forty-three

Someday They'll Come to You

Odessa, Texas was experiencing a sharp downturn in the oil business. The big "lay-off" hit Mac without warning, and he was out of a job. He decided to try selling vacuum cleaners, door to door, for the Kirby Company.

If he sold a Kirby, he would get a commission on the sale, but there wasn't much money in the sale of vacuum cleaners in Odessa. Kirby's district manager decided to relocate the company to Emporia, Kansas. They packed the Kirby operation into a horse trailer and included Mac and Jane's personal belongings. After that, Mac went door to door in Emporia.

Jane spent her days keeping house in the huge, old two-story rental, and going to garage sales, flea markets, and auctions. Both Mac and Jane enjoyed antiques and collectibles. They dreamed of opening an antique shop someday.

This hobby had all started for Jane with an Occupied Japan figurine. Before long, she had amassed quite a collection. Soon, she began refinishing furniture and preparing boxes of collectibles, which they stored in the upstairs of the big house. They even bought an old pickup truck to haul home their treasures.

On one of their forays, they stopped at an antique shop just off the highway outside New Strawn, Kansas. A sign on the door said, *Open 3:00 to 5:00 daily...If you need help, ask at the café.*

Mac and Jane were interested in looking around, so they decided to get a bite to eat. Then they asked if they could browse in the antique shop after lunch. The owner happened to be at the café, and they had an interesting visit with her.

"They are building a nuclear reactor above the dam," she told them. "We've been so busy with construction workers, that I am looking for someone to help me out."

She needed a manager for the service station, and someone to manage the motel. Whoever managed the motel would work in the antique shop a couple of hours a day, as well. She asked if they were interested in the jobs.

"We'll go talk it over," Mac said, as he led Jane out of the cafe toward the old pickup.

"I think we should take it," Jane told her husband. "You don't make very much money at Kirby and we sure could do better if we were both working. Besides, I'd love to work in the antique shop. It'd be good training for when we open ours."

It took a couple of days to quit the Kirby Company and move their belongings into the trailer house behind the motel. The antique store was in a converted red barn called the *Mouse House Antique Shop.* They stored their personal collectibles in the loft above the shop.

Their new boss was a very unusual person named Lynae Newsom. She had the look of someone rolling in money—someone who was used to the good life. Lynae Newsom had been an actress in Hollywood in her hey-day.

Now, in later life, she owned a four-acre square plot of land. In one corner stood her home, the only octagon-shaped house in a town full of trailer houses and whitewashed cracker-boxes. Needless to say, the house drew attention. The second corner of the lot had a barn which housed the Mouse House Antique Shop. An eight-unit motel stood on the third corner of the lot. The fourth corner was where the service station was located, with its attached café.

Mac opened the service station at six o'clock each morning. His job was to change tires, pump gas, and change oil for the customers. His only time off was for lunch, and even then, he was on call. The service station and café closed their doors for the night at 8:00 p.m.

Jane began her day waiting on tables in the café for the breakfast and lunch crowd, from six o'clock in the morning until 1:00. Then she ate lunch and went to the motel to clean the rooms and make the beds. Most of the rooms were rented by the week to the nuclear reactor construction crew. From 3:00 in the afternoon until 5:00, she worked in the antique shop. At five o'clock, she went to the motel and stayed until 8:00, when she switched on the *NO VACANCY* sign, and called it a day.

Lynae Newsom was a fiery redhead with a drinking problem. She was usually dripping in diamonds, and she kept a gold brick in the bottom of her big fish tank. Her house was festooned with original paintings and priceless antiques. An elephant foot, which had come from Africa, had been made into an end table. It was one of her prized possessions.

With their busy schedule, the six months they worked for Lynae Newsom just flew by. Early in December, Mac's mother wrote a letter saying that she was very ill. The letter left Jane and Mac with a feeling that his mother was in trouble. Her words made her seem desperate.

Lynae Newsom agreed to let them take two weeks off. Mac and Jane drove to Big Lake, Texas, to see what was up with Mac's mother. They stayed for a week and found her problem to be depression and loneliness.

"I'm so glad you came," she told them. "I just didn't feel like eating and I haven't been sleeping well, either. I feel so much better just seeing you."

"We'll come back and see you more often," Mac promised.

Mac and Jane left Big Lake and drove to Odessa to stay with old friends for a few days. On the drive back to Kansas, somewhere near Abilene, they ran into an ice storm which stranded them for several hours.

While they waited for the roads to clear, Mac decided they should go back to Odessa, and Jane agreed.

"We would be closer to your mother and we have been killing ourselves working such long hours," she said.

"We'll go back to Kansas later and get our things," Mac promised.

When the storm subsided and they could travel again, they turned around and went home to Odessa.

"We're back," Mac said to his friend when they knocked on the door again. "Can we stay with you until we find a place of our own?"

It took a couple of days to find a furnished house to rent, and for Mac to get a job. Lucky for them, the oil business had begun to boom again during the two years they had been living in Kansas.

Jane felt betrayed by Mac. He refused to live up to his part of the bargain and would not go back to Kansas to get their personal things. All of her treasured pictures of her children and letters from her brother and sister were left behind.

"Those are just possessions," Mac told her. "They don't mean anything."

"They might not mean anything to you, but they are very important to me," she cried.

Soon after their return from Kansas, Jane noticed that she was having abdominal cramping and heavy bleeding.

"I'd better go in for a PAP smear," she told Mac. "It's time for me to get a check-up anyway."

A few days later, a letter came in the mail. It said that she had a class 3 uterine cancer. Jane was scared to death. She ran across the street to her neighbor, Mickey, who was a cancer survivor.

"Get to the doctor and get treatment right away," Mickey said. "The earlier you get treatment, the more successful it will be."

"I can't do the surgery until you lose some weight. We need to stabilize your blood pressure," the doctor told her.

Mac didn't understand what Jane was going through. He began pulling away and grew distant. Jane saw that he was not on the same emotional level as she was. It hurt her that he was not empathetic.

The day of her surgery the doctor said, "We will do a procedure called a *cold knife slice* to see if the cancer has spread. If it is contained in the uterus, and we are able to get it all, you may not even need to go through chemotherapy."

Jane's cancer surgery was a success, but Mac grew even more distant after the surgery. Finally, Jane took matters into her own hands.

"We have to sit down and talk," she said.

"What's the problem?" he asked.

"I'm the one who had cancer, and you act like you're the one who is sick."

"I thought we would have a baby someday," Mac said with pain in his voice. "Now I know it will never happen."

On the heels of Jane's surgery, a letter arrived from the Chippewa County Welfare Agency. The letter stated that Jane was to be present at the Chippewa County Courthouse for a meeting with John Botsford, regarding the welfare of their children.

Mac scraped together enough money for Jane's airline ticket, and Ted and Hazel met her at the Eau Claire airport. There were no hugs this time. Since Mac was not along, there was no need for a performance.

Ted and Hazel sat stiffly on the bench outside the courtroom, while Jane and John went inside to face the judge. Jane learned many disturbing things from that meeting.

She learned that her parents had lied to her when the children were first taken away, and when she was trying desperately to find them. Ted and Hazel had always known the kids were with the Marionkowitz's in Stanley. John had contact with the children and saw them whenever he wanted. He had always known where they were, too. She discovered that when she ran away to her brother, Alan's house in Georgia, Jane was the only one who didn't know where Ronnie, Jonnie, Tammy and baby Todd were.

"We are here to make a determination for the four Botsford children. A decision has to be made as to whether they remain in the custody of the courts, or if some other living arrangements can be made," the judge began.

"Are you the mother of Ronald, John, Tammy and Todd Botsford?" the judge asked Jane.

"Yes, your honor," she answered.

Then he turned to John and asked, "Are you the father of Ronald, John, Tammy and Todd Botsford?"

"Yes," said John.

"At this time, you can choose to take the children with you. If you choose not to take them, they will remain wards of the court until they are eighteen. What is your decision?" asked the judge.

"I want them to stay in foster care," John answered immediately.

He liked the idea of seeing them when he wanted, without having any responsibility to them. He didn't have to pay child support or change his lifestyle, in order to spend time with his children.

Jane thought long and hard before she gave her answer. With all her heart, she wanted to take her children home with her. Having her kids back had always been her dream, but the circumstances of her life had not changed much in all of those years. She still didn't have a big enough house. She still didn't have money to support them. She still didn't have any way to get them to Texas. She couldn't move back to Wisconsin, now that she was married to Mac. She felt hopeless.

In her mind, she replayed a movie of her inadequacies. *She was a terrible person. She couldn't give her children the things they needed. The Marionkowitz's were wonderful parents, much better than she. Her children had a chance for a good life if they stayed where they were.*

Finally, in despair, Jane spoke up.

"I will sign them over to the court with one stipulation," she said firmly. "They have to remain with the Marionkowitz's, as a family, until they turn eighteen. I don't want them sent from one foster home to the other, and I don't want them separated."

"Then it is agreed," the judge stated. "They will remain in foster care until the age of eighteen, and you will give up your parental rights."

"Can I see them one more time?" Jane asked the judge.

"I'm sorry. Your rights as a parent have been terminated," the judge decreed.

The meeting lasted about fifteen minutes. When it was over, Jane was exhausted with grief. Sadly, she followed her parents out of the courthouse into the parking lot. There, in a car waiting for them, sat Mrs. Marionkowitz.

"Good news!" Hazel said to her, smiling broadly. "The kids are staying with you."

"Thank god!" said Mrs. Marionkowitz.

She nodded to them and drove away.

Hopelessness and depression set in with a vengeance. Jane cried silently in the back seat, as her parents drove back to Cornell.

"It's for the best," Hazel sighed loudly.

"They will be better off if they never see you again," Ted added nastily.

I know they will be better off without me, she thought dismally. *But, I will not be better off without them.*

Jane called Milwaukee to talk to her sister, Joyce.

"It's over," she cried. "They belong to somebody else now."

"Someday they will come to you," Joyce soothed. "You'll have another chance. Just wait and see."

Chapter Forty-four

Worry and Joy

Joyce was very worried about her husband, Jim. He had developed emphysema and was ill more often, as time went on. When he wasn't at work, he spent more and more time at home sitting on the couch, smoking cigarettes, and watching TV. The worse he felt, the crabbier he became.

"I'll take you to the doctor," Joyce coaxed again.

"Mind your own goddamned business," Jim growled as usual.

With all this friction, Joyce's oldest son, Robbie, chose the wrong time to announce that he had a new girlfriend.

Jim said, "You are not allowed to see that girl."

Of course, Robbie didn't listen and began spending time with Annette, behind his father's back.

Personally, Joyce was happy. She thought Robbie's new girlfriend was just beautiful, with her blonde hair and happy smile. Joyce also thought Annette was the smartest, most confident young woman she had ever met.

Confidence was something that Joyce admired in other women. She just wasn't equipped to be a strong confident woman herself, especially since she had never had a role model in that department.

She was not a strong and confident mother, either. She fulfilled her motherly duties by driving the boys where they needed to go, taking care of their basic needs, and loving them. Aside from that, she didn't pay much attention to what they were doing, and she ignored all signs of trouble.

In her heart, Joyce believed that Robbie and Randy were such good boys that they would never think of doing anything wrong. She was unaware of their activities, and unaware that Robbie and Annette were spending as much time together as they were. Unaware, that is, until one evening when Annette's father phoned to speak to her about the kids.

"If that kid gets my daughter pregnant, and messes up her life, I'll kill him," he told her.

Joyce was stunned.

After that call, Joyce was afraid for Robbie. She truly believed her son's life was in danger, but she was too afraid to confront him. She worried in silence. *What if Annette gets pregnant and her father carries out his threat? I'm a terrible mother,* Joyce lamented. *I don't even know what to do to protect my son.*

One day Robbie announced, "Annette's pregnant."

"Do her parents know?" Joyce asked in a panic.

"They know," Robbie answered.

A sigh of relief escaped her lips. *Robbie is standing here, so I guess Annette's father isn't going to kill him,* she thought.

Annette was so young and Joyce was devastated for her. She had suffered through being unmarried and pregnant herself, and she knew exactly what Annette would be up against.

"We're naming her Tonya Lynne," Robbie said with pride, when the baby was born.

"I don't know why he's so excited," Jim told Joyce. "That kid's probably not even his."

"She's beautiful," Joyce said. "I can't believe it. I never had a daughter, but now I have a granddaughter."

Joyce finally had something to be happy about.

Chapter Forty-five

Tammy and then Todd

Jane was living with the idea that things were going well for her children. She didn't know her oldest sons, Ronnie and Jonnie, had begun acting up. They had been caught shoplifting, and the "hot" goods were found stashed in their lockers at school.

The social worker called Jane to inform her of the situation, and to say that the Marionkowitz's wouldn't keep them any longer.

"The children will be placed in other homes," she said.

"In court, we all agreed that they wouldn't be split up," Jane said in a panic. "I don't want them sent from one foster home to another, and I want them to be together. I would take them, but we don't have a big enough house. I don't know how we would buy food for them. We don't even have a car right now. I still can't support them."

"They are wards of the court. You don't have parental rights," the social worker reminded Jane. "I am merely calling to inform you of the change in their living situation."

Jane plunged into a deep depression. That's when she noticed that Mac was not helping her. Mac didn't have the finances to get the kids back, and Jane knew she couldn't do it on her own. *Mac is brilliant but he doesn't apply himself,* Jane thought. *He doesn't want me to work, but he doesn't keep a job so we can get the kids back, either.*

As time marched forward, Jane continued to fight depression. Thoughts of suicide often crossed her mind. Though she felt secure in her husband's love, they continued to struggle financially. She continued to struggle with the reflections of her abusive past.

One warm spring day, an envelope came from the Chippewa County Welfare Department. The letter read,

Dear Mrs. McDaniel, We have decided to send your daughter, Tammy, to live with you. She will be sent to you for the summer. At the end of that time, she will decide whether she wishes to stay with you for the next school year. We will contact you by telephone with her travel arrangements."

The anticipation was almost too much for Jane, as she and Mac arrived at the airport to meet Tammy's plane.

"Finally, I will actually have one of my kids living with me," Jane told Mac.

From the beginning, Mac adored Tammy. He helped get her started on a stamp collection and loved having her around. A friend of his had a daughter named Debbie, who was about Tammy's age. The two girls became good friends.

Jane loved Tammy with all her heart, but their relationship was strained. To Tammy, Jane just wasn't her mother, and it was clear to both of them that they didn't see eye to eye.

One time, while they were shopping, Tammy told her mother, "I don't want any of this. You can't buy my love."

Late one afternoon, Jane and Tammy were sitting in the sun in the back yard.

Tammy looked at her mother with sad eyes, and said, "Mom, I'm going back home. I don't want to stay here any longer."

Jane didn't know what to say. She hadn't been what Tammy expected her to be. She had never been around kids this age, and didn't know how to act with them.

"You're not going to be mad at me, are you?" Tammy asked, almost shyly.

"No, honey, I'm not. I want you to be happy," Jane told her daughter.

They sat together on the lounger, side by side. Tammy drifted off to sleep in the warm sun and Jane put her arm around her daughter, kissed the top of her head, and cried.

"I am so sorry for the hurt that I have caused you," she whispered to the sleeping girl. "I wish I knew how to change so I could be what you need."

When Tammy woke up, they both went into the house to call the welfare agency. Tammy told her social worker she wanted to go home. She asked them to send an airline ticket. Jane was broken hearted, but in a way, it was a relief. She realized she just didn't know how to be a mother.

About a week after Tammy returned to Wisconsin, Jane received another letter from the Welfare Department.

Dear Mrs. McDaniel, Todd has expressed the desire to live with you. We will be sending him to start the school year. He will be arriving within the week. Since school will be starting shortly, we are sending his transcripts. You will need them to register him for school.

Mac and Jane met Todd's plane with more than a little apprehension. *Dear Lord,* Jane prayed as the plane landed. *It didn't work out with Tammy. Please let it be different with Todd.*

Todd had never known Jane as his mother. He was just a baby when he was taken away, and had only seen her a couple of times. He did have a picture of the woman his older brothers called Mama. Due to the stories his brothers told, Todd had a picture in his mind of how great things would be if he could only be with his mother.

So, when Todd got off the plane, he ran to Jane and jumped up to put his arms around her neck. Surprised, Jane hugged and kissed him. Her heart filled with love for her youngest son.

They had to wait at the baggage claim for Todd's bags.

"They're going to send my drum set and my bike by UPS," Todd told his mother.

He was too excited to stand still.

Jane helped Todd unpack his things, and then made supper. Later, they got an ice cream cone, and went for a walk around the neighborhood.

"It's time for bed," Jane told her son. "You've had a big day."

"He sure is happy to be with his mama," Mac laughed later, as he and Jane looked in on the boy, sleeping soundly in his new bed.

Todd started school in Odessa. Almost immediately, the teacher talked to Jane about the hard time he was having with his studies.

"The poor kid doesn't know what to do," Jane told Mac. "The teacher says he is behind. I think the schools here must be ahead of the ones in Wisconsin."

As the days went on, Jane realized that Todd was terribly unhappy at school, and he was becoming rebellious. He had started testing her at every turn, and she didn't know how to discipline him. Aside from taking him to flea markets and garage sales, she had no idea how to entertain him, either.

One day, Todd was riding his bike.

He came home and told his mother, "I wrecked my bike."

Jane took one look at the mangled bicycle and it scared her to death. *What if he hurts himself while he's here?* She thought. *What will the welfare think of me then?*

"I think the problem is, he doesn't have anybody to play with," Jane told Mac.

Jane found that she was blind when it came to seeing what her son needed from her. Life had become miserable, for all of them.

"For his own sake," Jane told Mac, "we have to send him back."

They all cried when Jane told Todd he was going back to Wisconsin, but she felt that, secretly, he was glad to be leaving.

As she watched her little boy fly away, Jane made a vow. *I'm going to get some help so I can get my life under control.*

Robin Gale Jasper was recommended as a good psychiatrist in the Odessa area. Jane began therapy and soon realized that she was a mess.

Being honest about her past had never come easy to Jane. She knew she was treated badly by all of her parents and that she had treated her children badly. Robin Gale helped Jane understand that this was the cycle of abuse.

"I need to learn how to control my emotions," said Jane. "Had I known my children would be taken away, I never would have signed myself into the mental ward at Sacred Heart Hospital. I didn't know that this was going to happen."

Robin Gale listened to Jane, and encouraged her to continue speaking.

"I just needed help dealing with John. I just couldn't stand to be let down by him again. Fight, fight, fight, and never knowing when I was going to get beaten up again," Jane continued. "When he started hitting the kids, I had to do something, but I didn't know what to do."

"It was never about the kids," Jane told the therapist. "I loved them but I was afraid for them. I needed to protect them, but I was so depressed and hopeless, that I became suicidal."

"Not being in control of my emotions got my kids taken away. I was their mother. I was supposed to handle everything, but I was weak. I didn't know how to be a good mother. My marriage to John was terrible, and he was even a worse father. I was a drunk. John was a drunk. We screwed up our lives. The worst part is, we screwed up our kid's lives, too," Jane sobbed to Robin Gale.

The therapist touched Jane's shoulder sympathetically, and encouraged her to continue.

"It might have been easier to have lost John to death instead of divorce," Jane continued. "We hurt so many people. We hurt the kids so badly. Death might have been better. They would have been hurt by their father's death, but not by his actions. He's still around, and I still see the demeaning things he continues to do."

"Death is final. Divorce is worse than death. I personally would rather have been a widow than a divorcee," Jane told Robin Gale, with certainty.

"I have never gotten over having my kids taken away from me."

Jane was crying harder.

"I'll never get over the guilt. There is no way to change what I've done."

"I didn't take care of my children. Ma and dad didn't take care of me. My adopted ma didn't protect me, and my adopted dad molested me. They didn't take care of me, either."

"I know," Robin Gale said. "It just keeps on going. It's a never-ending cycle that affects many people and many generations."

"I don't want to be this way," Jane said. "Most of the time, I just want to kill myself and be done with it."

"You have tried to commit suicide several times," Robin Gale said. "I'm glad you decided to get some help."

"I've waited over ten years to get my children back, but when they came, I found out I didn't know how to be a mother," Jane told the therapist. "I wish I hadn't had kids just to put them through all of this."

Jane had finally begun therapy sessions to try to understand her pain.

"I feel like I've lived in pain my whole life," she told Robin Gale.

Chapter Forty-six

Does the Skullduggery Never End?

"Mrs. Cellars?" the young woman's voice on the phone asked.

"Yes," answered Joyce hesitantly.

"This is Carrie from Appleton Electric. Jim has just been taken to the hospital. Can you meet him there?"

"What happened?" Joyce asked.

"He was having trouble breathing and he passed out. We called the ambulance and he is on his way to emergency."

Joyce grabbed her purse and took off for the hospital. *I just knew something like this would happen*, she thought. *He refuses to take care of himself.*

That was the last day that Jim ever worked in his life. He came home from the hospital with doctor's orders to quit smoking. From then on, he was on oxygen and under doctor's care for his emphysema.

If it was possible for things to get worse for Joyce, they just had. Jim was forced to go on disability, but he told Joyce about the $10,000 pension plan he had coming from work. As the months passed, and the medical bills mounted, Joyce found some relief in knowing there was a small fortune on its way to help them out.

"When is the money coming?" she asked. "We really need it bad."

"I don't know," Jim told her disgustedly. "I think they are trying to screw me out of it."

Robbie celebrated his eighteenth birthday several months after Jim became disabled. Joyce had decided to wait to tell Robbie that his grandpa Ted was his real father, until he was eighteen.

"I don't believe you," Robbie yelled. "You're nothing but a liar."

"Robbie, it's true," Joyce told him. "I didn't want to tell you until you were eighteen. I thought you would understand better, if you were older."

"Then why did you always say that you were raped when you lived in Rice Lake?" he wanted to know.

"Grandpa Ted made me say that, and I was scared to go against him," she answered truthfully.

"You are a liar," Robbie told her. "You are lying to me."

One day, the doctor called Jim and Joyce into his office for a medical consultation. He told them there was nothing more that could be done. The damage to Jim's lungs was just too great. He said Jim had one year, maybe two, if he was lucky.

"Get your affairs in order and try to enjoy the time you have left."

The news hit Joyce hard. *How are we supposed to survive? We can barely make ends meet now? I'll have to get a job, but I don't know how to do anything. I'll have to learn to handle the finances by myself, and I can barely add and subtract. How am I going to make decisions on my own? What am I going to do?*

She was grateful that she might have $10,000 to help her out, and another one of her concerns had eased. Robbie had moved in with Annette's parents. *Things are looking better for the kids. Red and Marlene are good role models for Robbie,* Joyce thought. *Red is teaching Robbie all the things Jim wouldn't.*

If Joyce had known what was transpiring in Cornell, she would have had a good reason to be worried.

Ted and Hazel had heard rumors that the mill was going to cut back. If it did, Ted would probably lose his job, and he was worried they wouldn't have enough money to live on.

"It's too bad the mill doesn't have a deal like Jim is getting from the place he works," Ted told his wife.

"What's that about?" Hazel asked.

"Jim told me that he is going to get $10,000 from his pension plan, now that he is disabled. That's quite a windfall," Ted explained.

"Actually, if you figure what we've done for those girls all these years, they owe us that money," Hazel said, planting the seed in her husband's mind. "He's going to die. What does he need the money for?"

Ted talked to Jim on the phone the next day.

After some heated words and long silences, Ted finally said, "What are you going to use it for anyway? It'll just go to Joyce. You'll be dead and she'll be living it up on your hard earned money. Besides, if everybody finds out you're a queer, they probably won't even come to your funeral."

Ted finished what he had to say and then let silence hang heavily on the phone line between them. Ted was good at playing the waiting game.

Jim thought of Joyce living the life of a rich widow on his money. He also realized the possibility of everyone gossiping about him after he died. Those two issues made him finally give in to Ted's demands. An agreement was reached. Jim would send Ted a check for $10,000. In exchange, Ted promised to keep Jim's secret, forever.

Adjustments sometimes have to be made in life. Jim had planned to leave the $10,000 to his friend, Donnie, but now it was gone. Then he had a brilliant idea. *I'll change my life insurance to make him the beneficiary of the policy,* Jim thought as he made his final plans. *Joyce is too stupid to figure it out and I can do what I want with it anyway. It's my money.*

"I'm canceling my life insurance," Jim told Joyce. "I can't afford to pay the premiums any longer. If I cancel the insurance policy, it'll give us a little more money to live on each month."

In the back of her mind, she wondered if it was the right thing to do. *He must know what he's doing,* Joyce decided. At any rate, she didn't think she had the right to question him about it.

"What about the $10,000 then?" Joyce asked once again.

"They won't give it to me because I was sick and left my job early," Jim lied.

No life insurance and no money. Joyce was really worried now. *I guess I'll just have to take one day at a time and do my best.*

Chapter Forty-seven

Something Has To Change

One day, Robbie told Joyce, "I'm going to Texas. Aunt Jane said I could stay with them, and Uncle Mac will help me get a job.

"What about Annette and the baby?" Joyce asked.

"I'll go down first and when I'm set up, I'll send for them," Rob answered.

Jane had misgivings about him coming, until Mac reminded her that Robbie was not their responsibility.

"There are openings at the oil company," Mac told her. "Looks like the kid can use a break."

Jane and Mac met Robbie at the Odessa airport. The next day, Robbie went to work for the oil company.

He came home and said, "That job isn't for me."

The next day he found a job at a fast food restaurant. Jane helped him find a trailer to rent in the trailer court down the street. A week later, they all went to the airport to pick up Annette and the baby.

"You're going to love it here," Jane told Annette when they met.

"I don't think so," Annette answered her.

Annette hated the trailer house and she hated Odessa, in general. She wanted to go back to Wisconsin, right from the start.

Jane was impressed with Robbie. She thought he was a hard worker, and he loved Annette and the baby.

One night, Robbie asked, "Is it true that Grandpa Ted molested my mother?"

"Yes, Robbie, it is true. Both you and Randy are your grandpa's children," Jane told him the truth.

"Then why did ma say that she was raped?"

"Because she was scared," Jane answered. "Grandpa threatened to kill her if she told. He made up the story and then made her tell it."

"She told me that grandpa was my father but I didn't believe it. He doesn't act like he'd do anything like that."

"I know, Robbie," Jane returned. "He molested me, too, and he always got away with it. That's why we couldn't do anything about it. He always told everybody that we were liars. We knew nobody would believe us."

Robbie didn't like the idea that his grandpa was really his father.

"I can't believe it, because I love my grandma and grandpa," Robbie said sadly. "Ma and I lived with them and they took good care of me. They didn't hurt me."

"I'm glad they didn't hurt you, but they did hurt us, and I think they hurt Roger, too," Jane added.

Annette said, "I believe it. Ted gives me the creeps. I wouldn't want to be alone with him, and I wouldn't want to leave Tonya alone with him, either."

Robbie and his family stayed in Odessa a few months. Annette was miserable the whole time.

"I'm going back," she finally told Robbie. "You can come with me or you can stay, but I'm leaving."

Robbie grew up a lot during his stay in Odessa. He and his Uncle Mac had many deep conversations about life and the best way to live it.

"I'm going to take Annette and Tonya back to Wisconsin," he told his uncle. "I don't want Annette to be unhappy, and I don't want to live here without her and the baby."

Annette and Robbie went back to Milwaukee and decided to get married. Jane was happy to have had the opportunity to get to know her nephew. *He had some good life lessons while he was here,* she thought.

Robbie, Annette and Tonya were now a family. Joyce was very happy about that, but she was unhappy with the struggle she was experiencing in her own life.

One morning, Jim woke up with an idea.

"Call Hazel and have her find us a place to live. We are moving back to Cornell. I want to be buried next to ma, and if I die here, you probably won't be smart enough to get me back there," Jim smirked at her.

"Don't you even trust me to do that?" Joyce asked, hurt and bewildered.

"Nope!" was all he said.

Hazel found them a place to rent, a few miles north of Cornell, in Holcombe. It was not much of a place but the rent was cheap.

Her youngest son, Randy, had dropped out of school and was working at a lawn and garden center in Milwaukee.

"We're moving to Holcombe," Joyce told him. "I want you to quit your job and move up there with us."

Jim, Joyce and Randy made the move to Holcombe. Joyce hated living there and constantly felt the sting of lonesomeness for Robbie, his little girl Tonya, and his wife, Annette. To Joyce, the only upside of living near Cornell was that Aunt Lydia and Uncle Tony were closer and she enjoyed their visits. The Cellars existed from hand to mouth, living on Jim's disability. Joyce was overcome with depression and panic. She had no idea what to do or where to turn for help. *Something has to change,* Joyce prayed.

Chapter Forty-eight

Welcome Home to Texas

Change was coming to Odessa, Texas

Ronnie, Jane's oldest child, had been living with his father, and stepmother, Carol. He was drinking, partying, and hanging with a rough crowd.

"I think it's time for that kid to go live with his mother," Carol told John. "If he doesn't get away from here, he's going to kill himself. Besides, the change will do all of us some good."

John called Texas to say he was sending Ron, and to give the travel information. Again, the McDaniels stood at the Odessa airport waiting, with apprehension, for one of Jane's children to land. It had been years since Jane had seen her little boy. She wasn't prepared for the tall skinny young man who stepped off the plane.

At first, she didn't recognize him with his baggy, worn-out clothes and his long, scraggly, uncombed hair. Then he flashed his famous "million dollar smile," She knew he was the boy she had always loved. *He looks so pitiful and forlorn*, she thought.

Mac and Jane were impressed when Ron immediately started looking for a job and found one at a fast food restaurant. He cut his hair and looked very nice and neat in the uniform he wore to work.

"He sure cleans up good," Jane said proudly.

"Me and some guys from work are going to rent that little house at the end of the block," Ron told his mother a couple of weeks later.

Jane bought him some better clothes at garage sales and picked up some kitchen utensils and dishes to help the guys set up housekeeping.

Ron kept in close contact with his mother. Sometimes he would meet Mac and Jane at the café for coffee in the mornings. Often they would have dinner together. He quit the restaurant and took a job working for a plumber. His new boss sent him to school, and his mother was proud.

Mac was finally making good money working in the oil fields. He decided it was time to become homeowners. He hated paying rent every month, and thought they could build up equity in a house of their own.

They took the first house the realtor showed them.

"I just love it," Jane said. "There's no point in looking around. This is the one I want."

The two-bedroom house had a nice garden and a fenced in back yard. There was a patio and a carport. Best of all, they had good neighbors, and it was only five blocks from the house where Ron lived.

Shortly after they moved into their new house, Tammy called to say she and Ron had been talking, and he urged her to move back to Odessa.

"She's a lot older now, and with Ron here, it probably will go better," Mac encouraged his wife.

"We have a bigger house with more room for the kids," Jane sounded pleased. "Let's fix a room for her in the den. It will be like a little apartment. She can even have a TV in there if she wants to. It has a door to the outside, so she wouldn't have to traipse through the whole house when she wanted to come and go."

Tammy drove to Texas all by herself in her little mustang. She had some car trouble in Kansas. Other than that, the trip went just fine. When she arrived, Jane had an embarrassingly big sign tacked across the living room wall that said, WELCOME HOME TO TEXAS.

In no time, Tammy had found employment at a clothing store, and also at Wendy's restaurant. She made friends easily and fell in love with her little white dog. The problem was, she didn't want to help with the chores around the house and she didn't like her mother. Mother and daughter fought like cats and dogs.

"You're too nosey and judgmental," Tammy yelled at Jane. "Just get off my back."

Jane saw Tammy making the same mistakes that she had made when she was young, and she wanted better for her daughter. She tried her hardest to be a parent to Tammy, but she was too late. Too much time had been lost. Tammy was already eighteen, and Jane was treating her as though she were eight.

It wasn't long after Tammy settled in that Jane's second son, Jonnie, arrived in Odessa, too. He moved into the spare bedroom at his mother's house. Jonnie was a much better helper than Tammy. He mowed the lawn and even helped vacuum and dust, if Jane asked him to. The next-door neighbors, Edna and John Adams, liked to visit with him, and hired him to mow their lawn.

Jonnie often sat in the back yard with his mother, playing with Tammy's dog and talking. He told Jane about the way the kids had been treated by the Marionkowitzs. Jane was shocked when she found out the kids were mistreated. She had always been told the Marionkowitzs were wonderful parents.

Jonnie was full of questions, too.

"Why did you give us up?" he wanted to know. "Why did you and dad get a divorce?"

Jane answered his questions truthfully, and they became closer as they talked things out. She felt so guilty about the lives her children were forced to live. She knew she had played a huge part in their misery. She just didn't know how to be what they needed.

Jonnie took a job at a clothing store as a shelf stocker. Then he went to Furr's Cafeteria and worked in the kitchen. A pattern soon began to develop, and Jane noticed that he didn't keep any job very long.

"He has inherited the 'job jumping gene' from his grandpa, Hale Colburn," Jane laughed to Mac.

Jonnie didn't have an outside door in his room like Tammy did, but that didn't stop him. He would just go out the window when he wanted to party with his friends. Jane and Mac thought he was asleep in his bedroom. They didn't know he was going out and getting into trouble.

Jane had given the kids a midnight curfew. Of course, since they were over eighteen, they never kept it. One night, Jane waited up for Tammy. When she came home, she was totally drunk.

"If you are going to live here, you have to follow the rules. Otherwise, you can just get out," Jane was screaming at her daughter.

"Good! I'm out of here!" Tammy yelled back.

Tammy called a friend, grabbed her purse, and went outside to sit on the curb and wait for her ride. Jane wanted to go out and tell her she was sorry. She wanted to tell her how much she wanted her to come back, but she didn't.

She hates me, Jane agonized in her mind. *She doesn't want anything to do with me now. I don't know what to do.*

Tammy left, and never went back to live with Mac and Jane. Eventually, she moved in with Ron. Shortly after that, Jonnie moved in with Ron and Tammy, too.

The house the kids lived in was next door to Brown Electric. One night while Jonnie was drinking and getting high, he decided to rob the electric place. He broke into the building and then broke into some of the trucks. During the robbery, he cut himself. When the police came, they were able to follow the blood trail to Ron's house. Jonnie was out cold, and he had the hot merchandise all around him. He was arrested and put in jail. When he came to, he didn't even remember that he had committed a robbery. He spent two and one-half years in prison before he was paroled, and he was put on probation when he got out.

He was released to Mac and Jane. To his mother's relief, he signed himself into the Midland Teen Center for rehab. That didn't last long. After a week or two, he signed himself out of the center, broke parole, and hitchhiked to California.

During that time, Tammy realized she was pregnant. She wasn't interested in marrying the father, so she decided to go back to Wisconsin to have the baby and put him up for adoption.

That was a time of grief for Jane. She mourned the heartache her children were experiencing, and she mourned her own failure as a mother.

After the birth and adoption of her baby, Tammy returned to Odessa, and took a job at a Mexican restaurant called, Jumburitto's. Soon, she met a nice young man named Tommy, and they started dating. Tommy was on social security disability for diabetes. His mother owned several rental trailer houses, and Tommy worked with her maintaining the property.

Eventually, Tammy and Tommy decided to get married.

"Can you come to my wedding?" Tammy asked her father, John, on the telephone. "I want Todd to come, too."

"We'll be there," John assured her.

Tammy's whole family, except for Jonnie, who was still in California, attended her wedding. Mac and Jane, John and Carol, Ron and Todd were all present for her big day.

"I'm so happy for her," Jane told Mac. "Who would have ever thought she would have her mother and father with her on her wedding day?"

Tammy's wedding was the first time that Jane had spent any time with John's wife, Carol. She didn't like her and she made no bones about it. All the kids knew their mother didn't like their stepmother. Even though she had issues with Carol, Jane thought she was a good person with good values. In a way, she felt sorry that Carol was stuck with John. She knew firsthand what kind of life that could be.

Carol died shortly after Tammy and Tommy were married, and Jane actually felt bad.

About this time, there was another sharp downturn in the oil business, and Mac lost his job. He found another one at the Red Door Antique Shop, but the pay was much less.

"I can't make the house payment on what I'm earning," Mac confided to Jane one evening. "I think we are going to have to let the bank take the house and go back to renting."

Sadly, Jane and Mac were forced to move again. *There's never enough money,* Jane cried to herself. *Everything I have ever had has been taken away.*

As Jane cried over the losses that lack of money had caused, her sister, Joyce, was about to become financially devastated.

Chapter Forty-nine

I Wonder What He's Hiding Now

About two years after moving to Holcombe, at four o'clock one morning, Joyce was sound asleep when Jim flopped over on her. She tried to push him off, but when her hand touched his skin, she realized he felt cold and clammy.

"Randy," she scream in a panic. "Come in here. Something is wrong with your dad."

Randy took one look at Jim, grabbed the phone, and called the doctor.

"He wants us to get dad to the hospital right away," he told his mother, as he called for an ambulance.

Randy drove as they followed the ambulance to St. Joseph's Hospital in Chippewa Falls.

At first, the emergency room doctors thought Jim had suffered a stroke, but further testing showed that he had had a massive heart attack. Immediately, he was transferred to Sacred Heart Hospital in Eau Claire, where he was put in intensive care.

"If it is necessary, do you want us to put him on life support?" the nurse asked.

"Yes," Joyce decided.

It proved to be necessary. Jim was in intensive care, on life support for nearly a month. Joyce and Randy went to the hospital to see him every day. They were only allowed in the room for ten minutes every hour. Those were long hard days, but Randy took care of his mother, and Joyce saw that he was actually developing a relationship with his sick father.

As the month went on, Jim grew strong enough to be moved into a private room, which made spending time at the hospital much easier. Joyce and Randy didn't have to leave his bedside every ten minutes, and he didn't have tubes and wires sticking out of every part of his body any longer.

Even though the doctors said he had improved, Joyce thought, *He doesn't look very good, and I can't understand him when he talks.* Randy, however, seemed to know exactly what his father was saying. It was Randy who always understood what his father needed.

Jim took a turn for the worse and the doctor met Joyce in the hall to tell her that he thought it was the end of the line.

"I don't think we're looking at more than a couple of days."

"You mean he's dying?" Joyce wanted clarification.

"Yes," the doctor told her. "I'm sorry."

On the day Jim died, Joyce and Randy made the trip to the hospital in the morning. Then they drove back to Holcombe around noon to have lunch. They called some of Jim's friends to tell them what to expect. Jess Luke wanted to see Jim one more time, so Randy and Joyce took him back to the hospital with them. Randy dropped everybody off at the door and went to park the car.

The doctor was just coming out of Jim's room as Joyce and Jess arrived.

"I'm afraid he's gone," the doctor said.

Randy came in from parking the car and saw Joyce standing in the hall crying.

"He's dead," she said.

The chaplain asked where they would like Jim's body sent.

"Take him to the funeral home in Cornell," Joyce told him.

Joyce saw that Randy had tears running down his cheeks. She couldn't believe the change in him. He and his dad had gotten so much closer.

Her sister Jane answered the phone on the first ring.

"It's over," Joyce said. "Jim died about an hour ago."

"I'll see what I can do to get there," Jane promised. "You know money's pretty short."

Mac was working at the Red Door Antique Shop in Odessa, Texas. He had a booth there where he sold military items. Jane had set up a booth in the shop as well, where she had collectibles and antique jewelry for sale.

"Jim died," Jane told her husband. "I'm not sure if I should even spend the money to go."

"He's your brother-in-law," Mac replied. "Your sister needs you more now than ever. If she didn't, she wouldn't have called you."

"I know, but mother says she doesn't want me around. In her last letter, she said that Joyce is embarrassed by me," Jane said sadly. "Besides, you can't leave, and I don't want to go without you."

"You'd better go," Mac told her. "You don't want to look back and regret that you didn't go to support your sister."

In the end, they decided that Mac would stay to tend the shop, while Jane went alone to Jim's funeral.

Money was short in Holcombe, as well. Jim's social security disability paid only $250.00 as a burial benefit. Joyce was told that amount would not give Jim a proper funeral, and she was penniless. She also learned that his disability died along with him. Jim had dropped his life insurance months before, and Joyce knew that the $10,000.00 pension check was only a dream.

"We don't have any money to give you," Hazel said, when Joyce told her parents how bad her financial situation was.

"I suppose you thought we would run right out and pay for his funeral?" Ted said, looking at his daughter with distain.

Joyce felt desperate and sad as she picked out the clothes she wanted Jim to wear in his casket.

"Aunt Lydia, this is Joyce. I wanted you to know that it's over. Jim is dead."

Joyce was crying.

"Are you all right?" Aunt Lydia asked.

"Not really," Joyce answered. "Social Security will only pay $250.00 for the funeral, and I don't have any other money. I guess I'll have to give him a pauper's burial."

"Oh, no, you won't," Aunt Lydia said emphatically. "He's getting a decent burial. Let us know how much it is, and we'll pay for it."

"I can't ask you to do that," Joyce began.

"You didn't ask. We want to do it," Aunt Lydia cut her off. "Just let us know what you need, and when the funeral is. We'll be there."

Joyce was very relieved about the money and anxious about her sister's arrival.

"I can't thank you enough," she told Aunt Lydia. "Jane is coming, too. She'll be so happy to see you."

Jane stayed with Joyce and Randy in Holcombe, for the week of Jim's funeral. Joyce wondered how she would have gotten through it all without her sister beside her, but there was a definite coolness between them.

A few days after the burial, Jane went to visit her parents. When she arrived, Ted and her brother Roger were not at home. Hazel was sitting at the kitchen table writing out a check. Jane stood behind her and noticed that there was a balance in their check register, of over $10,000.00. *That's funny*, she thought to herself. *I thought they told Joyce they didn't have any money to help pay for Jim's funeral.*

Ted and Roger walked into the kitchen just as Jane was thinking about the large amount of money in the account.

Ted let out a yell, "What in the hell are you letting her look at the checkbook for?"

"She didn't see anything," Hazel shot back.

Ted was livid.

"It's none of her business what we have in there," he roared.

I wonder what he's hiding. Jane thought to herself.

"What's there to eat?" Roger asked his mother.

"I didn't know when you were coming back, so I didn't fix anything yet," Hazel answered her son.

"You stupid, old woman. I want something to eat now!" Roger said menacingly.

Hazel stood up and nearly stumbled as she limped to the cupboard to start making lunch. Ted just kept walking into the living room. He didn't say anything to Roger about the way he had talked to his mother.

If I had talked to her that way, I'd be eating my teeth, Jane thought to herself. *Why does Roger get away with it?*

Later that day, Jane brought up her mother's stumbling, and Roger's disrespect while she was talking to Joyce.

"I don't know," Joyce said. "I've hardly seen them since we moved back. I've had to stay here and take care of Jim."

"Do you think Dad is abusing Roger, too?" Jane asked her sister. "Maybe that's why he's so bad to Ma. She doesn't protect him, either."

"All I know is, she lets him talk nasty to her and dad doesn't stop him," Joyce answered.

"Poor Mama," Jane said. "She can hardly walk, and they are so mean to her."

At the end of the week and with great relief, Jane flew back to Texas. She was worried about her sister, but the closeness they once shared was gone.

"Ma and Dad have over $10,000.00 in their checking account," Jane told Mac when she got back to Texas. "Dad got really mad because he thought I was looking at their check register. I wonder what he is hiding. It seems like he's always hiding something."

Hazel and Ted Buck

Joyce and Duane West

Jane and Mac McDaniel

Book Five…

Rise to Freedom

Chapter Fifty

Boy, He Must Be a Hippie

"Eighty-four thousand dollars!" Joyce screamed.

She dropped the piece of paper, and watched it float downward until it settled on the floor at her feet. All she had to her name was a $250.00 check from Jim's social security burial benefit. How did they ever expect her to pay an $84,000.00 hospital bill?

She called her friend Rosie in Milwaukee to tell her how miserable she was.

"Why don't you move back, and stay with me?" Rosie asked. "You can use that check to get down here, and I'll get your room ready."

This brought another problem to Joyce's already troubled world. What to do with Randy? He had a new girlfriend, had gotten a job at a service station, and he didn't want to move back to Milwaukee. *I can't just leave him,* Joyce agonized, *but I have to get out of here.* Then it came to her that if Randy stayed, he wouldn't get back with his wild friends in Milwaukee. *I guess he's better off here,* she conceded.

Joyce took the bus to Milwaukee and stayed with Rosie for several months. In no time, she realized how happy she had become. She had applied for welfare and the agency was sending her to school. To her delight, she was back in office practice class. To add to her happiness, she was living near Robbie, Annette, and the baby again.

The thorn in her otherwise comfortable existence was the hospital bill she received each month. She had no money to pay it, so she developed a habit of tossing the bill in the garbage. Then one month, the bill came from a collection agency, and the collection calls started coming in.

"I'm afraid to answer the phone anymore," she told Robbie.

"I'll talk to Annette's dad about it," he said.

"You probably should file bankruptcy," Red suggested. "I'll talk to a lawyer and find out what you need to do."

Joyce was grateful for his help. She had no idea what to do about the situation. She only knew she could never find $84,000.00 to pay the bill.

Red spoke to a lawyer, and let her know that she would need $400.00 upfront to start the action. *How in the world am I going to find $400.00?* Joyce worried.

Sleep was elusive for her that night. She lay in bed tossing and turning, thinking about where to get the $400.00. As though struck by a bolt of lightning, she sat up in bed with an idea in her head. She knew what she was going to do, and she had to do it before she lost her nerve. She watched the hands on the clock go round and round all night. *Wyoming is a two-hour difference in time,* she told herself. *I have to wait until at least ten o'clock in the morning to call.*

Hazel and Ted had mentioned many times that Roger's real mother, Kim, and her husband, Carl, had found oil on their land.

"They'll never have to worry about money again in their life," Ted had said with envy.

Joyce remembered how nice Kim had been to her and her sister, Jane, when they had taken their trip out west. Kim had lived with the Bucks in Cornell, while she waited for Roger to be born. Joyce was banking on that relationship.

"I am desperate," Joyce told Kim on the phone. "My husband died and left me with no money and an $84,000.00 hospital bill."

"That's terrible," Kim said.

"They told me to file bankruptcy, but I need $400.00 as a retainer fee. I was wondering if I could borrow it from you," Joyce asked, almost losing her nerve.

"What is your address?" Kim wanted to know. "I'll send you the money. Count it as a gift from me. You don't have to pay me back."

"Thank you," Joyce was crying.

"Take care of yourself," Kim said as she hung up the phone.

The check arrived at the end of the week, and Joyce used it to file bankruptcy. She was very relieved to know that the collection calls, regarding her dead husband's hospital bill, would soon stop.

This was a truly joyous time for Joyce. The hospital issue was finally being settled and Robbie told her that she was going to be a grandma again. To make it even better, Randy was happy in Holcombe, and his girlfriend, Krissy, was pregnant. Joyce hadn't known she would find so much happiness in being a grandmother.

In the spring, a not-so-young girl's thoughts turned to love. Rosie decided to get married. She asked Joyce to be her matron-of-honor.

"It looks like we have a wedding to plan, and I suppose I'd better find a different place to live," Joyce said.

Joyce thought the wedding was beautiful, and she loved living in her new apartment. Her roommate was Annette's sister, Char, and they got along very well.

Life was going better than she could have expected, until one day the social worker for the welfare agency said, "Joyce, I don't think you are making enough progress at school. I think it's time to have you tested."

The test results showed that she had a learning disability.

"We can't continue to pay for your education, but we will help you get a job," the social worker said.

The welfare agency put Joyce to work at the Butler City Hall. She was to do filing, address envelopes, and help the secretary in any way that was necessary.

It was spring cleaning time at the city hall. Joyce spotted a guy she had never seen around the building before, buffing the floors. He had a very long beard and she thought, *Boy, he must be a hippie.*

He walked by the table where she was working and stopped to chat.

"What's your name?" he asked.

He looked interesting to her.

"Joyce Cellars," she said with a smile.

"Mine's Duane West. Do you like dogs? I've got two Doberman Pinschers," he offered.

"I love dogs, but I have never seen a Doberman," Joyce confessed.

"Do you want to see them?" he asked.

Duane asked Joyce if she knew about the "Great Program." It was a program where people who wanted to get off welfare could go to look for jobs. They could get help filling out applications and bring their resumes up to date.

"I'd like to go, but I don't have a car, and I don't have the money to take a cab," Duane told her.

"How about I go and you can ride along with me?" she volunteered. "I'd like to see your dogs, too, sometime."

The trip to the Great Program was a success. Joyce found a job at Lamp Lighter Farms and Duane found one at Stein Garden Center.

Lamp Lighter Farms was her first real job, with a weekly paycheck. Joyce was finally off welfare, and she was in love. *Finally I get to choose the man I'm spending time with,* she beamed.

Nothing was ever easy for Joyce. To her dismay, Robbie did not like Duane.

"He looks like a motorcycle hood," he told his mother. "I don't trust his friends, either. They act like they're casing the place. Someday they will probably come back here and rob us."

Joyce tried to tell him that Duane was a good guy, but Robbie just didn't see it. He was afraid for his mother, and he thought Duane was using her because she had a car. He didn't like it that she was so trusting, and was willing to take Duane wherever he wanted to go.

Chapter Fifty One

Comparing Notes

Usually, time and maturity is what it takes to help people heal. Now that Tammy was a married woman, and time had passed, she and her mother could find a common ground. They were getting along better. One day, Tammy called to tell Jane she had received an invitation to her class reunion. One of her friends had asked if she wanted to go to Rock Fest, the same weekend. Tammy had lost a lot of weight and was feeling good about herself.

"Would you like to ride along with me to Wisconsin?" she asked her mother. "I can't afford to fly and Tommy doesn't want me to drive alone. I thought you might want to go to Cornell to visit Grandma and Grandpa Buck while I'm at my reunion."

Jane agreed to make the trip with her daughter. She didn't want Tammy to drive that far alone, either.

The two women made the long drive from Odessa, Texas, to Cornell, Wisconsin, together. When they arrived, Tammy went into the house while her mother got her suitcase out of the trunk.

"If she's here to cause trouble, you can just take her with you," Ted warned Tammy.

"She's not here to cause trouble. She just rode along so I wouldn't have to come alone, that's all," she answered.

Tammy stayed at her grandparent's house for about a half hour, and then she said her good-byes. She told them when she would be back and drove away, happily anticipating the fun she would have over the next few days.

Since Jane had not been in contact with her parents for some time, she was taken by surprise at her mother's condition.

The doctor had told Ted, "It's time for Hazel to go into a wheelchair. She will need help with everyday tasks. It might be best if you hire someone to come in to help take care of things."

"It's too expensive to have somebody in the house," Ted answered him. "I'm retired now and I can take care of everything."

From that moment on, the vulnerable woman began to live a life of horror.

Ted had retired, but he hated taking care of Hazel. He took a job at the Auto Stop gas station, to get out of the house. He left early in the morning, came home to give Hazel her lunch, and then stayed away until late at night.

What's he doing behind my back? Hazel asked herself often. She, of all people, knew what he was capable of.

Jane was totally disgusted by Ted's treatment of Hazel. She watched as her father poured a small bowl of steaming hot soup. Then he went over and literally grabbed Hazel from her rocker, and threw her into her wheelchair.

When Hazel cried out in pain, Ted yelled at her, "Shut up, you're not hurt."

He wheeled her up to the table so roughly that her fingers went into the scalding soup.

"Ouch," Hazel responded, and jerked her hand out of the hot liquid.

"I told you to shut up," Ted screamed at her. "You're not hurt. You're just trying to get people to feel sorry for you."

Jane was flabbergasted. She knew her father was a bad man, and this proved to her again exactly how truly evil he was.

"You treat mother like this again and I'll kill you," Jane threatened him.

"You shut up, too," Ted said menacingly through clenched teeth. "Just be glad you're not the one who has to take care of this old bag of shit."

Jane spent the next few days trying to help her mother as much as she could. She kept her distance from Ted, and did nothing to stir up his anger. Her visit was tense, to say the least, and she was relieved when Tammy came back to pick her up.

"Joyce," Jane said on the phone, when she was back in Odessa, "Ma looks just terrible. Dad is so abusive to her. I think we should call the police."

"Don't do that," Joyce answered. "He'll be so mad, he'll kill her, and then he'll come after us. I don't want it on my conscience if mother dies because of something we did."

Both Jane and Joyce hung up from that conversation feeling sad and hopeless. They had been brainwashed from the beginning, and they truly believed that it was not safe to cross Ted Buck.

"Ma, can you come up here?" Randy asked Joyce on the phone. "Krissy and I are getting married."

"Of course, I'll come," Joyce told her youngest son. "I wouldn't miss it for the world."

Joyce invited Duane to make the trip to Holcombe for Randy's wedding. Robbie and his family went too, and Joyce was ecstatic. She would have both of her sons together again. The problem was that neither of the boys liked Duane. However, when Randy's best man didn't show up for the ceremony, Duane stood in for him. Joyce was proud to be the mother of the groom and the girlfriend of the best man.

Grandma Joyce held the baby, while his parents got married. She sat in church and looked at her three beautiful grandchildren. *I should pinch myself to make sure this is real*, she thought.

Shortly after Randy and Krissy were married, Duane and Joyce decided to tie the knot. They were married in a civil service at the Waukesha courthouse. Joyce borrowed Rosie's dress and veil and asked her to be the matron of honor. Her wedding day was one of the "happiest days" of her life.

The newlyweds moved into an upstairs apartment at Timmerman Field.

"This is the nicest apartment I've ever lived in," she said to Duane. "I just love the balcony."

Very soon it was clear that Duane didn't know how to handle money any better than Joyce. The rent lapsed as Duane spent their money foolishly.

"That will never change," Rosie wisely told Joyce. "Be prepared to live this way as long as you are married to him."

Joyce and Randy were talking on the phone when she explained they were being evicted because they couldn't pay the rent.

"There's a job open at the Sheldon gas station, if Duane wants it. You could move back up here," he told his mother. "You could stay with me and Krissy for awhile."

They discussed Randy's offer and Duane decided that he would like to move out of Milwaukee. Krissy was pregnant again and still working at Walters Brothers Palate Factory in Holcombe. Happily, Joyce filled her days babysitting with her grandson.

The trailer house they all lived in began to feel pretty cramped once Krissy gave birth to another baby. One day, Randy's landlord, Dora Brown, stopped to talk to Joyce.

"The Lord has spoken to me," she said. "He told me you and Duane should move into the rental house that we just finished remodeling."

"We really should move and let Randy and Krissy have their whole place, now that they have the two boys," Joyce agreed. "Besides, if the Lord thinks we should, it must be all right."

She and Duane packed up and moved into Dora's rental.

It wasn't long and Joyce began to question the Lord's will. The rent was expensive and they couldn't afford to live there if they were going to buy food, too. Dora had a solution.

"We have another house on the property that isn't fixed up yet," she said. "Maybe the Lord meant that you should rent that one. It won't cost anywhere near as much money as the nice house does."

After the move, life progressed at a normal pace for several months, and then the bomb dropped. The gas station where Randy and Duane worked went out of business.

"Duane lost his job again," Joyce told her sister, Jane, on the phone. "It's really hard for him to find work around here."

"Why don't you two come to Texas?" Jane asked. "You and Duane could live with us while he looks for work."

Jane had not been able to help Joyce when Jim died, but she thought maybe she could help her sister now. Joyce and Duane arrived on Jane's doorstep the day before Thanksgiving.

The sisters were happy to see each other again, and they stayed up most of the night talking. This was the first Thanksgiving they'd spent together in years, and they both wished their brother, Alan, could be there with them.

"When we were little, we probably didn't eat anything but dried bread crumbs," Joyce said, laughing at the memory of Alan pulling bread out of his pocket to feed his sisters.

Jane's daughter, Tammy, and son, Ron, came to meet their Aunt Joyce.

"Tammy is just beautiful and Ronnie is so tall and handsome," Joyce told her sister. "I knew you'd get a second chance to be with your kids."

The West's lived with the McDaniel's for about four months, until they moved into a little cottage of their own. While Jane and Joyce were living together, they began comparing notes.

"I got this letter from mother," Jane said. "She said that you didn't love me and you didn't want me around."

"That's not true," Joyce told her sister. "I never said anything like that. Actually, mother wrote to me several times and told me that you were happy living in Texas, so you wouldn't have to put up with me anymore. She told me that you didn't love me."

"I never stopped loving you or Alan," Jane said.

"Me, either," Joyce told her. "But it hurt me because I just couldn't understand why you would tell Mama that you didn't love me."

Joyce and Jane finally figured out that Hazel had been playing a game by pitting them against each other. The reality of their mother's deceit hit them like a hammer. Immediately, the coldness that had grown between them over the years disappeared, and the warm feelings they had always had for each other resurfaced.

Hazel's game had not really worked, anyway. Even when they were unsure of each other's love, they always did their best to be together and support each other during the hard times.

"I guess Ma lost that game," Jane said, and Joyce agreed.

Tammy and Ronnie grew to love their Aunt Joyce. Once in awhile, Ron would stop in on his way home from work to see her. She thought he was one of the nicest young men she had ever met. Joyce visited with Tammy and always marveled at how smart and pretty she was. *Thank you for bringing Jane's children back to her*, Joyce offered a silent prayer of gratitude.

Chapter Fifty-two

Feels Like Heaven to Me

During the time they were together, Jane convinced Joyce to go with her to see her therapist. Joyce had never been to a psychiatrist or counselor before, so she was apprehensive.

"I can't afford it, and Duane will have a fit," Joyce answered.

"She might be able to help you understand why you feel the way you do," Jane countered. "Besides, Duane spends money on what he wants."

On her first visit, the therapist, Robin Gale Jasper, led Joyce to a sandbox where she had laid out several different items for Joyce to "play" with. It took a few minutes for her to relax and get the hang of what Robin Gale wanted her to do with the items. Finally, Joyce sat down and began to play. She put a house in the corner, and then she dug a river and put a bridge over it. Next, she set a barn on the other side of the bridge.

"This is fun," Joyce said. "But, what does it mean?"

"It means that you want to get away. The house represents bad memories. The bridge represents escape. The barn represents safety," the therapist told her.

"I feel like I want to cross the bridge and never go back," Joyce told the counselor.

Then she began to cry.

Robin Gale was very gentle and allowed Joyce to cry on her shoulder.

"What has happened to you is not your fault. No child is to blame for being abused and neglected."

Joyce left her first counseling session with a glimmer of understanding, and the desire to look inside herself to begin dealing with her past.

Jane's kids were happy to get to know their Aunt Joyce. One day, Tammy took her out to see the place where she and her husband Tommy lived.

"Oh, my," Joyce said. "Ducks, chickens, goats and dogs. This is paradise."

"I need a dog of my own," Joyce decided. "I've always loved animals, especially dogs."

So Cricket, a darling white miniature Spitz, moved in with the West's.

Immediately, little "Crickee" became the apple of Joyce's eye, and set about becoming lord and master of the house.

"She loves that dog more than she does me," Duane teased.

Life was going well for the sisters. Joyce had just received word that Randy and Krissy were expecting baby number three, and Jane had good news from Ron. He and his girlfriend, Susan, were expecting a baby and had decided to get married.

"Ron sounded so happy," Jane told her sister. "I just love to see him this way."

Ron seemed happy that his dad had agreed to come to Odessa for the wedding. His stepmother, Carol, had died earlier, so his dad would be coming alone. Jane was always apprehensive when she knew John would be around.

"I sure hope he doesn't start anything," she told Joyce.

The wedding and the reception were held at the Hilton Hotel in one of the ballrooms.

"Ooh, it's just beautiful in here," Joyce said as she walked into the room with Jane and Mac.

Duane was not with them since he was a night watchman and had to work.

"I don't think I've ever been to a more beautiful wedding," Jane told Mac and Joyce.

They were all thrilled for Ron and Susan as they left the Hilton to attend an informal reception being held at the kid's favorite bar.

John was already at the bar when they arrived. After a few beers, he started acting up and talking mushy. He blatantly flirted with Jane and Joyce. After awhile, Mac looked as if he was standing under a storm cloud.

"I think it's time we go," Mac said.

The next day, John unexpectedly stopped over at Jane's house. Joyce and Duane were there but had to leave so Duane could get to work on time. Jane was about to go pick Mac up from work, so she asked John if he wanted to ride along.

"Sure," John said, and they walked out to the car.

Jane looked over at her ex-husband and saw him leaning toward her for a kiss. She leaned forward and met him halfway, kissing him full on the mouth. Stunned at her own behavior, she quietly drove away with John sitting beside her in the passenger seat.

I guess I'll chalk that up to old time's sake, she thought, ridden with guilt.

John moved from the front into the back seat when Mac came out of work. Jane was mute, as she drove home. Her heart was thumping inside her ears, and she was sick to her stomach. Without a word, she jumped out of the car and ran into the house. *I'm going to have to tell Mac the truth. I can't believe I did that.* Through the window, Jane could see the two men standing together, beside the car.

Mac looked devastated when he came through the kitchen door.

"Mac," Jane confessed, "I kissed John. It didn't mean anything and I know it was wrong, but I did it."

"You went to bed with him this afternoon, too, didn't you?" Mac accused.

"No! We did not go to bed together," Jane denied. "He kissed me and that's all. I promised you I'd never cheat on you, and I haven't. You are my husband, and I love you."

Mac was not convinced, and at that moment, he stopped talking to his wife. The silent treatment he imposed on her lasted for more than two months. During that time, Mac went to work, came home for supper, and sat watching TV. He wouldn't say a word or touch Jane in any way.

The day after the kiss, Tammy called her mother.

"Can you come over? Dad has something he wants to say to you," she said.

Jane was upset that her beloved husband would actually believe she would cheat on him. She decided to get even with Mac and go meet with John.

"I told Mac that we never had sex. I told him that he might think we did, but we didn't," John said to her.

"Oh, great," Jane said, "Thanks a lot. Now he really believes we went to bed together."

"Will you leave him and come back to Wisconsin with me?" John pleaded. "We could get married. That's what the kids have always wanted," he added.

"Mac is my husband and I love him," Jane said. "I suppose I love you, too, but in a different way. I don't want to be married to you."

John left and went back to Eau Claire, Wisconsin, and Jane tried to pick up the pieces of her life. As Mac got more and more depressed, Jane became afraid for him and for their marriage. After about six weeks of silence, Jane left and went to stay with Mac's mother in Big Lake, Texas. She couldn't think of anywhere else to go. She was convinced that Mac wanted a divorce and she was crushed. After much soul searching and nighttime agony, she realized she would have to be the one to set things straight. She got in the car and drove home.

"All right, let's sit down and talk," she said to Mac when she got there. "We have to get this out in the open and get it over with. Do you want a divorce, or do you want to settle this?" Jane asked him point blank.

"I do not want a divorce," Mac answered. "What do you want?"

"I want us to stop this silence. I want you to talk to me. I want to be your angel again," she said crying. "I want you to believe me that I did not have sex with John. I'm sorry I kissed him, but that's all I did."

"I'm sorry, too," Mac said. "Don't cry. It'll be okay. I love you."

They finally made up.

One day Mac came home from work with exciting news. His friend, George, was opening a military memorabilia and record shop in Dallas, Texas, and he had offered Mac a job. They would have to move to Dallas, but the pay would be twice what he made at the Red Door Antique Shop.

"I told him I'd talk to you and we'd think it over. He's going to call me back when he gets his plans finalized," Mac finished.

As luck would have it, during the time Mac waited for George to call them back, Duane got laid off from his job at the oil company. The West's began to think they should probably go back home. Joyce was lonesome for the grandkids and she didn't want to stay in Odessa, if Jane was moving to Dallas.

"It's too hot down here and I want to go somewhere that has good fishing," Duane told Joyce.

Money was always a problem. Joyce had never been taught to handle it, and neither had Duane. At the end of their eight months in Texas, it was the same old story. They had no money and Duane was without a job.

"I think the Lord planned for us to move here so we could figure out what mother was doing to us, with her letters. Now that I know you still love me, I don't care about anything else," Joyce told her sister.

"I know what you mean," Jane answered. "What did we ever do to make her so angry with us that she would try to destroy our relationship?"

"I don't think it's what we did," Joyce answered. "I think it's what daddy did. He was having sex with us while he was married to her, and she's mad."

"She knows he's the father of Robbie and Randy, but she's scared to get even with him, so she's out to get us," Jane added.

"I don't know what to do. We need money to move, and I can't ask them for any," Joyce said. "Some people have parents who love them and would help them. I guess we just didn't luck out."

"Maybe Robbie would lend you the money to move back," Jane suggested.

Joyce called and asked Robbie for the money. He sent $200.00 to help them get back to Holcombe. Joyce and Duane stayed with Randy for a few weeks, until they found a place of their own.

"I have two wonderful boys," Joyce declared. "They take good care of me."

Mac and Jane received the call from George and began preparing to leave Odessa. They gave notice to their boss at the Red Door, and sold their belongings. Actually, they asked for very little money for their things, and gave most of it away.

Their big dreams of military expos and big money didn't pan out. After only two months, the dream evaporated into thin air.

"We might as well go back to Odessa," Mac said sadly. "I think we can get our jobs back at the Red Door, and find another house to rent.

Mac was able to return to work at the Red Door, but within a few weeks, the boss retired and closed the antique shop for good. Luckily, Mac found a job right away with another oil company. His boss was a Mormon with a strong work ethic, and Mac was impressed with his sense of fairness.

Mac liked his job, and Jane was happy to be back in Odessa with her family. On Christmas Eve, Tammy and Tommy, and Ron, Susan, and the baby joined Mac and Jane for the best holiday Jane had ever experienced. It was an evening where everyone seemed to love and appreciate each other.

"This is what I've prayed for ever since my children were taken away," Jane cried in Mac's arms, after the kids all went home. "This feels like heaven on earth to me."

Chapter Fifty-three

I'd Rather Sleep in the Camper

When she returned from living in Texas, Joyce couldn't believe how much her mother had failed. To her, Hazel looked as though she were a shrunken woman. She was appalled at how rough Ted treated her. While she was visiting, he opened a can of peaches and put some in a small dish. He wheeled Hazel to the table and got her leg caught between the table leg and the wheel chair.

"Ouch!" Hazel complained.

"There, goddamn it!" Ted yelled. "You're not hurt. Eat now or you won't get any!"

"Is that all you're going to give her?" Joyce asked.

"That's all she eats. She don't want any more," was Ted's harsh reply.

I think he's trying to starve her to death, Joyce thought sadly. *He's probably trying to get rid of her.*

Ted saw the look on his daughter's face.

"Don't judge me," he said belligerently. "You never come around to help, so you don't have anything to say about it. Now get out of here. She doesn't need your sympathy."

Joyce went home feeling very sorry for her mother. She didn't know what to do or how to help her, so she just didn't go to the house anymore.

Duane heard about a paper route, delivering the St. Paul Pioneer Press. He thought it might be a fun job, but he wanted Joyce to help him deliver the papers. So at three o'clock in the morning each weekday, they'd pick up the papers in Bruce, and deliver them to subscribers in

Ladysmith and Hawkins. Fortunately, they had a company car and the gasoline was provided. They put on more than 300 miles every day, six days a week. On the seventh day, they'd start out at midnight to drive to Cameron to get ready to deliver the Sunday paper.

"You have to find a different job," Joyce said. "We only make twenty-five dollars a week and we can't pay the rent and buy food on that."

"I like this one," Duane whined.

"Then we'll have to go back on welfare so we can get food stamps," Joyce reasoned.

To try to make ends meet, she began cleaning the boss's house, and then took on the added task of inserting the advertising flyers into the papers before they delivered them. With those added duties, Joyce was able to increase their income to $135.00 per week.

One morning, Joyce woke up with a very funny feeling.

"Something is wrong with mother," she said to Duane.

She knew she wasn't welcome but she decided to call her parent's house and just check it out for herself.

"She's at the hospital," Ted said. "She's had a stroke."

"Can I see her?" she asked her father hesitantly.

"She doesn't want to see you. She wants you to stay away," he said in a nasty voice.

Randy's wife, Krissy, knew her mother-in-law was afraid to go to the hospital alone, so she offered to take her. The two women went to see Hazel. As Joyce feared, her mother didn't acknowledge her. She wondered if Hazel knew she was even in the room.

Joyce visited her mother a time or two once she was transferred to the nursing home in Cornell. She felt sad for her mother, and in spite of everything, she still loved her. After all, Hazel had adopted her and had been kind to her in the beginning. She also knew what her mother had suffered at the hands of her father.

Though Hazel was ill, one of the nurses helped Ted plan a big splash for their fiftieth wedding anniversary. The party was held at the Care Center.

"I'll go with you, if you want me to," Krissy came to Joyce's rescue again.

Krissy and the grandkids attended the celebration with Joyce, however, they were treated like strangers.

"Well, that was a waste of time," Krissy exclaimed. "I don't think grandma even knew there was a party going on."

Joyce agreed that it had been fruitless for her to be there. It was a waste of her emotions and energy, as well. A week after the party, Joyce and Duane stopped at her father's house to pick up a copy of the anniversary picture.

Ted said, "Sorry, I threw the negative away."

Joyce and Duane walked out of the house without saying another word to her father. Joyce's face was hot with anger and humiliation.

A few days later, it was a different kind of hot in Odessa, Texas. Jane was up early since it was too hot to sleep.

"Hello," Jane answered the phone when it rang.

"Ma just died," Roger said tersely on the other end.

"I'll catch a plane and be there as soon as I can," Jane told her brother.

"I don't think Dad wants you to come," Roger said.

"Let me talk to him," Jane insisted.

"I'm going to try to fly out today," Jane told her father. "I'll call when I have the tickets and let you know what time I get in."

"What for?" was Ted's question. "She's dead and there isn't anything for you to come home for."

"She's my mother and I want to come," Jane was defiant.

Ted said, "No one wants you here," and then he hung up.

Jane called Joyce to tell her about the exchange with Ted, and to ask if she and Duane would pick her up at the airport. The trip to Wisconsin was emotional for Jane. She was lonesome for her sister, and felt bad that her mother was dead. Mostly, she was sad that things had turned out the way they had for the Buck family.

Now that she's dead, I don't have to protect her anymore, Jane raged silently as she flew toward her mother's funeral. *I can tell people what that bastard did to us. He should spend the rest of his life in prison.*

Joyce and Jane were very happy to see each other. Tears flowed freely between them. They rested a few hours, and then went to the Cornell Funeral Home to attend their mother's wake. Several people offered condolences to Joyce and Jane, but their father and brother totally ignored them.

The funeral was held at the Presbyterian church, and the family was scheduled to meet in the fellowship hall prior to the service. The celebration of Hazel's life was cold and impersonal, as though she were a stranger to the minister and everyone in attendance. Joyce and Jane sat with Ted and Roger, but not one word was exchanged between them.

The sisters expected to ride in the front of the funeral procession with their family. Instead, Ted told them to take their own car, and they were nearly last in the parade to the cemetery.

Following the interment, a depressing feeling settled over them as they walked into the church dining room. The Ruth Circle was in charge of the luncheon. Ted and Roger had already sat down at one of the long tables, leaving no room for Joyce, Duane, or Jane. People commented on how far from Ted the girls were sitting.

One person said, "I thought family sat together at these things."

Hazel's nurse sat next to Ted. She made a show of taking care of Ted's every need.

"I bet he's having sex with her," Jane whispered to Joyce. "With mother out of the house all this time, there's been nothing to stop him."

"Nothing ever stopped him from getting what he wanted," Joyce whispered, knowingly.

On the way back to the house, the sisters continued their conversation.

"We don't have to worry about mother anymore," Jane said. "I think we should call the cops and tell them what he did to us."

"I don't think we should do that, yet," Joyce answered. "He's still alive and he will find a way to hurt us."

"I won't do anything if you don't want me to, but someday he should pay for what he's done," Jane told her.

"Someday he'll get what's coming to him. He'll spend eternity in hell," Joyce stated.

"I told Jeannie Hebert a little bit about our life. She thinks we have a good story to tell," Jane continued. "I think she might be willing to write it for us."

"I'm not ready yet," Joyce pleaded.

After Hazel's death, the sisters had virtually no contact with their father. Roger worked at a window factory in Bloomer, and Ted was still working part-time at the Auto Stop, in Cornell. Joyce and Jane were so hurt by the treatment they received at their mother's funeral that even after Jane went back to Texas, Joyce simply stayed away.

One night Joyce and Duane were listening to their police and fire scanner. They heard the call go out for volunteers. There was a fire in the basement at Ted's address. Joyce got in the car and went to her father's house to see what was happening. The EMT's were just loading Ted into the ambulance when she arrived. He was in his underwear and he looked away as Joyce came to talk to him.

"You and Roger can stay with us for the night, if you need to," she offered.

"No!" Ted stated emphatically. "We'd rather sleep in the camper."

That fire and the resulting smoke inhalation was the beginning of health problems for Ted Buck. From that time on, he was in and out of the hospital with one ailment after the other.

Chapter Fifty-four

Dark Days

Jane felt blessed that she lived as far away from her father as she did. She flew back to Texas from her mother's funeral, with gratitude in her heart. She loved her husband, her children were near, and she loved her life in Odessa.

One morning, Mac went to work, as usual. Business was pretty slow, so he did what was necessary and then called Jane.

"Why don't you meet me at the coffee shop?" he asked. "I'm going to take a little break and I could use a cup of coffee."

"Okay," she answered, "I'll be there shortly."

They sat talking over a cup of coffee when Mac suddenly complained of an upset stomach.

"I think I should go home," he said.

When they walked into the kitchen, Jane asked him, "Do you want me to fix you something to eat?"

"A poached egg sounds good. I think it will feel good in my stomach," he answered.

While Jane was poaching his egg, his boss called to ask him to take a load of pipe somewhere.

"I can't do it," Mac told him, "I'm just not feeling good enough, right now."

Mac ate his egg, turned on a football game and asked Jane to scratch his back. Shortly, he got up from the couch to go to the bathroom.

He gave Jane a kiss and said, "I love you," as he left the room.

Then suddenly she heard a strange thud and ran to the bathroom where she found Mac slumped on the floor. She pulled him out of the bathroom and called 911. Jane knew, by looking at him, that he was dead. The EMT's confirmed that he was gone, but they followed procedure and transported him to the hospital.

Ron and Tammy joined Jane at the hospital and waited with her for the doctor.

"He died of a massive heart attack," the doctor told them. "It went so fast that he didn't suffer. There was nothing anybody could do."

"I know you are in heaven," Jane told Mac as she stood crying beside his coffin. "Now you know the truth. I did not sleep with John after Ron's wedding. Now you know that I kept my promise to you. I never cheated on you. I love you."

The loss of her beloved Mac was a very, very, very deep journey for Jane. She was a mess. Everyone she knew was worried about her. As she sank deeper into depression, she again turned to drinking and men.

Tammy went to Jane's house one morning, and asked, "Do you think it would help if I tried to get hold of dad? Maybe he could come down here."

"I don't care," Jane answered.

The truth was that she was mentally and emotionally ill, and she didn't care about anything, least of all John Botsford.

Years before, when John had married Carol, he had started a construction company. Carol was the financial backer, and the businesswoman who took care of the financial end of the company. Now that she was dead, John had begun drinking heavily and mismanaging the finances. The business had fallen to ruin.

Some people always seem to be in the wrong place at the wrong time. Jane's second son seemed to be one of those people. Jonnie had the bad fortune to be working with his father when the business failed. Checks were written on the account, when there was not enough money in the bank to cover them. John had given Jonnie the authority to write checks and sign his name.

John always told him, "Don't worry, I'll cover the checks."

As soon as John realized his business was in trouble with the law, he skipped the country. He went to stay with his real father in Nebraska, but he didn't tell Jonnie he was going. He just ran off and left his son holding the bag.

Tammy had been in touch with her grandfather in Nebraska, so she knew how to get in touch with John.

"Hi, Dad," Tammy said on the phone. "Mom's right here, and she wants to talk to you."

"Mac died," Jane said sadly. "Tammy thinks you should come down here."

"I could do that, but I don't have money for the bus ticket," John answered.

"I'll get a ticket for you," Jane promised.

In reality, Jane was afraid to have John come to Odessa because she had the feeling that she would be cheating on Mac, if her ex-husband were around. The other men she slept with didn't count since they didn't mean anything to her.

Somehow Jane realized she was not thinking clearly, but she couldn't help herself. Somewhere in her despondent mind, she thought maybe she and John could get back together, since that was what the kids seemed to want. She was in survival mode and grasping at anything she could, to just hang on and not float away.

John arrived in Odessa a couple of days later and went straight to Jane's house. At first, things went pretty well, except Jane did not trust him. She began to worry that he might come into her bedroom and force himself on her, or hurt her, while she was sleeping.

"Tammy, can your dad come and stay with you?" Jane asked her daughter.

"Yes, he can move out here," Tammy answered.

Jane felt much better after John went to live near Tammy.

John got a job painting a new building that Ron's boss was constructing. Until he got his first paycheck, Jane bought his cigarettes and Tammy provided his food. Jane's brakes needed to be replaced. John did that and then changed the oil in her car. He also helped make several repairs to Tammy and Tommy's trailer house.

Jane and John got along pretty well for several weeks. Then one night, Jane, Tammy, and Tommy were at John's trailer house playing cards. Tammy answered the ringing phone. Jonnie was on the other end and he began telling Tammy what was happening in Eau Claire, since his dad left.

"The cops are after me because of several checks I wrote on dad's account," Jonnie said. "Now they are trying to arrest me for forgery because dad and I have the same name. They think I'm trying to forge his signature. The checks are hot, too, because dad said he was going to cover the account, but he didn't. He needs to call them and get this straightened out, or I'm going to jail."

"Dad," Tammy said, as she was about to hand the phone to John, "you have to talk to Jonnie. He's in trouble with the law for those bad checks. It's your fault, and not his."

"Naw," John said. "It's his fault, not mine. I didn't write those checks. He did."

"But you told him he could write those checks and sign your name," Tammy's voice was rising. "He didn't know that he was committing forgery when he did that. You have to call the authorities and tell them it was you and not Jonnie who did this."

Finally, John took the phone and talked to his son.

"Don't worry about it," he said. "They can't prove anything. I will get in touch with them and let them know. Your name is John Dale Botsford and mine is John Wayne Botsford. The business is in my name, not yours. They can't do anything to you."

By the time they hung up, Jonnie thought his father was going to handle everything and he believed he was off the hook. Jane and Tammy thought John would live up to his promise and call the authorities in Eau Claire, Wisconsin, to explain the situation. They were wrong. John lied to his son, and eventually Jonnie would pay the ultimate price for that deception.

On Mothers Day, Jane got a call from Jonnie.

"Happy Mothers Day, Mom," he said.

"Well, thank you, honey. You sound happy," Jane answered.

"Linda and I have been talking about getting married," he told his mother.

They talked a while and then Jonnie said, "Well, good-bye, Mom. I love you."

Jane said, "I love you, too. Take care of yourself. Good-bye."

The next day, Linda called to tell Jane that Jonnie had been in an accident the night before. Jane felt panic rise in her throat, as she listened to the details. The police had chased Jonnie through Eau Claire

County for over an hour at high rates of speed. He finally was arrested for eluding an officer, and booked for drunk driving. He was in jail when he started spitting up blood, so the authorities transferred him to the emergency room at Luther Hospital. They left him alone for a few minutes, and he went into the bathroom and hung himself.

"He's still alive, but the doctors don't think he will last very long. You'd better get here right away," Linda said, crying.

When it finally sunk in what Linda was saying, that Jonnie was dying, Jane couldn't move. She sat in shock and disbelief. Somewhere, she found the strength to get off her chair and walk out to her car. She drove to Ron's workplace with tears blinding her, and a crushing pain in her chest. Together, Jane and Ron went to Tammy's. Jane tried to relate what Linda had said.

"We have to call Linda," she finally told them. "I can't remember everything."

Tammy called Linda, and she encouraged Tammy to come right away.

"Jonnie is on life support and a decision has to be made as to whether or not to keep him on it," Linda told her. "They won't let me make the decision because I'm not his wife. You and your brothers have to make the decision."

The family made plans to drive to Wisconsin. Todd called from Wisconsin, later in the evening, to find out what their travel arrangements were. He was relieved they all were coming.

After the call, Jane and Tammy went looking for John. They went to every bar they could think of until they found him. It was clear that he had been drinking heavily.

"Jonnie tried to kill himself, and they don't think he will live very long," Tammy told her father.

John didn't seem very interested in what she had to say.

"This is disgusting," Tammy told her dad. "I had to track you down in a bar to tell you that your son is dying."

"I'm over twenty-one," John said. "You just leave me the hell alone. I can do as I damn well please."

"Are you coming or not?" Tammy yelled.

John went along with them and when they got to his place, Tammy lit into her father.

"I'm so mad that you were in the bar. You make me sick. You never were a father. All you ever think about is yourself and your booze. I'm done. It's over. I can't take it anymore."

Then she turned to include both John and Jane.

"You two can just go to hell. You can take yourselves to Wisconsin. You can drink and screw around all the way up there, if you want to. You gave us away, and you never were our parents. I've had it!"

On her way home, Jane stopped at the Baptist church to meet with Pastor Woods. She asked that he put the family on their prayer list. That night she went to bed and wept. She prayed and begged God to take her, instead of her child.

The next day around ten o'clock, Jane took her suitcase over to Tammy's house.

Tammy came flying out of the back door screaming, "Get off my property. If you want to go to Wisconsin, go with dad."

Tammy kicked the car door shut and stood glaring at her mother.

"Get the hell out of here," she yelled.

Jane knew that Tammy was upset and hurting, but she figured she was just blowing off steam. She had to go to the town of Big Springs, to get some money from Mac's friend, George, for selling Mac's military items. Jane figured Tammy would be calmed down by the time she returned.

She was gone for about an hour and a half.

When she got back to Tammy's, Tommy came out to the car and said, "Tammy, Ron and Susan have already taken off for Wisconsin."

Jane was devastated. She didn't know what to do so she went to John's trailer house. He asked her for gas money and she gave him a one hundred dollar bill.

"I'm not going," she sobbed.

Joyce began to cry when Jane called to tell her about Jonnie. They talked about the situation with the kids, and Jane decided that she just couldn't stay away. She had to go to Wisconsin after all. She called Joyce back with her travel arrangements.

"I can't get out until tomorrow and I can't get into Eau Claire. I have to go to Milwaukee," she told her sister a few hours later. "Do you think you and Duane could drive down to Milwaukee and pick me up at the airport?"

"We'll leave today and drive down to Robbie and Annette's. We can stay overnight there and be ready to pick you up and drive back to Eau Claire, as soon as you get in," Joyce planned.

When they finally arrived at Luther Hospital, Jane and Joyce went to the emergency room. The nurse wasn't going to let them in.

"I'm sorry, but you are not on the list. We have a written order here. Neither you nor his father are to be allowed in to see him," Jane was told.

Jane was crushed.

"But I came all the way from Texas to see him," she told the nurse with tears flooding her eyes.

"The rest of the family is gone right now. I suppose it wouldn't do any harm," the nurse told her. "He is in intensive care. You will only have five minutes."

The nurse took Jane to Jonnies' room. When she saw him lying there, her heart almost stopped. His face was terribly swollen and he was on life support.

Jane went to the bed. She leaned over, kissed his face, and took his hand.

"Mama's here. Wake up. Everything is going to be okay," she told him. "Remember, I love you."

She stood there holding Jonnie's hand, grieving the loss of her husband and her son, when the nurse came to tell her it was time to leave. Jane's heart broke completely that day.

Joyce and Jane were outside the hospital in the parking lot, when Tammy, Todd, Ron, Susan and Linda arrived. Tammy was visibly surprised to see her mother and her aunt. No one said a word, except Todd.

"Hi," he began.

"Come on," Tammy tossed the words over her shoulder.

Todd gave Jane a quick kiss on the cheek, turned his back, and followed the rest of them into the hospital.

Jane and Joyce cried on the way back to Joyce's house. They cried for Jonnie and were hurt by the way the other kids treated them.

"There's nothing we can do about it," Jane said. "I've hurt them so much. They are just getting back at me."

Later in the week, before she was scheduled to go back to Odessa, Jane called Linda.

"Can I see Jonnie one more time before I go?" she asked.

"Everybody has gone back to Texas," Linda said. "If you come down, I'll meet you and we can go in together."

Jane flew back to Odessa and began soul searching. She had been a weak mother who lost her children, and never found a way to get them back. She had married John to get away from the hellish life she and Joyce were forced to live, under the rule of Ted Buck. She had fallen into the same lifestyle as her real parents, Hale and Esther Colburn. By doing so, she had exposed her own children to abuse and neglect. Once they were taken away, the neglect and abuse continued in foster care. She found that she just wasn't her children's mother. She and the kids did not have a bond. *I can't change the past and suddenly be the matriarch of the family*, she thought to herself.

She had lived a lifestyle and made choices that kept her in financial crisis her entire life. She finally understood that she had become a victim. She was the only one who could change things. She realized that she had spent too much time at Tammy's after Mac died. She couldn't help herself. Mac's ghost was everywhere and she wasn't mentally strong enough to cope with it. She had worn Tammy out by being so needy. She began to understand that her children could not count on her or John, because they had let them down too many times. Anything she could do now was just too little, and too late.

When Jonnie died, Jane did not go to Wisconsin for his funeral. She was at peace with her decision. She had said her goodbyes at the hospital.

Chapter Fifty-Five

I Think I'm Going Crazy

Sometimes, when things get just so bad, the only thing a person wants to do is run. Jane began to think that it would be best if she moved out of Odessa. Her life there, had turned to mush. Mac was dead, and she was consumed by loss and fear. Her son, Jonnie, was dead, and her other children were terribly disappointed in her. She felt she couldn't face any part of her life in Odessa.

After a particularly bad night, Jane called Mac's friend, Fred, and asked him if he would help her pack and drive her to Wisconsin if she rented a U-Haul.

Joyce was worried about her sister. Once she knew Jane was coming, she just couldn't wait. She was anxious to see for herself if Jane was okay. But Jane was not okay.

Jane and Fred arrived, and unloaded her belongings from the U-haul. The next morning it was evident to Joyce that her sister was not thinking clearly. Jane had decided to go back and get the U-Haul.

"I'm just not ready to move up here yet," she said. "Mac is not dead to me. He's waiting for me in Odessa."

Fred just shook his head, and helped Jane reload the trailer, while Joyce tried her best to talk her sister out of going back.

Shortly after Jane returned to Odessa, she ran into an acquaintance who owned the Hide-Away Bar.

"Why don't you stop in and I'll buy you a drink?" Bruce asked.

"I'll just have to do that," Jane replied.

Bruce became a source of free drinks for Jane. She found that alcohol helped her forget her troubles, for a little while anyway. She continued going out with guys and doing things that she knew Mac wouldn't have wanted her to do. One night she met a guy named George, at the bar. She liked him and soon they had a "thing" going. George and Jane spent a lot of their time at the bar. He helped ease her loneliness, and the alcohol helped ease her pain.

Tammy's husband, Tommy, had been ill with diabetes for many years. This time, he didn't survive. Jane knew the devastation Tammy was feeling. She fully understood how deep the pain could go.

This family has had so much loss, Jane thought. *It seems like we are being punished for something. I don't know if I can stand it anymore.*

Joyce decided to take the bus to Odessa. Jane had sounded so desperate on the phone, that Joyce was worried she'd try to commit suicide again.

"You'd better call her and tell her you're coming," Duane told Joyce. "She could stand to hear some good news for a change."

During the first week of Joyce's visit, Jane complained of unbearable pain in her stomach.

"I bet you're having a gall bladder attack," Joyce told her. "When I had mine, it was the worst pain I ever had in my life."

Joyce was right. The doctor told Jane she needed to have surgery right away. Joyce called Tammy and Ron to let them know their mother was in the hospital. When both kids showed up, Jane was surprised, overjoyed, and grateful that they came.

"I'll call Duane and tell him that I'm going to stay a couple of weeks longer," Joyce said. "You'll need some help when you get home."

Joyce's two-week trip to Texas turned into a month. She took care of her sister and watched as her spirits rose.

The doctor had not given Jane the okay to drive yet, so when it was time for Joyce to leave, she was relieved when her friend, Fritzi volunteered to take Joyce to the bus station. As soon as they left, Jane thought, *I can't let Joyce go back this way.* She defied the doctor's orders, got in her car, and drove to meet Fritzi and Joyce at the depot.

"I just couldn't let you get on the bus without me," she said when she met up with them.

"Last night you said you weren't coming. Don't you even trust me enough to take her to the bus station?" Fritzi asked defensively.

"That's not it," Jane tried to explain. "I just needed to see my sister one more time. I couldn't have her get on the bus without me being here."

After the kids visited her at the hospital, Jane's relationship with them seemed to be improving steadily, but her health didn't follow suit. Within the next few days, infection set in the surgery site.

Her friend Darlene lived in the same apartment complex a couple of doors down. Darlene offered to help Jane. She packed the incision site three times a day, waited on her, and practically lived with her for a month.

"I don't know what I would have done without you," Jane told Darlene. "You are a life saver."

Fritzi and Darlene visited with Jane and kept her company while she recuperated. She felt blessed to have two such good friends.

One day, Jane and Fritzi were talking on the phone.

"The doctor says I can drive again. How about I come over, and we'll go to the Catfish for a cup of coffee?" Jane asked Fritzi.

"Great," Fritzi answered. "I'll be ready."

As Jane walked out to the car, Darlene saw her and hollered, "Where are you going?"

"Fritzi and I are going to the Catfish for a cup of coffee. Do you want to come along?" Jane yelled back.

"I'll be right there," Darlene answered.

The three friends enjoyed their coffee, and some good conversation. Jane knew most of the people at the Catfish, since she and Mac used to be regulars there. It felt wonderful to be out and about with so many people who knew her.

The phone was ringing when she walked through the door into her house.

"This is Fritzi. You paid for Darlene's coffee and you didn't pay for mine—after all I did for you, when your sister was here. I even took her out to eat, and paid for her meal. I spent my gas money hauling her around, and she didn't even say thank you. I never want to talk to you again," Fritzi was screaming when she slammed the receiver in Jane's ear.

Jane had been hanging on by a thread since Mac and Jonnie died. This phone call, from someone she thought was a friend, put her over the edge.

She went to the dresser, got Mac's handgun and loaded it. She sat looking at the gun in her hand, and decided to join Mac and Jonnie.

Then a thread of sanity appeared.

"If I don't get help," she said out loud, "I'm going to kill myself, and then what would Joyce be left with?"

She picked up the phone to dial her therapist's number.

"I have a gun in my hand and I am afraid that I am going to use it," Jane told Robin Gale Jasper. "I don't know what to do. If I can't even keep a friend, I might as well kill myself."

"Come right over," Robin Gale said. "Right now! Don't even stop to lock your door. Just come."

Robin Gale listened patiently while Jane talked.

"I think I should get out of town. I'll call my sister and ask her if I can stay with her. She's my rock and I think I need her. So much has happened to me in a very short period of time that I think I'm going crazy. I guess it's time to go home, to Joyce."

Having finally made a decision, gave Jane strength. She hugged Robin Gale and thanked her. With new resolve, she drove home and called Joyce.

"I'm coming home for good," she told her sister.

"I can take you to Wisconsin," Tammy told her mother. "I'm going to my class reunion again, but we have to do this thing right away. I have to be on the road in a couple of days. If you want to go with me, we'll have to hustle."

Jane was desperate to change her life. She sold practically everything she owned. A few days later, she and Tammy were sailing down the highway toward home.

Chapter Fifty-six

The End of the Reign Of Terror

Jane stayed with Joyce and Duane until she found a cute apartment in Cornell. She quit drinking, and began making a life for herself, near her trusted sister.

Joyce had some good news for her sister, once she was all settled in.

"Alan and Tina are coming here for a vacation," she said. "They have a motor home and they'll be here in a few days."

"Oh, my God," Jane cried. "I haven't seen Alan for so long. It's been years, and I've missed him so much."

For the first time in a very long time, Sharon, Shirley, and Alan Colburn were together again. They laughed, talked about old times, ate good food, and took lots of pictures.

"We'll have these pictures to look at whenever we get lonesome for each other," Joyce told her brother and sister.

"All these years have gone by, and we're still here," Jane said.

"We are survivors," Alan added.

When it was time to go, Shirley, Sharon, and Alan stood together remembering.

All through the years, though miles had separated them, they had remained a family. In spite of it all, they loved and cared for each other. Against all odds, the Colburn family had survived.

The love they felt for each other contrasted sharply with the hate the girls felt for their adopted father, Ted Buck.

Jane hadn't seen Ted or her brother Roger for a long time and she was curious.

"Let's go see dad. I've been kind of wondering how he's doing," Jane suggested to Joyce.

"I'll go if you go, but I'm not going alone," was Joyce's answer.

When they got there, Ted made coffee and offered them each a cup. They noticed their graduation pictures had been taken down, and replaced with a picture of a little girl.

"Who's that a picture of?" Jane asked her father.

"The nurse who took care of your mother. It's her kid. She was more like a daughter to me than you ever were," he announced.

We know what he does to his daughters, and that's probably his kid, Jane thought to herself.

Oh, he's gotten another girl pregnant, Joyce was thinking, at the same time. She remembered how the woman hung on Ted and took care of him at Hazel's funeral.

Jane decided to ask her father about the antique, "Tree of Life," broach she had once given Hazel for a Christmas gift. She wondered if her father still had it.

"Do you still have the broach I gave mother?" Jane asked.

"Nope," Ted said with a shrug. "There's no jewelry here. All her stuff is gone. I gave it all away."

"Why didn't you save it for me?" Jane glared at him. "I gave it to her. It should have been mine, after she died."

Ted looked at her as if she were from outer space. Then he slammed his fist on the table, stood up, and shuffled down the hall to the bedroom.

While Ted was out of the room, Roger came home. When he saw his sisters, he raised one eyebrow with a look that said, "W*hat do you want now?"*

"Hi," he mumbled and walked through the kitchen, without waiting for a reply.

Roger and his father passed each other in the doorway, as Ted returned and threw the piece of jewelry onto the table. Jane picked it up and held it in her hand for a moment. Then she threw it back on the table.

"Why did you lie to me about this?" she asked her father.

"You were never my daughters! I gave you everything and all you ever did was cause me trouble! Get out of here! I never want to see you again! Ever! And you'd better keep your mouths shut or I'll kill you!" he screamed, shaking with rage.

It was all so uncomfortable that they left, and never saw Ted again, alive.

"When I see him, I have the urge to kill him," Jane told her sister.

"I know what you mean," Joyce answered. "He has ruined so many lives. He is just plain evil."

"I have to find a way to forgive him before I actually kill him, and end up in prison for the rest of my life," Jane told her sister.

Jane knew she needed help if she was going to find a way to forgive Ted. A therapist in Ladysmith was recommended to her, and she was eager to start working with him.

"I have an appointment with Virgil Walks," Jane told her sister. "I haven't seen anyone since I told Robin Gale I was moving home.

"Let me know how you like him," Joyce said. "If you like him, I might make an appointment with him, too."

Jane was happy with his understanding, non-judgmental approach to her mental health problems. She felt that she was finally on the right track and getting the kind of help she needed.

Then one day Joyce called Jane, and said, "John is in town. He just called and asked me to see if you would meet him at Red's Café."

"What does he want?" Jane asked.

"He wants to see you. That's all he told me," Joyce answered.

When Jane opened the door to Red's Café, John Botsford was standing there, waiting for her, with a grin on his face.

"What do you want?" she asked as she entered.

"Can I stay for awhile?" he asked. "I miss you and I was thinking that we should get remarried. I quit drinking and I'm ready to settle down. I love you."

"Well, I don't know," Jane began.

"I thought we could live together for a while, and I'll make you a happy woman," he promised her. "I'll prove to you that we should get remarried."

Jane wanted to find happiness again, and somewhere deep down, there was a place that had always loved John. As she looked at him, standing there smiling at her, she forgot about the mess he always helped her make of her life.

"You can't drink in my house," she told him. "If you do, you will have to leave."

He stayed about a week and then he left. He went down to LaCrosse, where he had been living, and got the rest of his things. He came back with his clothes and a big TV set.

Jane had high hopes. She knew he had stopped drinking and had worked while he was married to Carol. She wanted to believe that he would do the same if he were remarried to her.

John's friend, Dan, helped him move his things into her apartment. Jane didn't like Dan very much, and she soon saw a pattern developing. When Dan was gone, John did very well. She saw shreds of the happiness he had promised her. But when Dan was there, it was another story. On those days, John would go through a whole case of beer.

Jane began to accept that John would be drunk when Dan was around. Then things started going off in her head. "He's a drunk. I don't need him. I don't want him. I don't want to live like this again."

Virgil helped Jane find the strength to realize she would be better off if she were rid of John, once and for all.

"The landlord wants you out, and I'm not going to lose my apartment because of you," Jane told John. "Call Dan and tell him to come and get you—TODAY!"

John left and never returned.

"Did you see the paper today?" Joyce asked Jane, sometime later.

"No, what's in it?" Jane wanted to know.

"It says here that John Botsford has been charged with raping a girl that he was babysitting for. He's going to jail, and he will have to register as a sex offender," Joyce finished.

"He has always gotten away with everything bad that he ever did," Jane remarked. "Finally, they got him for something."

"I guess it was just a matter of time," Joyce said.

"Thank God, I'm finally rid of him and he's out of my life, forever!" Jane declared.

One morning, Joyce woke to thunder booming, and white bolts of lightning shooting across the gray sky.

"Oh, it feels like a good day to stay in bed," Joyce told Duane. "When I was younger, I was afraid of thunderstorms. Dad told us the storms were our fault. He said God was angry because we were such bad girls," she added.

"I wonder what God's mad at today?" Duane said. "Maybe he's mad at Ted."

Just then the phone rang, and Joyce heard Duane say, "Hon, it's for you. It's Roger."

"Dad died. I'm still at the hospital. I'll call you after I get the funeral arrangements made."

They hung up and Roger made the same call to Jane.

A few hours later, Roger contacted them again to tell them the viewing would be at four o'clock the next day, and the funeral would be the day after that.

"I'll let my kids know," Jane said to her brother. "They probably should at least be told their grandpa is dead."

"Do what you want," Roger said as he hung up. "It don't make no difference to me what you do."

Jane phoned Tammy and Ron in Texas, and then she called Todd in Wisconsin.

Todd said, "I'll be there. Thanks for the call, Mom."

"Annette and I will come," Rob told Joyce when she called him. "We'll get a room at the River Edge Motel."

Krissy answered the phone when Joyce called.

"We'll be there tomorrow night, as early as we can," she said. "Are you okay with all of this?"

Krissy understood what Joyce had gone through all her life, and she felt sorry for her. She always wished Joyce's life had been happier.

"Yes, I am," Joyce answered. "Now that he's dead, I feel much safer."

Jane drove to Joyce's house to make sure her sister was okay.

"Now that he's gone, I'm not worried that he will kill me anymore," Joyce said, almost in a whisper. "I just want people who are abused to know they are not alone. Maybe if we tell our story, it can help other kids so they don't have to go through life like we did—always afraid, always feeling threatened, always feeling inferior, always wanting someone to love us, always hungry, and always angry."

"I've been thinking about this since Roger called to say dad was dead. I think you should call Jeannie Hebert," Joyce told her sister.

"My dad passed away," Jane said into the phone. "Can you come?"

"Of course, I'll come," Jeannie answered. "I'll be at the funeral home tomorrow night. I'll see you then."

Joyce, Jane, and Duane arrived at Ted's wake promptly at four o'clock. Roger was already there, sitting in a corner of the room. The sisters went to the coffin and stood together. They silently looked down at the man who had adopted them so many years before.

In her heart, Jane was glad that it was over, and that Ted was dead. For the first time in over fifty years, she wasn't afraid of what her father would do or say to hurt them. *Thank you, Lord,* Jane prayed. *Finally, Joyce can feel safe, too.*

Jane was fascinated by Ted's mouth. In death, his lips were set in a straight thin line. Gone was the curled sneer that once invoked terror as it spewed evil insults, broken promises, wet sloppy kisses, and vile threats. In death, Ted Buck was no more than a weak, pathetic looking little *dead man.*

Relief, anger, and an unexpected feeling of love, surged through her as she stood together with her sister, quietly remembering.

"I have to go sit down," Jane said. "I can't stand to be here."

Joyce nodded in agreement. They sat beside Duane and waited.

When Jeannie arrived, Jane smiled and walked toward her. Together, they approached the coffin, to look at the man who had done so much harm.

"Do you see that son-of-a-bitch?" Jane asked. "He's dead now. He can't hurt us anymore."

Sadly, Jeannie took Jane's hand and stood silently, giving strength and support to her friend. Hand in hand they turned their backs to the coffin, and slowly moved toward the place where Joyce sat, looking down at her folded hands.

As they approached, Joyce looked up at Jeannie and said, "It's time to tell our story."

Printed in the United States
115883LV00003B/40/P

9 781434 373663